THE ROMAN MOTHER

THE
ROMAN
MOTHER

SUZANNE DIXON

CROOM HELM
London & Sydney

© 1988 Suzanne Dixon
Croom Helm Ltd, Provident House,
Burrell Row, Beckenham, Kent BR3 1AT

Croom Helm Australia, 44-50 Waterloo Road,
North Ryde, 2113, New South Wales

British Library Cataloguing in Publication Data

Dixon, Suzanne
  The Roman mother.
  1. Motherhood — Rome
  I. Title
  306.8'743'0937   HQ759

  ISBN 0-7099-4511-6

Typeset in 10pt Baskerville by Leaper & Gard Ltd, Bristol England
Printed and bound in Great Britain by Mackays of Chatham Ltd, Kent

PATRICIAE MATRI CARISSIMAE

Contents

Plates

1. A relief panel from the Augustan Ara Pacis enclosure.
   DAI Neg. No. 32-1744.

2. Part of the sacrifice frieze on the Ara Pacis enclosure,
   showing the adults and children of Augustus' family.
   DAI Neg. No. 72-2403.

3. Trajan distributing largess to poor children: relief panel.
   Alinari No. 11496.

4. Marcus (Aurelius) benefiting the children of the poor.
   Alinari No. 2541.

5. Coin issues showing the Empress Sabina as Pietas, Julia
   Domna, wife of Septimius Severus and her sister, Julia
   Maesa, grandmother of the Emperors Elagabalus and
   Alexander Severus.
   (*RIC* Hadrian 1041) ANU 69.02; (*RIC* Septimius Severus
   555) U/Q 91; (*RIC* Elagabalus 263) U/Q 93.

6. Terracotta relief of a childbirth scene from Ostia.
   Museo Ostiense Inv. 5204.

7. Fragment from a sarcophagus showing a baby immediately
   after birth and as a youth or child.
   DAI Neg. No. 42-101.

8. Childhood stages on a marble sarcophagus from Trier.
   Marburg Archiv No. 180249.

9. Commemoration of the nurse Severina, shown with a
   swaddled baby.
   Rheinisches Bildarchiv, Köln 120 328.

10. Baby's feeding bottle.
    U/Q Classics Inv. 73/6.

Picture identification codes:

DAI: Deutsches Archäologisches Institut, Rom (German Archaeological Institute in Rome)
U/Q: The University of Queensland Antiquities Museum
ANU: The Australian National University Classics Department Museum

Photographic Sources

The University of Queensland Antiquities Museum permitted the use of plates 5(c) (U/Q 91); 5(d) (U/Q 93); 10 (U/Q 73.6).
Mr D.S. Barrett provided the negatives for plates 5(c), (d) from his book *Greek and Roman Coins in the University of Queensland* (1982 rev. ed., Brisbane), which has full descriptions of these coins. For plate 10, see M.G. Kanowski *The Antiquities Collection. Department of Classics and Ancient History, University of Queensland* (Brisbane, 1978).

The Australian National University Classics Department Museum gave permission for the use of plates 5(a), (b) (ANU 69.02) and the Instructional Resources Unit supplied the photographs. For additional detail about these plates, see J.R. Green *Antiquities. A Description of the Classics Department Museum in the Australian National University, Canberra,* particularly the section on coins by B. Rawson (Canberra, 1981).

The Deutsches Archäologisches Institut of Rome supplied plates 1 (DAI neg. 32-1744); 2 (DAI neg. 72.2403); 7 (DAI 42.101). Pl. 7 is described in greater detail by N. Kampen *Image and Status. Working Women in Ostia* (Berlin, 1981). On the Ara Pacis plates, see Kleiner (1978).

Archivi Alinari supplied plates 3 (Alinari no. 11496); 4 (Alinari no. 2541).

Professor S.M. Treggiari supplied plate 6 (Museo Ostiense Inv. 5204, also discussed by Kampen (1981)), a photograph taken by Professor M.F. Kilmer, with the permission of the Soprintendenza Archeologica di Ostia.

Rheinisches Bildarchiv, Cologne supplied plate 9 (RBA no. 1200328; Römisch-germanisches Museum, Cologne Inv. no. 122.1). (See Kampen 1981).

Bildarchiv Foto Marburg supplied plate 8 (Arch. no. 180249) (See Kampen 1981).

Acknowledgements

This book began its life as a doctoral thesis at the Australian National University under the supervision of Dr B.M. Rawson, who kindly took time from her pressing duties as Dean to give me the benefit of her extensive knowledge of the Roman family. Professors P.R.C. Weaver, K.R. Bradley and R.A. Bauman examined the thesis and made many helpful comments and criticisms which improved the published version. Professor Bradley continued to provide advice and support in correspondence throughout the publication process. My own views frequently diverge from theirs and the responsibility for any errors or wrongheadedness naturally lies at my own door.

The work of turning the thesis into a book was made possible by a grant from the Australian Research Grants Scheme and made pleasurable by the cheerful and stunningly competent assistance of Mrs Penny Peel. Mrs Joanna Slater was also of great help in extending the inscriptional data base and Miss Louise Mellick in typing the script. The University of Queensland provided me with computing facilities for systematic analysis of tombstone inscriptions. Mr Richard Stoneman, Humanities Editor of Croom Helm, was patient and helpful throughout the production process.

I have listed photographic sources, with inventory and negative codes, at the end of the List of Plates. For the pictures and permission to use them, I owe special thanks to Mr B.A. Gollan, Director, the Department of Classics and Ancient History Antiquities Museum, University of Queensland; Dr A. Moffatt, Curator, Australian National University Classics Department Museum; Dr C. Weber-Lehmann, Deutsches Archäologisches Institut, Rome. Mr D.S. Barrett, Dean of the Faculty of Arts, University of Queensland, kindly allowed me to use his own negatives of the coin pictures from the Antiquities Museum and Professor M.F. Kilmer generously allowed me to use his slide of a relief sculpture taken with the permission of the Soprintendenza Archeologica di Ostia. Mr C.R. Leigh, Senior Photographer of the University of Queensland, willingly gave of his considerable professional expertise.

Dr Donald M. Watt's careful reading of the typescript has inproved the final product and saved me from the public commission of errors and solecisms.

Above all, I must thank my mother, Patricia Harris Dixon, to whom this work is dedicated. *Her* maternal style has always been forceful, affectionate, unfailingly dependable and selfless. However bizarre my ambitions and whatever their cost to her, she has supported them without hesitation.

Suzanne Dixon
University of Queensland

Preface

In politics, motherhood is notoriously a flag-waver, a concept to which everyone pays lip-service but which means little. It is difficult to imagine a society which does not laud motherhood but the associations can differ greatly. My interest in this topic was aroused by the contrast between the ideal mother of Latin literature and the Christian ideal of the Virgin Mary, interceding in her mercy for sinners, often depicted as a radiant young mother with her divine child. Classic examples of intercession by Roman mothers include Volumnia, who, with her daughter-in-law and grandchildren, confronted her son Coriolanus in his treasonable march on Rome and diverted him from his course; Cornelia, mother of the Gracchi (*mater Gracchorum*), interceded with her son Gaius to spare his political enemy the humiliation of being barred from public office; Julia, mother of Antonius (Mark Anthony), insisted that he spare her brother in the civil war following Caesar's death. These intercessions ran counter to the sons' wishes and even their interests but they were obliged to accede to them.

The emphasis on maternal forcefulness and its exercise by the widowed mother on her *adult* son is typical of the literary image of the Roman mother. It reflects the aristocratic ideal of the late Roman Republic and early Empire. The salient role of the women portrayed admiringly in Latin literature was as disciplinarians, custodians of Roman culture and traditional morality. The familiar modern contrast between the authoritative father-figure and the gentle (and powerless) mother is strikingly absent. The ideal mother of Latin literature was a formidable figure. The chief concession to the 'softer' side of motherhood was in the image of the anxious mother worrying about an absent child or maternal grief at the death of a child.

My stress on ideals and stereotypes is imposed by the nature of the sources: the model mothers of literature and the terse and conventional epitaphs from the vicinity of Rome. This places obvious limitations on a study of the complex area of family relations but I have attempted none the less to explore the relationship between ideals, norms and actual behaviour by supplementing the literary and inscriptional material with iconographic, legal and numismatic evidence. My working hypothesis has been that the most rarefied ideals can reveal basic values, while examples of actual behaviour and the construction placed on them by ancient authors indicate conventional views of everyday obligation. My aim was to determine the *defining characteristics* of the maternal role within the city of Rome from the early second century BC (after the Second Punic War) to the early third century AD (the end of the Severan rule) among citizens.

The result was an authoritative image of motherhood akin to the Roman paternal stereotype. This makes sense in its context. Filial piety was valued and reinforced at Rome by the institution of *patria potestas* ('paternal power') which kept upper-class children in a state of protracted financial dependence until the death of the father, the *paterfamilias*, which caused the children in his power (*in patria potestate*) to become *sui iuris* or independent. A grasp of this fundamental aspect of Roman family law is essential for any discussion of family relations. I have tried not to overwhelm the reader with technical legal terms but this much is unavoidable. The relationship between law and practice is explored in Chapter 3, 'The maternal relationship and Roman law'. The position of the mother can be related to the prevalence of widowhood (an honoured status at Rome) and her ability to dispose of considerable wealth by the bestowal of dowry or by testament. Her position was bolstered by a general regard for parenthood and age but it lacked the firm legal foundation of the father's. An analysis of conflict between mothers and adult sons in Chapter 7 exposes the limits of maternal power.

It will be evident that these observations and standards were more applicable to the Roman ruling class which possessed wealth, sought political power and had great numbers of servants to perform the tasks associated with modern motherhood. I have made a consistent effort to extend the social base of the study, chiefly by the use of inscriptions. Their yield has been limited but I believe they support my general contention that Roman mothers were not associated more closely than fathers with tenderness. Nor were lower class children reared exclusively by their mothers. Foster-parents are attested for children who were not orphans. So in different social groups, Roman childhood seems to have been characterised by a variety of relations with adults. This is quite different from the modern urban condition and I have examined the general social and psychological implications in Chapters 5 and 6.

Throughout this work I have used two comparison points for

assessing the position of the Roman mother: the Roman father and the modern mother. The latter is necessarily an over-simplified stereotype of modern culture but I found it a useful analytic tool for testing modern theories of child development (which I regard as culture-bound). I have tried to avoid over-generalising from modern observation and assumptions and over-reacting to Roman variations from currently favoured practice. Upper-class Roman mothers apparently spent less time with their infant children than we regard as normal (Chapter 5) and bossed their adult children far more than my peers (Chapters 7 and 8) but I do not think it legitimate to moralise about this in a historical work.

People tend to regard their own unexamined ideas about family relations as universals. It comes as something of a shock to learn, for example, that elite Roman women did not wash and change their own babies and that fathers usually retained the children of divorcees. Yet the modern customs are of very recent date. The Roman procedure is more in line with European tra-dition and the practice of some contemporary societies. Children usually remain with the father after an Islamic divorce, for example, and in many Third World countries even mothers of slender means are able to relegate basic infant care to young relations or servants. It might seem to the modern reader that the loss of a child on divorce would have influenced the attitude of a Roman mother to the dissolution of marriage (cf. Rawson 1986b: 35), but I have reservations about the extent to which Roman mothers shared modern notions of close and continual contact between mother and child, especially in the early years. In the absence of testimony from mothers of the ancient world, I have preferred to supply the information available and scrutinize it, but to leave it to the reader to speculate about the emotional implications. By modern standards of maternal involvement and the work ethic, the elite Roman woman might seem idle and sel-fish. In fact, pre-industrial domestic production and processing of food and clothing was arduous and time-consuming, even for the elite woman with many servants to do the basic work (Balsdon 1962: 270-281; and cf. 200-208). We know that some distin-guished matrons did wool-work with their own hands, while supervision alone must have constituted an involvement akin to the tasks of modern factory managers and restaurant owners, in addition to the matrons' social and religious obligations.

It is particularly difficult for a student of the family to preserve fundamental standards of scholarship without side-stepping the dangerous but vital area of feelings and values. Recent work on the history of childhood highlights the problem. Scholars are divided between those who claim that parents in the past cannot have loved their children and those who counter that they felt much as 'we' do about our children. Certainly brutality and love are both attested and both merit as much historical attention as the court intrigues and territorial games which have usually pre-occupied historians but, like it or not, the subject seems to engage our feelings and prejudices more violently. The tone of the con-tinuing controversy is often emotional.

My compromise solution has been to deal with thinly docu-mented areas and to speculate about feelings and implications but to be explicit about the character of the evidence and the speculative nature of my own conclusions. Young children (Chapter 5), lower-class families (esp. Chapters 2 and 6) and relations between mothers and daughters (Chapter 8) receive scant attention from the ancient sources but are too important — and interesting — to be excluded altogether. Some areas, such as adultery (and, by implication, bastardy), abortion, infanticide and the Augustan marriage laws have been dealt with in less detail than some might have wished and subordinated to the topic in hand. My criterion throughout has been the relevance of specific issues to motherhood. I have provided bibliographical information on current controversies but did not wish to be side-tracked from an integrated treatment of Roman motherhood.

I was concerned to keep the domestic details of the imperial families in perspective and so resisted the temptation to dwell on Tacitus' account of the conflict between Agrippina the younger and her son Nero. I have also spared readers my more whimsical imaginative flights from the sepulchral inscriptions. Some will doubtless find the result unsatisfyingly stodgy while others will feel I have transgressed the standards of academic distance. Still others might wonder whether the wide chronological sweep and the heterogeneous character of the sources have obscured vari-ation over time and across the social barriers. I can only say that I have conscientiously alerted the reader throughout to the particu-lar slant of each source. Apart from a greater sentimental interest in young children and in the pleasures of family life (which I discuss in Chapter 2), I found few significant historical develop-ments within the family and no appreciable change in the per-ception of motherhood, in spite of official moves to encourage marriage and procreation and to celebrate the mothers of the imperial family, which I detail in Chapter 4.

I have included translations in the body of the text and sometimes in the footnotes as well, where I judged this to be necessary. I regard footnotes as the tools of the specialist scholar and have made fewer concessions in them to the lay reader. In all my translations I have inclined to the literal for the benefit of the reader without classical training. I have avoided tidying up the expression of inscriptions, which are not usually accessible to the general reader. It proved awkward to identify at each appearance people like Julia Procilla, Julia Soaemias and Murdia, who recur frequently but may not be instantly recognisable. I have made allowance for this in the text. Indeed, I have acknowledged that some readers will dip into chapters of particular interest to them and have often repeated short identifying formulae for women like Cornelia, mother of the Gracchi, or incidents like Servilia's *consilium* at Antium, but the reader will need at times to resort to the 'Appendix of Family Trees' and to the 'Index', which has been arranged to explain terms and personalities, as well as to cite their incidence.

1

Sources and Parameters

Severa mater: the argument

The notion of the mother as soft-hearted ally of her children and
the father as disciplinarian is deeply embedded in our cultural
tradition. It can be unfolded in art — as in de Maupassant's 'La
vie d'une femme', or, for comic purposes, in the blonde of the
half-hour American TV comedy who cutely deceives the (slightly)
sterner father to gain some concession for their child. It can be
exploited for gain, as in the advertisement depicting the young
mother lovingly applying a patented product to her smiling baby.
It can be idealised in religious teaching, as the merciful Holy
Mother interceding for humankind with a just, paternal god. All
of these cultural symbols share a common foundation: the
mother who cares with unfailing patience for the infant and
whose tenderness inclines her ever after to indulgent favour of the
child she once nurtured during its total dependence. The other
side of this picture is that of the father as the family's authority
figure, more inclined to judge transgressions for their content and
less given to capricious forgiveness, the keeper of purse-strings
and purveyor of discipline.

So pervasive is this dual conception that it might appear to be
universal, and yet this is not the case. Anthropologists can adduce
cultures in which the structure is reversed — the children view
their father with affection, their mother as the disciplinarian.
This, according to Richards (1950: 217), is the case with the
matrilineal and uxorilocal Mayombe, where the father, though
able to secure the obedience of his children by devices, can have
his authority checked by his wife or his brother-in-law, since the
children belong to their lineage, not his. In that system, the

children are more inclined to view the father affectionately, while the mother is an authority figure. In most systems, both parents will exercise some discipline and demonstrate some affection, but the relative weight of the characteristics would seem to be contingent on such factors as residence, economics and lineage.

The peculiar character of *patria potestas*, acknowledged even by the Romans themselves (Gai. 1.55, Aul. Gell. *NA* 2.2), has focused attention on the supreme authority of the Roman *paterfamilias*, but the expected corollary, of the soft-hearted mother, seldom emerges from the ancient sources. There are some indications that the juxtaposition was known, and could be appealed to in philosophic analogy[1] or for comic purposes,[2] but it was not a commonplace of Latin literature. The mothers who won praise from Roman biographers and moralists were those who instilled traditional virtue in their children, particularly their sons. There is little stress on the softer side of such women as Volumnia, Cornelia or Aurelia. Rather, mothers were praised for diverting their sons from unsuitable courses — Atia supervised the young Octavian's social life (Nicolaus 6, 10) and Agricola's mother (Tac. *Agric.*4), like Nero's (Suet. *Nero* 52), kept her son from an excessive interest in philosophy.

This work focuses on Roman citizens from the city of Rome and on the period from the end of the Second Punic War to the end of Severan rule. The source material is unevenly distributed across this time frame. There is more literary evidence for the last fifty years of the Republic and the first century of the Principate, while the epigraphic evidence tends to be concentrated in the first centuries of the imperial period. The combination can be awkward, since these sources represent different aspects of experience. It is therefore particularly interesting that they combine to demonstrate a consistent and growing emphasis on ideals of conjugal and familial love from the late Republic and throughout the period studied. By the late Republic, there was a decline in the proportion of women who passed on marriage into the *manus* ('control') of the husband and thus into the inheritance network and legal membership of his kin group, which included her own children. In spite of this formal weakening of ties between a matron and her conjugal group, it seems to have been expected that a married woman would leave her estate to her children and perhaps to her husband rather than to the 'blood' relations who were her intestate heirs. Married love was celebrated not only in tombstones [3] but in stories handed down within families (Plin.

Ep. 3.16) and even in poetry (Ovid *Tristia* 3.3, Statius *Silvae* 3.5, Sulpicia *passim*). Although the virtue of wives in the distant past became a literary *topos*, it was in the late Republic and early Empire that wives were prepared to die for or with their husbands.[4]

The last two centuries of our era have seen analogous developments in the sentimental ideal of the family. One of the attractions of reading Cicero's letters or Statius' tribute to his wife is the familiar tone adopted between spouses and the affectionate concern for children. The modern development has been associated with an interest in the child — especially the young child — and an emphasis on the bond between it and its mother. This element does not seem to have been pronounced in Roman society. Although sentimental attachment to young children is expressed in inscriptions and literary sources, the small child was not accorded as much attention by ancient moralists as by modern educational theorists (Manson 1983), nor was the association between mother and infant as automatic as in our own culture. It was conventional to advocate maternal breast-feeding and to invoke it as an admirable custom of the virtuous past (Aul. Gell. *NA* 12.1; Tac. *Dial.* 28; cf. Plut. *De Am. Prolis* 3; *De Lib. Educ.* 5). Yet it is clear from literary and medical writings that wet-nursing was the norm in upper-class circles from the late Republic at least and that fostering was practised in the lower classes. The implications of this are explored in Chapters 5 and 6, 'The Roman mother and the young child' and 'Mother substitutes'.

The young child was of interest to the ancient authors chiefly as a potential orator, and some passages in which early training in grammar and morals are discussed raise the role of the mother. Thus authors as different as Cicero, Quintilian and Tacitus, either directly or through literary *personae*, mention the mother as a formative influence. Yet in each case she is cited as simply one of several influences on the small child, not to be put before the father.[5] These authors neither assume nor advocate maternal intimacy with the child. Rather, such *indulgentia* is associated with servants. The famous mothers named in these passages are admired for their *disciplina ac severitas* — their vigilance and high standards — rather than the 'softer' qualities of patience or tenderness (Tac. *Dial.* 28.6-7). This model of maternal virtue is scarcely distinguishable from notions of proper paternal guidance. It is, indeed, a contention of this study that

3

the role of the two parents, even in its most rarefied ideal form, is seldom differentiated clearly. Fathers, too, involved themselves actively in the sons' education.[6] Fathers and mothers were assumed to be equally affectionate towards children.[7] Only in the mourning of children is there a distinction in the stereotype: to mourn at all was *muliebris* (womanly); to mourn with abandon was particularly the lot of the bereft mother (Tac. *Agric.* 29.1; Cic. *Fam.* 9.20.3; Sen. *ad Marciam* 2.3-4, 7.3; cf. Plut. *Cons. ad Uxorem* 4). Yet in practice both parents dedicated epitaphs to children, particularly adult children, while the conventional adjectives applied to parents in inscriptional commemorations varied little between father, mother and the two parents treated as a unit.

The idealising or prescriptive character of much of the material available forces a disproportionate emphasis on images rather than observed behaviour. Even accounts which purport to describe events are often shaped to a moral purpose — as in Tacitus' *Agricola*, or Suetonius' biography of Caesar, where the mother of the subject forms in each case an exemplary *topos*. Yet a society's view of what its standards are or ought to be is revealing in itself and the most unrealistic moralists unconsciously reveal practice — as in the too vigorous advocacy of breast-feeding. Mothers in our society are not uniformly patient with small children, but the ideal is a significant element of our culture.

In 1964, Minturn and Lambert published a study testing the hypothesis that ethical values attached to maternity in any given society are actually rationalisations of existing social and economic circumstances. The hypothesis is a variation of the general materialist view of society stressing cultural relativity over the assumption of a universal maternal instinct, for example. According to such a view, the attendance of mothers on small children in our own culture is advocated largely because it is expedient rather than for any intrinsic benefit to the child. We place great emphasis on making sacrifices 'for the children' where traditional Chinese society would stress children's duty to their parents. At a time when domesticity was being celebrated in British popular songs of the late nineteenth century, the seven-year-old sons of the wealthy were taken from their nannies and sent to boarding schools for their own good, to develop independence. The same governments which established child-care centres and drew women into war work in the early 1940s thrust married women out of paid employment in 1946 with pious homilies about the importance of home life.

I proceed from this general presumption that the mother's behaviour and position in any society is based on economic and social contingencies. I argue that the expectation of *pietas* to parents was linked to the control of property by the older generation in Rome. The fact that the mother could hold property and had the power to transmit it conferred on her a position of authority within the family which she held for life. In our own culture, children typically earn their living from about the age of eighteen and often live apart from their parents. Adulthood is associated with independence and continuing deference to either parent is discouraged. The expression 'mother's boy' is derogatory even of a child — it is particularly opprobrious if applied to a grown man. Not so at Rome, where obedience and respect to parents were valued even in adults. The virtue could be enforced, if necessary, by the threat of exheredation or, more drastically, by the supreme powers conferred by ancient law on the Roman father. Unless they were emancipated or adopted or underwent *capitis deminutio* for marriage or some other purpose, children remained in the *potestas* ('power') of their father until his death. This power was tempered by custom and eventually by statute but it did exist and must have underpinned relations with fathers throughout the ranks of Roman citizens (Crook 1967a: 107-111; 1967b).

The position of the mother was different. In spite of formal limitations on her ability to own and transmit property, the Roman woman appears to have been free in practice to make her own dispositions. In Chapter 3 we shall examine the extent to which she exercised authority within the family by customary means and the gradual recognition at formal law of her right to administer her children's property or arrange their marriages. So the power of the father was enshrined in the law but tempered by custom. That of the mother was recognized by convention but had little institutional basis. Mothers could arrange marriages and divorces for children, as Caecilia Metella and Sassia were said to have done,[8] or preside over political conclaves, as Servilia did,[9] or support a son's political candidacy, as Helvia did for Seneca.[10] Children would reckon descent from both parents in attracting marriage partners or votes[11] and if the maternal line were more distinguished it was not impossible to assume the maternal name, as in the case of Poppaea Sabina's adoption of her maternal grandfather's name.

5

It is notable that many of the mothers cited for their great qualities were widowed while their children were young. Given the age differential between Roman marriage partners, women who survived the dangers of reproduction were likely to outlive their husbands. While this made it probable that a mother would take on additional responsibility for her children's education, it is by no means self-evident that widowhood would enhance her authority. In ancient Athens, Demosthenes' mother was left destitute on her husband's death, although he had made provision for widow and orphaned son in his will. She was helpless to gain redress against the fraudulent executors until her son attained adulthood and eloquence. At Rome a widowed mother had greater financial independence yet her children were by definition *sui iuris* ('independent') and therefore subject to fewer strictly legal constraints than children in the paternal power, *in patria potestate.* The mother would be drawing on the force of custom and her own character to assert herself. There is evidence aplenty of such assertion and of the affectionate respect accorded mothers by their adult children. Yet, in the last analysis, the mother did not have a legal sanction corresponding to *patria potestas* to enforce her authority if it were challenged. In Chapter 7, 'The Roman mother and the adolescent or adult son', we review examples of sons' revolting against maternal authority — sometimes mildly, sometimes violently. Such revolts expose the limits of the mothers' rights. The fact that there are fewer instances of daughters' rebellion might suggest that the conflicts concerned the proper boundaries of masculine and feminine spheres, but could equally reflect the lack of knowledge or interest of the ancient authors in purely female relations.

In Rome, as in most societies, motherhood enhanced a woman's status. The achievements of her children, once grown, reflected on a mother, just as her moral reputation and inherited distinction conferred status on them. Widowed mothers who chose not to remarry occupied a position of particular esteem. The respect in which a mother was held would therefore rest on a complex of factors: her responsibility as sole parent on the death (or absence on military service) of her husband, her standing as an independent economic agent capable of enriching her children if they retained her favour, her greater age and experience in the social realm and the accumulation of influence which this might have brought. All of these elements combined to produce a formidable stereotype, strongest within the aristocratic echelons, of the unbending moral mentor, guardian of traditional virtue and object of a lifelong respect comparable with, though not equal to, that accorded a *paterfamilias*. The object of patronising affection common to Greek New Comedy and Dagwood comics was far removed from this figure.

Limitations and problems of using the ancient evidence

The ancients saw history primarily as the chronicle of political and military events. Children and family life did not fit the elevated character of the genre. In writing to Tacitus, Pliny contrasted the content of oratory and history:

> Both oratory and history unfold a narrative, but in different ways. Oratory is drawn for the most part from the lowly, everyday, trivial aspects of life, while history combines its profound, glorious and exalted experiences.
>
> (*Ep.* 5.8.9)

The social historian is therefore driven to ransack a variety of sources, each with its own limitations and problems, in an attempt to piece together a picture of life outside the senate and the battlefield. Art, tombstone inscriptions, the law, official coin issues and satire all have something to contribute. Speeches, letters and biographies are among the most fruitful sources. Biography could contain less uplifting details, such as information about an emperor's childhood, although it needs cautious assessment. For example, we might not believe that imperial infants had miraculous powers but the account of Augustus' movement from his cot (Suet. *Aug.* 94; cf. *Nero* 6) informs us that even the privileged babies of the ancient world were not constantly watched as their modern Western counterparts are.[12]

The part of the lower-class mother must be retrieved almost entirely from epitaphs, which unfortunately drew heavily on stock formulae. Even the upper-class mother, praised in inspirational references to Cornelia (Cic. *Brutus* 211; Tac. *Dial.* 28) or panegyrics of great men (Tac. *Agric.* 4), is viewed in ideal terms. We do not hear the mother's point of view or many details of her daily experience: we hear rather what adult male statesmen, philosophers and doctors thought she ought to be. The factual elements have generally been included incidentally. In his desire to pass on to posterity Favorinus' beautifully argued commendation of maternal breast-feeding, Aulus Gellius unwittingly gives us a glimpse of the social ritual attending the birth of a Roman child (*NA* 12.1.1-4).

The resulting picture is therefore disproportionately weighted towards the aristocratic Roman ideal of motherhood. It is assembled from discrete and ill-matched parts scavenged from odd points of a wide time frame. Although I can discern some development in the acknowledgement at law of the rights and duties of maternal inheritance, this study as a whole presents a synchronous view of the maternal ideal which might simply reflect the imperfections of the sources rather than continuity, although there is some appeal in the view of the French *annalistes* that social structures are essentially stable within a given environment. The aristocratic bias of the sources makes it difficult to generalise about the authoritative position of the mother throughout her children's life cycle in the lower social group which had no property to transmit. The epigraphic evidence for fostering within the lower orders and the lack of distinctive epithets for deceased mothers across the social spectrum supports the idea that the mother's role was not associated as closely with tenderness and the exclusive care of dependent infants as it is in prosperous countries today (cf. Bradley 1985a; 1986).

Modern research and the politics of motherhood

Mothers and children as such have excited little interest amongst historians until recently. Yet the Roman family was the subject of considerable scholarship from the mid-nineteenth until the mid-twentieth century. The concentration of that scholarship was on the archaic family and its underlying structures. It was based on findings of nineteenth century ethnographers and elements of early Roman law, which were fused to form a picture of the 'joint patriarchal family' of *paterfamilias* co-resident with married sons, their wives and children — all those in his *potestas* or *manus*. Such studies (Westrup 1934/1939/1941; Lévy-Bruhl 1947; Koschaker 1937) emanated from the belief that there was such a thing as a universal primitive family and in particular that there was a common Indo-European prototypical family form, the nature of which could be determined by examination of kinship terminology within the relevant language groups and vestigial traces of the early forms in subsequent laws and customs. Recent scholarship has favoured the view that the nuclear family has universally been the most common structure and that the rambling three-generational household is either a myth or a historical rarity (Murdock 1949, 1967; P. Laslett and Wall 1972; P. Laslett, Wachter and R. Laslett 1978). Classical scholars now tend to assume that the chief Roman residential unit was the nuclear family (Crook 1967b; Saller and Shaw 1984; Rawson 1986b), but it is important to note that kinship ties are not limited by residence any more than they are by rules of inheritance. Young and Wilmott's classic (1957) study of East London working-class families showed the close relations maintained with their mothers by women after they married and formed separate residences. My own material and that of Phillips (1978) and Hallett (1984) suggest that this was also the case at Rome and that the ties between women and their married children did not significantly weaken.

In general, I argue that the obligations attached to motherhood in Roman society were not contingent on co-residence or early bonding so much as the fact of the maternal relationship. A mother who had been separated from her child after its birth because of a divorce or exile was still expected to behave dutifully towards the child — to include it in her will, or stand by if the child suffered disgrace or misfortune as an adult. This seems to me to differ radically from the prevailing modern view which puts the emphasis on the relationship between mother and infant as the foundation of all subsequent interaction. Thus Africa's (1978) identification of a 'Coriolanus complex' in Roman men who showed particular regard for their mothers' views strikes me as suspect — based, like Hillard's (1983) analysis of Roman women in politics, on modern masculine repugance for maternal interference. The deference shown by adult Romans to their parents, like the style of early child-rearing, is best viewed in its own social context. Our standards of normal maternal behaviour towards infant or adult children are not necessarily those of the Romans. Some authors have directly related child-rearing techniques to national character or 'cultural personality' (Gorer 1948; Muensterberger 1951). There is an intrinsic attraction in the idea that a culture might foster a particular kind of personality by early training, and examples of conscious attempts to do this are not far to seek: modern girls encouraged to play with dolls and domestic toys, Spartan boys of the warrior class inured to pain and outdoor living from an early age. Roman writings on education link early training and later careers — the moral and grammatical attentions from their mothers allegedly contributed to the political development of the Gracchi and Julius Caesar. Unfortunately, our knowledge is not sufficient to allow a thorough correlation of early training with the ideal Roman character.

The history of the European family has received considerable attention in the last twenty years. Ariès' (1960) work on French childhood and Stone's (1977) study of English families have both aroused much debate and stimulated further research. Ariès' contention that there was no concept of childhood as a separate stage of human development has provoked particular comment. I believe that there is evidence for Roman recognition of childhood by the very late Republic (cf. Manson 1983) and that, like the modern development, it was linked with a sentimental view of the pleasures of family life and high expectations of marital happiness. This is a controversial view, which I shall substantiate in later chapters.

In considering these important questions, I have read widely in the literature of psychoanalysis, history and demography of the family, cognitive and linguistic development as well as ethnography. I have not always drawn directly on such sources in this book, but the ideas and examples produced by such disparate authors as Freud, Gorer, Murdock, Mead, Bowlby, Stone, Shorter, Flandrin, Goody, Piaget, the Whitings, Le Roy Ladurie and Minturn and Lambert have stimulated me to look at the Roman material in ways which might not have occurred to me without their inspiration. In general, I reject psychoanalytic interpretations, but our twentieth-century assumptions about the role of the mother are so influenced by post-Freudian authors like Bowlby and Spock that any treatment of the subject is bound to consider concepts such as infant bonding (object relations), maternal deprivation and the Oedipus complex, however unsympathetically. Although I find the work of Freud and Bowlby impressive, I am bound to view many of their conclusions as culture-bound and (perhaps unwittingly) misogynist. I perceive the development of recent models of the Western family as tied to historical trends, particularly the individualist wage-based economy, which have largely excluded children and married women from the paid work-force. The consequences have included the devaluation of landed property and the greater

10

independence of the wage-earning younger generation from its elders, but a lengthier 'childhood' even in the lower classes since the extension of formal schooling and a greater stress on the mother's role, especially in the early years of childhood dependence. The moral prescriptions which have proliferated about maternal duty differ in content from those which Roman men voiced as freely as their modern counterparts. In this book I examine the ideals they expressed and the practice in different social groups throughout the life cycle of the child in ancient Rome in the late Republic and early Empire.

Notes

1. As in Sen. *Dial.* 1.2.5:
'non vides quanto aliter patres, aliter matres indulgeant? ... matres fovere in sinu, continere in umbra volunt, nunquam contristari, nunquam flere, nunquam laborare.'
'Do you not observe how differently mothers and fathers express their affection? ... Mothers want to coddle children, keeping them in the shade, wishing them never to feel grief, or cry, or experience hardship.'
2. As in Plautus' *Asinaria*, e.g. 509:
hoccine est pietatem colere, matris imperium minuere?
'And is this a proper way to behave, diminishing a mother's rule?' — where the joke is that a mother has no such authority.
3. E.g. *CIL* VI. 13528; 20569 — or the famous '*laudatio* Turiae', *CIL* VI. 1527, a = 37053.
4. Val. Max. 6.7 contains several such examples. Compare Appian *BC* 4.23; Plin *Ep.* 3.16 (cited above); Tac. *Ann.* 15.63.
5. Cic. *Brutus* 211; Quint. *Inst. Or.* 1.1.6; Tac. *Dial.* 28-9. These passages are discussed at length in Chapter 5. Plutarch (e.g. *De Amore Prolis*) and pseudo-Plutarch (*De Liberis Educandis*), both stressing the moral education of the young child and youth, give even less attention to the mother's role, as one might expect of Greek sources.
6. Plut. *Cat. mai.* 20; Aul. Gell. *pr.* 23; Cic. *Att.* 6.1.12; Quint. *Inst. Or.* 6 *pr.*
7. E.g. Cic. *Rosc. Am.* 53; *Verr.* II.i.112; compare the letters exchanged by Fronto and Marcus Antoninus, e.g. *ad M. Caes.* 5.42 (57) (= Naber p. 88) and 5.53 (68) (= Naber p. 91) — very similar to the otherwise dissimilar letters of Cicero to Atticus in the references to children.
8. Plut. *Pomp.* 9.1-2 for Caecilia Metella's arrangement of her daughter's divorce and remarriage to suit the plans of her own husband, Sulla; Cic. *Clu.* 35 for Sassia's behaviour in insisting that her daughter divorce her husband so that Sassia could marry him. See Philips (1978) and Hallett (1984). Cf. Erdmann (1939) on Greek mothers and their daughters' marriages.
9. Cic. *Att.* 15.11 Cf. Nicolaus 52-4 for Octavian's consultation of

his mother Atia on Caesar's death.

10. Sen. *ad Helviam* 14.3; 19.2 and cf. *ad Marciam* 24.3 on the early election of Marcia's son to a priesthood.

11. Cf. Plin. *Ep.* 1.14 on the respectability of the potential groom's descent and his grandmother's virtue. Caesar boasted of his maternal descent as well as that of his father's line in the funeral *laudatio* he delivered for his Aunt Julia — Suet. *Iul.* 6.1.

12. Compare the material of Hanawalt's (1977) study of medieval English practices or the aunt in the nineteenth-century novel *A Blue Stocking* by Mrs. Edwardes (London, 1877: pp. 16-18) who sees no need for the modern custom of watching over small children, even at a beach:

'But I am, of course, ready to watch over him in your absence, if you consider watching necessary. When I was a child,' adds Theodora devoutly, 'people of education believed the world to be under a moral government. Parents had faith in Providence.'
'So have I,' cries Daphne Chester [the mother of the three-year-old], 'when the tide is going out.' p. 16.

2
Roman Family Relations

Defining the family

The word 'family' or its equivalent has a certain flexibility in many languages. In Latin the term *familia* could mean the agnatic lineage, as in the juristic statement of the status of the woman:

for a woman is the beginning and end of her own family

mulier autem familiae suae et caput et finis est
(Ulpian *Dig.* 50.16.195.4)

or it could mean the household, including — or even stressing — the slaves and freed slaves attached to it.[1] Needless to say, everyday usage was less precise, but usually clear enough from the context. This study focuses on a particular relationship within the family: that between a mother and her children. Yet, to understand that, it is necessary to set it in the context of other family relationships.

In our own society, the common application of the term 'family' is to the residential group of parents and children. With the significant difference that the household at Rome included slaves and their families, this was also the basic unit of ancient society, at least in the best attested period[2] when marriage seems usually to have occasioned a new residence for the married couple (Rawson 1986b). Exceptions to this general pattern are noted as such by the sources. Thus the Aelii Tuberones of the second century BC were even then practising a quaint and archaic system in continuing to live in a joint agnatic household: married brothers with their wives and children under the same roof as their father (Val. Max. 4.4.9; Plut. *Aem P.* 5). The brothers Licinii Crassi continued to live in the parental home after marriage (Plut. *Crass.* 1; cf. Tellegen 1980). Cato (*Uticensis*) spent his childhood with his half-relations because the adults of the family had been reduced by the Civil War of the eighties (Plut. *Cat. min.* 1). Less exceptional is the occasional mention of a parent living with a young married couple. We hear of Aurelia's residence in Julius Caesar's home in connection with two anecdotes (Plut. *Caes.* 7;9). In that case, the widowed mother seems to be described as living in the son's home — the second-century example of Cato censor residing with his married son is different, because the young couple are seen as living in *his* home. Since the son was necessarily dependent on his father, this difference is not surprising. A widow's son was by definition *sui iuris* ('independent') and able to own his own household, although there would be nothing to prevent him from living on his mother's property, if that suited them both.

For most purposes, we may take the residential unit of 'the Roman family' to include parents and unmarried children (Saller 1984b; Rawson 1986b), while *familia* would usually extend to the slaves attached to that household, and even slaves on other holdings of the husband and wife.[3] Henrion's (1940) study of the origin and applications of the world '*familia*' is still an important supplement to modern scholarship. It is notable that the French word '*famille*' long signified the wider household (Flandrin 1976: 6-9) rather than the conjugal unit. Even now, when 'family' generally denotes the nuclear unit, husbands and wives will speak in certain contexts of natal kin outside that unit as 'your' and 'my family' or 'my side of the family'. We know from Cicero's remarks about Caelius Rufus (*Cael.* 18) and his financial arrangements for his own son (*Att.* 15.20.4) that young men of the upper class commonly ran their own establishments by the very late Republic on an allowance from their fathers. The young men therefore ceased to be part of the residential group at about age eighteen, while daughters probably left it at an earlier age, on marriage.[4]

It need not follow that these practices have any bearing on the customs of the poorer classes in the city or the countryside. To say that the nuclear family was the norm does not mean that it was the only residential form. Even among the rich, natural death or warfare might have necessitated *ad hoc* arrangements whereby children were reared by their grandparents or other relations.[5] It is necessary to go beyond the residential group to gain a notion of how family relations and reciprocal obligations varied through the life cycle. Married daughters and sons in bachelor apartments or on military duty were still very much part of the family. As we shall see, the maternal role in the Roman upper class did not have the same close association it bears in our own culture with the very young child. Ideally, the young Roman is represented as 'reared in his mother's lap' (Cic. *Brut.* 211), but even if — as was more likely — he was raised by slaves or separated at an early age from a divorced or widowed mother, the requirements of the relationship held: visits, attention to funeral rites, help in adversity and so on.

This point is worth stressing. Studies in the past have sometimes exaggerated the implications of the technical, legal aspects of Roman relationship as if they reflected actual behaviour. Buck (1949:93) insisted that in-law relations through a wife were less significant and the terminology for these relations consequently developed at a slower pace than the corresponding terms for the wife's relations with her in-laws.[6] Others have placed undue stress on *agnatio*, the principle of relationship through the male line which determined intestate succession.[7] Males adopted into another family, or women in the control ('hand') of the husband, *in manu mariti*, lost their 'natural' agnates and gained a new set at law (Gai. 2.139; Crook 1967a: 103). Yet there is abundant evidence that adopted males, married women and even Vestals — who had no agnates[8] — showed a great awareness of their 'natural' affiliations. Thus Scipio Aemilianus continued to honour his obligations to his natural parents after his adoption (Polyb. 31.26; 18.35.6). Lucretia, raped by Tarquin, summoned both her husband and father to hear her case (Liv. 1.58). The Vestal Claudia mounted her father's chariot in 143 BC to enable him to celebrate an unauthorised triumph in the face of tribunician opposition.[9] For legal purposes, Roman names passed through the paternal line, but descent was reckoned for many purposes from both sides of a family — especially if the maternal side were particularly distinguished.[10]

The general term *cognatio*, which encompassed all relationships, 'blood' and legal, came to be used predominantly of those which did not have legal priority, such as relations with maternal connections[11] or with a daughter or sister who had undergone *conventio in manum* ('transfer to the husband's control') at marriage and thereby entered a distinct agnatic network. '*Agnatus*' came to be applied to the more distant patrilineal relations. *Sui heredes* (children/grandchildren *in potestate* and wives *in manu*) and *consanguinei/ae* (brothers and sisters), the first two categories of intestate heirs, were, strictly speaking, also agnatic relations. The Twelve Tables ruling that where there was no *suus heres*, the 'next agnate' should succeed (*Tab.* 5.4; cf. Gai. 1.155ff on *tutela*), led to the term being applied chiefly to other relations. Compare our own use of 'relations', which usually denotes relations *beyond* the immediate degree of brothers, sisters, parents and children — or 'descendants' to mean descendants beyond the degree of grandchildren. The primary significance of agnatic relationship was for the formal transmission of property. It was the basis of awarding hereditary succession to the estate of an intestate or of determining the *tutor* of a woman or child whose father had not named one in his will. This formal aspect seems to have had little bearing on the way in which people measured the closeness of their relationship and the obligations they acknowledged. Hallett (1984) provides ample instances of close relationships through the maternal line. Although I believe she over-argues the cultural primacy of such relationships, she does demonstrate that maternal uncles and grandfathers took a strong, affectionate interest in the children of their married sisters and daughters.

Sepulchral inscriptions and tombs supply some notion of how the family was defined in Roman eyes. The great Monumentum Liviae, for example, provided a place for the remains of the members of her *familia*, in the sense of her slaves — apparently her skilled and favoured slaves — or freed slaves. Other inscriptions were set up to a particular family member, to the dedicator in due course, and to the children, descendants and freed slaves, sometimes (theoretically) in perpetuity, as in *CIL* VI 14105, erected by Umidia Onesime to her brother, uncle, mother (*COGNATIS SVIS*) and to her freedmen and freedwomen and their descendants; or *CIL* VI 24452, erected by L. Pompeius Eratus to his daughter, his (or her) mother and himself and to their freedmen and freedwomen and their descendants. It is difficult to know where to draw the line. Slaves, *libertini* and their descendants, though attached to the family of such a dedicator, were not, strictly speaking, 'family', but their inclusion suggests that the system of attachment and obligation resembled family feeling (Cf. Hainsworth (1986) on the seventeenth-century

English household). We must keep reminding ourselves of the configurations and relationships imposed by the life chances of the ancient world: the nurses, foster-mothers and other surrogates (discussed in Chapter 6) who formed a quasi-family, were an outcome of maternal mortality as well as the social hierarchy. The basic family unit of single mother and children, common at all social levels, might have been particularly so in the upper class, where early marriage with older men created young widows.

The conditions of slavery imposed obvious strains on family life. Slaves are generally excluded from this study, which focuses on Roman citizens, but the *libertini* population, so well[12] represented in sepulchral inscriptions from Rome, began its life in slavery and the lower class of shopkeepers and labouring proletariat sometimes had families of mixed status (Rawson 1966; Weaver 1986). The slave population of Rome was largely imported from diverse parts of the empire and the urban lower class could have drawn on different ethnic models of family life, but there are few signs of these in the meagre family histories yielded by our chief source, the sepulchral inscriptions of *CIL* VI and *IG* XIV. It was once the fashion to blame slaves and foreigners for the 'decline' of the family at Rome[13] but recent scholarship has generally demonstrated the persistence of family ties. Slaves and freed slaves were not always able to form co-resident nuclear groups, but some clung to their blood ties in spite of hardship and others formed family-like associations with their fellows.

A slave woman's child was necessarily the property of her owner who could sell, expose or send elsewhere the child, the mother and — if he was also a slave of the same owner — the child's father. Rawson's (1966) study of 1500 early imperial epitaphs reveals that this did, indeed, happen. She cites several instances of children who were freed at an early age in a household other than that of the parents. One child, Antestia Glycera, had been freed by the time of her death at the age of three. In the same period, her mother had attained freedom from a different patron, while her father came from another household again (Rawson 1966: 78-9; cf. Flory 1975: 42-3). This suggests that children were bought and separated from their mothers when quite young.[14] As Rawson observes (1966: 79-80), this shows not only the disregard of slave family ties by owners, but the strength of family ties among the slaves. The parents' opportunities for forming lasting unions were limited by the possibility of separation through sale. That they would go to the trouble of combining from separate households to scrape up the necessary sum to commemorate a child who had died in a third household — that is, a child with whom they had had little regular contact — in a society which theoretically frowned on mourning for young children argues a touching determination to uphold that most human of institutions, the family.

Yet there must have been cases in which separation and its likelihood weakened ties. The slave father certainly had little incentive for acknowledging the children of brief liaisons. Unlike the citizen parent, he gained little kudos from paternity, since the children belonged to the mother's *familia* and bore no legal relation to him. His feeling for his children might have been closely linked with his relationship with the mother, as it tends to be in modern Western societies, where divorce typically weakens paternal responsibility. Rawson (1966: 75-7) cites examples of solidarity in families of mixed status which reflect the impact of circumstances on such groups and Flory (1975: 44) insists that death more than slavery broke up families but Treggiari (1969: 212-13) has noted a tendency for freedmen to commemorate only those children born to them after manumission. The mother-child unit regarded by many as the fundamental element of the family (Radcliffe-Brown 1950: 77) might often have constituted the whole slave or lower-class family (cf. Rawson 1966: 77 on *CIL* VI 13410 and Smith 1956 on the matrifocal West Indian and Afro-American family).

The fact that children of unions not classified by Roman law as proper marriages generally took their status from their mother (Weaver 1986), might have encouraged a matrifocal tendency in the lower-class family, but even the maternal relationship could be eroded by slavery. Martial taunted a freedman who had the legal capacity to sire free-born citizen children, but could never have a mother or father acknowledged at law (*Epig.* 11.12). The formal position and the vicissitudes of slavery must have affected maternal attachment. One despairs of reconstructing the feelings of a slave woman rewarded for repeated reproduction for the benefit of an owner's purse (Columella *RR* 1.8.19). Within the *familia*, especially a large one, there would be such a variety of relationships that the mother-child bond could have been fairly weak (Bradley 1984: Chapter 3). One cannot even assume that slave mothers breast-fed their own babies. As early as Plautus, the 'nurse who suckles the *vernae*' (slaves born within the *familia*) is referred to casually, as a stock household figure[15] and the

18

mammae and *tatae* — possibly foster-parents of young children — figure also in inscriptions for slave and *libertini* families.[16] A foster-parent might even be given priority over mothers and fathers.[17] Considerations of status and sentiment must both have played their part. Some parents worked to free slave children (*CIL* VI 22423, 14529, 34936) while others might have considered children born in slavery as lost to them (cf. Rawson 1966: 77).

The abandonment of newly born or very young children is referred to as a fact of life in the ancient sources (Musonius Rufus 15; Plin. *Pan* 26.5; Plut. *De Am. Prolis* 497E) and suggests that parental responsibility and affection could be overcome by external circumstances. Even free-born children, once abandoned, could be treated as slaves by those who took them up, although legal complications could eventually ensue (Rawson 1986c). We hear of one Melissus, fortunate enough to be trained in the imperial household after his desertion as a child. When his mother attempted to reclaim him many years later, he chose to remain instead in privileged slavery (Suet. *Gramm.* 21). The bond between brothers and sisters sometimes survived the vicissitudes of slavery.[18] There are a few instances of freed slaves 'buying out' brothers or sisters (*CIL* VI 22423) or erecting epitaphs to each other during or following on their slavery (*CIL* VI 12564). *CIL* VI 9868 was set up by the freedman Quintus Philomusus to his *colliberta* (freed slave from the same *familia*) Cornelia Daphne and her sister Cornelia Nymphe: that is, the two sisters had maintained ties which the friend acknowledged. There are also instances of the inclusion in epitaphs set up by a patron of a brother or sister of a former slave, although the relative was not a member of the same *familia*. These people must have made special requests or paid for the favour of inclusion, which implies a general recognition of the importance of this family tie by fellow slaves and owners as well as the individuals concerned.[19]

Rawson (1966: 83) and Flory (1975: esp. Chapters 2 and 3) have both noted the strong sense of solidarity, resembling kinship, observed by members of the same *familia*.[20] Flory cites the example of Aulus Memmius Charus, commemorated in *CIL* VI 22355a by his *collibertus* of many years standing, Aulus Memmius Urbanus. She makes the point that *collibertus* was often used as if it were a kinship term.[21] Flory (1975: 50, n 20) rightly draws a distinction between the formal designation of *colliberti* as confined to those freed by the same patron and its normal, wider usage, denoting people who had ever shared the same household.

Flory insists that this 'kinship'of members of the same *familia* was not merely a substitute for real kinship. Both types of tie could be observed at the same time. She cites examples of kin and fellow slaves combining to erect epitaphs, as in *CIL* VI 26629 and 12564.[22] Sometimes, too, relations of former slaves of a particular household, although they themselves had never served in it (Flory 1975: 29-30), were included in the *familia* plot.

Kinship and patronage must have been important buffers against the insecurity and hardships of life for members of the Roman lower classes. Hopkins' study of burial clubs (1983: 211-17) suggests that these groups performed a similar function for those who could not call on such ties. The burial clubs provided more than the obvious kin-like office of obsequies. The regular meetings, usually of a social character, and the fact that members would celebrate deceased friends' birthdays, all argue an interest in one another resembling that of kin. Other associations might have been formed on the basis of religion, ethnicity, a common craft, common (past or present) membership of a *familia* or simple need (as in the case of burial clubs), which provided the material and emotional support usually expected of kin. The early Christians appear to have based whole sub-communities on ties of that kind. Such groups must have supplemented kinship ties in many cases, but for those deprived by death or the circumstances of poverty and slavery of their "blood" relatives, these associations must have been their families for all intents and purposes.

On the whole, the closest family relations seem to have been within the group in which our own culture expects their concentration: between parents and children, brothers and sisters. Rawson (1986a) draws this conclusion from a review of the ancient evidence and modern scholarship. Saller's (1984b) analysis of the terms '*familia*' and '*domus*' in Latin literature and legal writings and the study by Saller and Shaw (1984) of relationships commemorated in tombstones throughout the Roman empire (cf. Shaw 1984 on the *later* Roman empire) have been landmarks in this field. Roman notions of what constituted 'the family' would vary slightly according to context. In Lucretius 3.894-6, Tac. *Ann.* 3.33-4 or Cic. *Att.* 1.18.1, 'family life' is clearly the life of the conjugal, residential unit. For those, especially in the nobility, thinking in the long term, the family was the lineage.[23] Augustus' rejection of the two Julias (his errant daughter and grand-daughter) entailed not only immediate punishment but their exclusion from the family tomb. In a sense they were thereby expelled from the enduring symbol of family unity, but they apparently remained during their lifetimes in his *potestas*; for it was in his capacity as *paterfamilias* that he exiled them and had Julia (minor)'s child exposed (Suet. *Aug.* 65). The family could thus be contracted or extended by strong feelings or external circumstances. Perhaps the most important point is that 'family' was not exactly the same as the residential or blood-kin group, nor were formal ties the most significant. In the chapter following, we shall see the gradual legal recognition of the importance of the tie between mother and child even where the connection was slight in formal, agnatic terms. Similarly, the reciprocal obligations of the relationship between mother and child altered through the life cycle, but did not disappear. In Chapters 7 and 8 below, we shall examine the kind of duties adult sons and daughters observed to their mothers.

Roman attitudes to children and family life

Two blocks of legislation were passed under Augustus' aegis in 18 BC and AD 9 which penalised celibacy, childlessness and adultery and offered certain benefits to Roman citizens who married and produced legitimate children. There was some talk of replenishing the depleted Italian stock which was traditionally regarded as the backbone of the Roman army (cf. Hor. *Carm.* 3.6, esp. 33 ff; Prop. 2.7.13), but the incentives and penalties laid down by the so-called 'Augustan marriage laws' really applied to the wealthy and politically ambitious.[24]

Wealthy men demonstrated against the laws. Augustus reproached them by appearing in the imperial box at the games with his great grandchildren (Suet. *Aug.* 34). He also addressed members of the equestrian order *en masse*, upbraiding the bachelors and praising the married men (Dio 56.1-10). He was fond of quoting from speeches of an earlier age to show that marriage had always been deemed a civic duty (*RG* 8.5; Liv. *per.* 59). Yet the saying which proved most memorable was the highly quotable aphorism of Metellus (Macedonicus), censor in 102 BC, that 'since nature has decreed that we cannot live at all comfortably with our wives, or live at all without them, we should consider the long-term benefit rather than immediate happiness' (Aul. Gell. *NA* 1.6.2: but cf. McDonnell (1987) on the identification with Numidicus).

21

Augustus' reported speeches proceed from the assumption that people were deliberately avoiding marriage and parenthood to such an extent that the continuity of the ruling class was at risk (cf. Cic. *pro Marcello* 23; but see Hopkins 1983: 126-7). Augustus represented himself as reviving traditional morals but his attempts to compel widows to re-marry were themselves at odds with the long-standing Roman ideal of the *univira*, the woman who had only one husband in her lifetime. The origin of this tradition was probably sacral and material rather than senti-mental (Lightman and Zeisel 1977, Dixon 1985: 358, 360), but it came to be associated with the love and loyalty of a widow for her husband. By the late Republic it was very common for divorcees and widows to re-marry, but the ideal persisted (e.g. *CIL* VI 13303; 31711 and see Frey 1930). The inconsistency between marital ideals and practice is a common one and modern parallels are easily found. The significance for this study of the ideal of the *univira* is confined to any possible relationship it might bear to the image of the widowed mother who devoted herself to her children's interests. The two stereotypes do not quite co-incide. Cornelia (mater Gracchorum) was praised for rejecting wealthy suitors in her widowhood (Plut. *Tib. Gr.* 1.7), but her daughter was long since married by then and her sons dead. Augustus' widowed mother Atia did re-marry (Nicolaus 3.5), but was still a model of the conscientious and influential Roman mother (Nicolaus 3.6; 4.10). On the whole, the re-marriage of a widowed mother was deemed dangerous to her children's interests (see the following chapter), but does not seem to be directly related to any intrinsic stress on widowhood in the Christian sense (see again Lightman and Zeisel). We cannot know how many widows actually resisted family and legal pres-sures (if they were childless) to re-marry because of loyalty to the ideal or to an individual spouse. Within the imperial family, Antonia (mother of Germanicus and the emperor Claudius) declined to re-marry (Val. Max.) but Agrippina the elder, a model wife and mother, wished to do so and was reputedly thwarted by Tiberius (T. *Ann.* 4.53). The pressure for women to re-marry and the prevalence of bachelors might both have stemmed from a shortage of marriageable women in some social groups (Dio 54.16.2; Brunt 1971: 558).

Resistance to marriage was in any case not the same as resistance to having children. Ancient authors assumed that even married couples avoided procreation. The childless old widow or widower courted by the gifts and attentions of legacy-hunters became a stock literary figure (Hor. *Sat.* 2.5; Juv. 1.37-9; Tac. *Ann.* 15.19; Martial *Ep.* 6.62). One must allow for comic and moralising hyperbole, but there are sober, casual references to the economic and emotional burdens of child-rearing which suggest that parenthood was not universally viewed as desirable.

Family limitation, particularly by the exposure of new-borns, was probably practised by the very poor (Plin. *Pan.* 26.5; Tac. *Germania* 19; cf. Plut. *Mor.* 497E). Even the wealthy took the view that children were a source of anxiety and long-term expense to their parents. Suetonius (*Tib.* 47) cited the example of Hortensius Hortalus, a member of a distinguished family whose very status was at risk because he had four children in patriotic response to Augustus' call to procreate.[25] Pliny, childless in spite of himself after three marriages and adopted as a youth in the will of his childless uncle, praised a friend for producing several children in an age where even one child could discourage legacy-hunters (*Ep.* 4.15.3).

Whether the rich actually exposed healthy, legitimate infants is uncertain (cf. Sen. *de Ira* 1.15; Musonius 15; Hopkins 1983: 226 n33) and accusations that some women sought abortions for the sake of their figures (Sen. *ad Helviam* 16.3; Aul. Gell. *NA* 12.1.8, citing Favorinus; Juvenal 6.592 ff) might be little more than malicious fantasy but exposure, abortion and contraceptive methods (of varying efficacy — Hopkins 1965b) were available options. Certainly the wealthy seem to have restricted the size of their families much as prosperous communities and social groups tend to do in the twentieth century.[26] But family limitation of this type does not imply an antipathy to children as such. It tends, if anything, to be associated with a strong sentimental attachment to children and a serious view of the parental role.

DeMause (1974) has argued that children were viewed in past societies as mere extensions of their parents. There is some truth in this, but I suggest that it is seldom a simple matter to distinguish emotional and economic parental investments from more general expectations. It could be argued that one of the fundamental functions of the family is the provision of food and care for the very young and the old or incapable and this leads naturally to the idea, explicit in some cultures but surely present in most, that children 'owe' parents security in old age as a return for care in their own dependent years (Bradley 1985b: 327-9; Lambert 1982: 53-4). The relationship between parental contri-

butions and their eventual return was not always so direct.
Certainly Roman nobles looked to sons to continue the family
name (Plautus *Mil. Glor.* 703-4; Sen. *de Matrimonio* 58). Parents
generally hoped their children would perform their funeral rites
and maintain the family cult (*CIL* VI 19914; 22066; 28644; Cic.
Mur. 27; cf. Lattimore 1942: 187-91). Cicero's liberality to his son
Marcus, studying abroad, was designed to enhance Cicero's own
standing (*Att.* 15.20) and the education would eventually bring
credit to the family once the young man exhibited its fruits at
Rome. At a much lower social level, Horace's father, a freed
slave, worked hard to ensure that his gifted son should enjoy a
liberal education — which would surely bring the father reflected
glory rather than a specific return such as support in old age. A
daughter would foster her family's honour by displaying both her
formal education and the skills learned in the home (cf. Plin. *Ep.*
4.19) and by bearing and rearing children who would bring glory
to their paternal and maternal lines (Plut. *Tib. Gr.* 1 and 8).

In urging upon the recalcitrant bachelors the joys of marriage
and parenthood, Augustus (according to Dio 56.3.4) asked:

> Is it not a delight to rear and educate a child born of you
> both — an image of your own appearance and character, so
> that you might live on in him?

This could be viewed as selfish projection, but it would arouse
echoes in many modern breasts. DeMause (1974) tends to distinguish between self-interested parental hopes vested in children
and the appreciation of children's individual qualities, but the
two are not mutually exclusive. Bereaved parents doubtless suffer
from self-pity, as he suggests, but this does not preclude the
possibility that they miss their dead children as personalities. The
death of young children must have been a commonplace in
Roman society and the practice of mourning them was not
encouraged (Hopkins 1983: 125-6), which suggests a much less
sentimental approach than our own to small children in general.
The strongest laments were for children who died as young
adults. Yet some parents made a point of commemorating the
deaths of very young children in a way which leaves little doubt of
their attitude. Consider, for example, *CIL* VI 34421:

> Her most unhappy parents, Faenomenus and Helpis, set
> up the dedication to Anteis Chrysostom — sweet prattler

and chatterbox — who lived three years, five months and three days, our dearly beloved, well behaved daughter, with her piping voice. Porcius Maximus and Porcia Charita and Porcia Helias and Sardonyx and Menophilus who tended her to the day of her death also commemorate her.

Apart from mourning practices, there is general support for the idea that family life and conjugal happiness were prized in the early imperial period in spite of the alleged resistance to marriage. In the late Republic, Lucretius' picture of a typical funeral includes a stock lament that the young man being buried will never again return to his happy home and his wife or have his children run to him to be kissed and lifted to his breast (Lucretius 3.895-6). Home life symbolises for the mourners the essence of what life has to offer. Cicero — admittedly in rather melo-dramatic, self-pitying vein — lamented that his worldly friend-ships were a sham and his only sincere happiness was in the time spent with his wife and young children (*Att.* 1.18.1). Such images are idealised, but show a value on family life akin to the western notion of the family as a 'haven in a heartless world' (Lasch 1977) which modern historians of the family tend to see as a relatively recent development.

It was to be expected that the imperial family would stress family solidarity, to reinforce Augustus' programme and display the stability of the regime by showing that the succession was ensured. It also seems to have been true that Livia and Augustus, Germanicus and Agrippina, and Drusus and Livilla were happily married. The wives commonly accompanied the husbands on public service in the provinces, sometimes taking their children as well, a custom which developed under the Principate and became general among governors' families (Raepsaet-Charlier 1982; cf. Marshall 1975). When the practice was called into ques-tion by one of the more conservative senators in Tiberius' reign, others argued that provincial governors should not be deprived of the companionship of their wives for the term of their public service (Tac. *Ann.* 3.34). This had not been usual in the Republic and does, I believe, reflect a growing stress on marital and familial 'togetherness'. Like our modern ideal of family life, it might not always have been achieved and it existed (like our own) in a period of frequent divorce and consequent splintering of the nuclear family. To our eyes, this was one of many apparently contradictory Roman attitudes to marriage and parenthood.

Romans expected to develop affectionate relationships within marriage *after* the match had been arranged with a view to status, material and political considerations (Dixon 1985b: 366-7; Treggiari 1982: 35; 1984) in contrast to the modern (but by no means universal) association of romantic choice and conjugal love. Parents who possibly exposed unwanted babies and sold off slaves' children became attached to those children they did rear.

The historian is left with the difficult task of juggling such information: a task made no easier by our ignorance of basic data such as the proportion of new-born children who *were* reared or the age at which most Roman men and women married. When it comes to plotting feelings, which are difficult enough to assess in contemporaries, historical resconstruction is beset with difficulties. Debates rage among historians of the family on the conclusions which are to be drawn from the limited information available (Pollock 1983; Thompson 1973; MacFarlane 1979; Ariès 1960; deMause 1974; Stone 1977). Sometimes we are too ready to assume on slight evidence that people in past eras felt much as we do on a range of subjects. Ariès' firm statement that the concept of childhood as a special stage of life was a relatively modern invention shocked social historians into a salutary review of their own assumptions. It is as easy to fall into the contrary trap of concluding that people whose expectations and behaviour differ radically from our own could not possibly share our sentiments: hence the refusal of some to accept the possibility of conjugal affection in arranged marriages. Pollock (1983) argues that scholars like deMause have exaggerated the cruelty and coldness of parents in the past, but it is genuinely difficult to balance apparently conflicting pieces of evidence.

Roman fatherhood poses problems. The Roman *paterfamilias* has been the subject of many works, the usual concentration being on the daunting legal authority he could exercise over his children, who remained in his power (*in patria potestate*) throughout his lifetime unless he chose to release them by emancipation or approved their transfer to another family and the power of a new *paterfamilias* — for example, by adoption or, in the case of a daughter, by the type of marriage (less common from the late Republic on) which committed her to the *manus* (literally, 'hand') of her husband.[27] On the whole, those Roman citizens with a living father remained in his *potestas*, which gave him complete authority over them. This included the right of life and death (*ius vitae necisque*) and therefore the ability to impose his will on them, the power to make and break their marriages and the capacity to hold and administer any property which fell to them, since children (of whatever age) *in patria potestate* had no power to own, dispose of or pledge any property in their own right (Rabello 1979; Crook 1967b). These fearsome powers were somewhat tempered by usage: the *ius vitae necisque* amounted in practice to the right to decide whether new-born children should be reared.[28]

Children, especially sons, had some right to protest against an unwelcome choice of marriage partner[29] and the father's power to end a harmonious marriage was eventually denied,[30] while adult children gradually gained some effective control over money they had earned themselves, especially through military service.[31] None the less, the rights of the *paterfamilias* were formidable and could be exercised by a tyrannical father without regard to convention.[32] It has been suggested (Rawson 1986b: 14) that the potentially oppressive nature of the relationship was averted only by the neo-local character of Roman marriage — that is, the formation of a new household on marriage — which enabled the young adult generation some freedom from the paternal presence. Veyne (1978: esp. 37) argues, rather, that pre-industrial mortality saved most from the burden of a father who survived to their own adulthood, and that the citizen population at Rome was divided into the groups of those happy individuals *sui iuris* whose fathers had died and those unfortunates who chafed into middle age under enforced dependence.

Individual variation must have been great. Yet it is notable that the examples of severity which have been preserved (e.g. Val. Max. 5.4.5; 5.8; Suet. *Aug.* 65) were recorded as oddities. There are inscriptions showing extravagant paternal grief and Latin literature yields diverse instances of fatherly behaviour, cited as typical or normative. Cato censor regularly attended his infant son's bath unless public duty called him away (Plut. *Cat. mai.* 20.4). Dedicated as he was to his studies, Aulus Gellius regarded them as, in some sense, a luxury to which he could devote only such time as remained from his more pressing duties of maintaining the family estate and attending to his children's education (*NA Praef.* 23). In Ovid's *Metamorphoses*, Apollo — admittedly not an ideal father — cries out that he shows his true parenthood by his anxiety for Phaethon's safety (2.91-2). Himself gravely ill, Caecina Paetus repeatedly questioned his wife Arria about their son's health.[33] Young Quintus Cicero caused his parents great anxiety but his father appears to have used pleading rather than paternal authority to persuade him to accept the parental choice of marriage partner (e.g. Cic. *Att.* 13. 42). The orator Cicero criticised his brother's *indulgentia,*while young Quintus accused his uncle of bullying *his* son, young Marcus[34] — demonstrating that there could be different styles of fatherhood even within the same family. The orator referred in his speeches to juries to the particular love fathers bore daughters (e.g. *Verr.* II.1. 112; *Mur.* 23) — a sentiment evident in himself, Atticus and Julius Caesar. In his speech for Roscius of Ameria, he scorned the suggestion that Roscius' father had ever intended to disinherit his son on the ground that the accusers had failed to enumerate sins of sufficient magnitude to drive a father to go against nature — to drive from his spirit that deeply instilled love — in a word, to forget that he was a father.[35] Even allowing for his rhetorical purpose, Cicero must have been appealing to a sentimental stereotype acceptable to the jurors.

This collection presents a more complex — and surely more plausible — picture of fatherhood than that of the stern *paterfamilias* exercising his full legal authority over children whom he could bind over to others or even kill. One of the striking aspects of the instances cited as typically fatherly behaviour is the resemblance to modern notions of motherly behaviour: anxiety, forgiveness, indulgence, involvement in children's education. The attribution of emotional functions was no more likely to follow modern notions of appropriate allocation than the division of labour or authority. The Roman father certainly had the full means of discipline to hand and the power of economic control over his children, but the upper-class mother seems to have shared in the disciplinary role and to have held a position of considerable authority within the family, perhaps related to her command of her own fortune and its disposition. Vipstanus Messala in Tacitus *Dialogus* (29.1-2) was made to voice criticism of contemporary parental laxity. There was no suggestion that either parent was more prone to this vice.

It is trite to observe that parents and children alike tend to develop strong feelings of affection for each other. These become inextricably linked with notions of duty and obligation. Thus Cicero associated the duty of a *paterfamilias* to pass property down the family line with 'that deeply instilled love' *amor ille penitus insitus (Rosc. Am.* 53). He also spoke of his nephew Quintus' affection for his mother (whom Cicero disliked) as proper — that is, both expected and dutiful.[36] A son's betrayal of a father was shocking in the same way that treason or blasphemy was, but with the additional dimension that filial behaviour should be impelled by affection as well as duty. The examples of Appian *BC* 4.11-18 were notable for this reason: although some wives betrayed their husbands in the civil war during the triumviral proscriptions, few children or parents betrayed each other. *Pietas* towards parents was stressed in the Roman value system, which vested so much formal authority in the older generation, particularly the father. If Veyne's analysis of Roman male psychology is correct, and adult males bitterly resented the power of their fathers (Veyne 1978: 36-7; cf. Baldwin 1976) we should expect a civil war to furnish a great number of betrayals of fathers by children. Yet the story of the two Quinti Cicerones seems more characteristic. They had had numerous conflicts in their lifetime but, faced with death, asked only to be spared the sight of the other's murder (Appian *BC* 4.20; cf. Shackleton Bailey 1960).

Perhaps conflict and support between the generations were related to stages of the life cycle. Thus a son might oppose his parents on the choice of a spouse or at a stage of his political career.[37] In the end, however, harmony would generally have prevailed, partly because the strength of family relations lies in their permanence — they are not really dissoluble, as marriages and friendships can be — and partly, within the upper class, because political honours required the full support of all connections. Thus Servilia, who had opposed her son Brutus' marriage to Porcia, and had bad relations with this new daughter-in-law (who was also her own niece), showed complete solidarity with their interests after Caesar's assassination and the resultant political uncertainty.[38] The needs of both generations would also have varied at different stages. A daughter might have needed her mother's practical help and advice on the birth of a first child but provided help for her widowed mother in her turn some few years later. Bradley (1985b: 237-330) has rightly stressed the importance for lower-class parents of income from their children's employment, especially when old age rendered the parents dependent. Indeed, family duty could extend beyond the life cycle proper. Within the political arena a young man could perform an act of filial piety and advance his own career at a stroke by prosecuting a former enemy of his father, whether the father were alive or dead. Cato censor is reported to have said to such a young man that these were the best kind of offerings to make to dead parents, superior even to the usual rites of remembrance (Plut. *Cat. mai.* 15). Duty and sentiment would often have gone hand in hand.

Life chances and the family

There have been several attempts to calculate patterns of mortality in ancient Rome from tombstones which record the age of death of the person commemorated. This involves methodological problems, for many groups are under-represented in epitaphs — children, women, and the poor who could not afford any memorial (Burn 1953: 45; Hopkins 1966: 261-2). Nor was the age of the deceased at death always provided. The Roman practice of erecting a memorial to oneself in one's own lifetime also complicates such exercises. These problems have not deterred successive generations from making the attempt to calculate the average life span in ancient Rome (Beloch 1886; MacDonnell 1913; Willcox 1937; Henry 1957; Durand 1960). The recent trend has been to look for the median life span (Burn 1953; Hopkins 1966; 1983: 147), to avoid the artificiality of averages distorted by a few very long lives. Thus Burn pointed out that life expectations at birth were much lower than at age ten.[39]

There is still considerable disagreement among experts on methods and results, but a broad consensus exists on the ancient life span, which was short by modern industrial standards. These trends have implications for many aspects of family relations. It is accepted that women had a lower median expectation of life than men, but that their expectations were higher if they survived the dangerous reproductive years. This in turn could be influenced by the age of women at (first) marriage, which is a subject of continuing debate. We know from the literary sources that there was often a considerable difference in age between husband and wife in the propertied classes, so that young women who survived childbearing could expect to outlive their husbands: Cornelia (*mat. Gracchorum*) bore her much older husband eleven children whom she effectively reared alone,[40] while Cato censor's second wife survived him with an infant (Plut. *Cat. mai.* 24). Pliny was unable to produce a full-term child with his young wife Calpurnia before his death in Bithynia. Yet in an age of frequent remarriage, this did not necessarily protect women from a death which was early by our standards, as in the case of Cicero's daughter Tullia, who outlived her first husband and divorced her second but died as a result of childbirth at about the age of thirty soon after divorcing her third husband (Plut. *Cic.* 41.7). While Hopkins contests the basis of Burn's calculation of a median age of death of 27 for women in the Roman empire,[41] he does not dispute that this was approximately correct.

Hopkins' (1965a) study established that upper-class girls generally married very young, usually before they were sixteen. It is not known whether peasant and poor urban girls married so early. Isolated inscriptions — like *CIL* VI 16592, to the nurse Crispina, dead at thirty, erected by her husband Albus in commemoration of their seventeen years of married life — show that early marriage was known in the lower classes, but there are suggestions that poor girls generally married in their later teens.[42] Early mortality meant that Roman society must have abounded in widows and widowers, who would have been quite young by our standards. Spouses proudly proclaimed the length of their marriages on tombstones, not only because they had avoided divorce but because they had cheated death for so much longer than they had any right to expect. Ideals of conjugal loyalty and harmony were seldom put to the test of time imposed by modern Western longevity. Ten or fifteen years of marriage constituted a great proportion of the ancient life span.

Relations between parents and children could be radically affected by life chances. A bride who survived the dangers of reproduction until her husband's death might have greatly increased her life expectancy, especially if she did not remarry.[43] In a society where prestige accumulated with age, this could leave the mother in a position of authority within her family. It is perhaps no coincidence that the mothers held up for admiration by Roman authors — Volumnia, Cornelia, Aurelia, Julia Procilla[44] — were widows. Such women could have been the medium for redistributing wealth between the generations. As we shall see in Chapter 3 ('The maternal relationship and Roman law'), the mother would pass on her own property to her children eventually, in the form of dowry or inheritance, but might in some cases have been the heir of her husband's property, so that she enjoyed its use for her lifetime before passing it on at her death to their common children. This would necessarily enhance the authority of a mother well into her adult children's life.

Scholars from other disciplines have speculated on the implications for inheritance practices of probable patterns of life expectancy and reproduction within families.[45] Hopkins (1983: 245) and Veyne (1978: 36) have pointed out the significance for a Roman of the timing of a father's death. Those citizens whose fathers survived into their sixties might have had a lengthy period of economic dependence which affected other relations, while many Romans must have become *sui iuris* ('independent') at an early age, so that property would be administered by a *tutor* until they attained puberty.[46]

The timing of a mother's death would also make a great difference to a child's upbringing. The fact that childbirth was so dangerous also meant that many Romans grew up without a natural mother from birth or early childhood. Again, literature provides several instances: Cicero's grandson Lentulus,[47] Seneca's mother Helvia (*ad Helviam* 2.4) and Pliny's wife Calpurnia (e.g. Plin. *Ep.* 4.19.1; 8.11.1). Where the mother died at birth or soon after, a wet-nurse — usually employed in 'respectable' society in any case (Bradley 1986) — became essential for the new baby's survival. So even if the nuclear household was the norm, Romans must in fact have known a variety of family forms and children probably became attached to a number of individuals at successive stages of their lives. Quintilian, gratified that his (then deceased) son had preferred his father to any others, enumerated those who figured in the motherless child's life (*Inst. Or.* 6 *pr.* 8). When Seneca wrote to a friend whose infant son had died, he reproached the friend for mourning a baby as yet better known to his nurse than his own father (*Ep. Mor.* 99.14). Others, like Seneca's mother Helvia, were reared from childhood by a stepmother and perhaps grew up with half-siblings.

Tombstones likewise testify to the number and diversity of relationships available to Roman children. *Tatae* and *mammae* — possibly foster-parents — figure alone or with natural parents as dedicators and as objects of dedications.[48] Children could be celebrated by a relation (other than a parent) and a nurse:[49] one imagines that if the child had lived it would have been reared by them, or at least by the relation, even if the nurse were not regarded as permanent. The role of other figures, termed variously *nutricii, nutritores* or *educatores*,[50] is not always clear but indicates the variety of arrangements which might be invoked if a child could not conveniently be reared by its natural parents.

It would be unwise to speculate too freely on the emotional implications of this diversity. Wet-nursing appears to have been enmeshed in the system of patronage and most upper-class children, however attached to their nurses as infants, will have learned quite early to view them from a social distance (cf. Gathorne-Hardy 1972: 78-9), often tinged with affection and a sense of condescension. The provisions made for their nurses by Pliny (*Ep.* 6.3) and others (*CIL* VI 10229) suggest this patronal role, as does the inclusion of a nurse in the tomb of the Cornelii Scipiones (*CIL* VI 16128). Fronto's contemptuous picture of the typical nurse, who prefers her charge to remain young and dependent (*Ep. ad Ant.* 1.5.2 — Naber p. 102), reflects this social distance, while the faithful ministrations of Nero's nurses to his remains (Suet. *Nero* 50) confirm the nurse's viewpoint as affectionate *clientela*. It was the social status, not the nurturance, which determined the future relationship. Cato censor intended his slave's children, nursed by their mistress, to be particularly bound to his son as they grew up.[51]

It is difficult to generalise from the types of arrangements to the emotional character of bonds between the parties. Even blood relations could vary in their attitudes to children assigned to them. Phillips (1978: 74-5) has pointed out the contrast between the letter written by Pliny to his wife's aunt and the one to her grandfather after the young bride's miscarriage. Calpurnia seems to have spent most of her life with her paternal aunt and grandfather, presumably after her parents' death or divorce. To judge from the two letters (*Ep.* 8.10 and 11), Pliny expected the aunt to be concerned about the young woman's health and the grandfather to be requiring an explanation for her failure to complete the pregnancy satisfactorily. In that case, the aunt seems to have been the responsible but affectionate figure, while the grandfather performed a more distant role as guardian of family continuity.[52] Livia and Augustus, who apparently maintained close contact with their grandchildren, extravagantly mourned the loss of their favourite at an early age and dedicated a statue of him to a temple on the Capitol.[53] As grandmother of Claudius, on the other hand, Livia made no secret of her cold contempt for him (Suet. *Claudius* 3), while Augustus unhesitatingly banished his adulterous grand-daughter Julia and had her child exposed at birth (Suet. *Aug.* 65).

The vagaries of existence made it likely that a Roman child might grow up with mother or father or both disappearing at some stage, to be replaced by a relation or step-parent as the adult who took primary responsibility for its upbringing. There seems no rule of thumb for determining the attitude of such adults to their charges. Divorce, warfare, provincial commands and exile or sale (at opposing ends of the social scale) could also introduce abrupt changes to the life of a child. In terms of modern notions of emotional security this may seem ominous but the large household inhabited by the aristocratic or slave child might have provided some compensations by its very size and internal diversity. The sternest mother, *paedagogus* or grandparent could be offset by an indulgent cook or aunt. Life must have been grimmer for the orphaned or unwanted children of the free-born poor, though even they were sometimes absorbed into households and relations which veered between the patronal and the familial.[54] The history of C. Melissus, exposed as an infant, who eventually became director of the two libraries in the porticus Octaviae,[55] provides a success story which was surely rare. Exposure was the obvious recourse for the improverished. Other children left undefended on the death of one or both parents would simply be left to die or absorbed into less promising housholds and put to work, for we know that poor children commonly worked from an early age even if they were free-born and had both parents living (Bradley 1985b: esp. 326-9).

Conclusion

Kinship obligations at Rome varied somewhat between the social classes but the basic residential unit of the nuclear family was the primary focus of obligation. At the same time, demographic factors — particularly mortality patterns — and the circumstances of slave life imposed a certain flexibility on Roman family patterns. It would seem that the Roman child, even within the lower social echelons, often had a variety of relationships available. That is, the mother-child bond was seldom as predominant as in modern Western practice. Although mothers seem to have retained stronger links with children than fathers in slave families, there is no evidence of an overriding regard for the bond between mother and child which might have limited the sale of young slave children. Nor is there any indication that slave mothers were particularly likely to breast-feed their own children. Again, this suggests that the intimate association between mothers and infants or very young children taken for granted in our own society was not necessarily the basis of the maternal bond in ancient Rome.

At the same time, family feeling is evident in all social groups. Slaves and freed slaves sometimes went to considerable lengths to commemorate relations from whom they had been separated by sale (Rawson 1966: 79), and parents lamented the premature death of small children, in spite of a general tendency to view infant death as normal. Yet circumstances could affect the expression of family solidarity: infant exposure seems to have been practised fairly casually; some *libertini* fathers might not have commemorated their slave-born children (Treggiari 1969: 212-13) and many parents went uncommemorated by their children. Women, especially as wives, were under-represented on sepulchral inscriptions, as were dead infants (Burn 1953: 45; Hopkins 1966: 261-2: Huttunen 1974: 59-61). There was great variation in the practice and interpretation of *pietas* to the dead and there are numerous exceptions to these general tendencies. There is ample evidence from inscriptions that parents were fond of their children and regarded it as a great blow to be predeceased by them. Literature also shows that family life was prized and children appreciated at least from the very late Republic. Yet these attitudes seem to have been contemporaneous with a resistance to marriage in the upper class which Augustus saw fit to combat with legislation, and a chronic difficulty of the lower class in rearing children.

The Roman family thus consisted of a range of people: mother, father and children comprised the basic unit, but it readily stretched to include foster-parents, slaves or friends where circumstances required it. The system of reciprocal obligation and affection within these groups was determined by a range of factors, material and sentimental, and linked with the status of the parties and their stage of the life cycle. Thus the child Pliny might have had a very different relationship with his nurse from that of the adult patron who bestowed a farm on her; and Cato's son might have played as a boy with the slave *collactei* (foster-brothers) who owed him respect in their adulthood; while adult children separated from an aristocratic mother by marriage or military service continued to pay her respectful and affectionate visits. The mother's position within the upper class would often have been enhanced by her widowed status and command of property. In the slave family, the mother might have been the focus of family feelings of solidarity. Mothers seem to have had an important role, but probably not the specialised and exclusive care of small children.

Notes

1. As in Cic. *Fam.* 14.4.4 *de familia liberata*, on the sale of slaves. Cf. Solidoro (1981). Crook (1967a: 98) points out that *familia* could signify the slaves of a business outside the domestic sphere proper, as in the expression *familia publicanorum*, although the distinction between 'domestic' and 'business' is seldom a strict one in non-industrial societies. Thomas (1976: 411-12) also discusses the different meanings of family, concentrating on the juristically significant unit of the *paterfamilias* and those in his power. Saller (1984b) is important for the social definition of *'familia'*.

2. Some have argued that the archaic Roman family consisted of the joint agnatic household of three generations, notably Westrup (1939, 1941).

3. *Dig.* 29.5.1.15 (Ulpian) records the ruling that if either husband or wife were murdered by a slave of their household, the slaves of both must be held to account 'because the *familia* is mixed up and constitutes one household': *quia commixta familia est et una domus.* The *Senatus Consulta Silanum* and *Claudianum* discussed in Chapter 5 of *Dig.* 29 specified that punishment applied only to those slaves 'beneath the same roof' — *sub eodem tecto* (29.5.1.26-7: Ulpian) — obviously *familia* could have been interpreted as including slaves on widely separated estates.

4. Perhaps also with an allowance. Cf. Cic. *Att.* 11.2 on Tullia as a young matron. For the age of women at first marriage, see Hopkins (1965a) and Lawler (1929), although recent work by Saller and Shaw suggests that lower class girls in the Roman empire married somewhat later than their élite counterparts. Literary evidence such as Cic. *Att.* 1.3 and Plin. *Ep.* 1.16.6 supports an early age at first marriage for upper-class girls in Rome.

5. As Octavian was — Nicolaus 5. Pliny's third wife was reared by her paternal aunt in her grandfather's home — Plin. *Ep.* 4.19.

6. Cf. Goody's remarks (1969: 234-9) on this line of reasoning.

7. Vinogradoff (1920 vol. 1, Chapters 5 to 7, esp. pp. 204-5, 256); de Zulueta (1953: II. 36). Pomeroy (1976) shows a better appreciation of the 'dual loyalties' which coexisted with agnation.

8. As demonstrated by their liberation from 'paternal power', *patria potestas* and the fact that they did not occupy a place in any network of intestate succession — Gai. 1.145; Aul. Gell. *NA* 1.12.

9. Suet. *Tib.* 2 (who says it was her brother's triumph). Cf. Cic. *Cael.* 34; Val. Max. 5.4.6.

10. Plut. *Cat. min.* 3.1 has the story of children accepting Sulla's son as leader because of their regard for his mother, Caecilia Metella; Tacitus *Agric.* 4 reckons his father-in-law's distinction from the male and female side.

11. One's father's brother was an *agnatus*, one's mother's brother a *cognatus* — Gai.1.156.

12. Some would say, over-represented — Frank (1916); Taylor (1961) — but cf. Rawson (1966: esp. p. 83) and Brunt (1971: 121-2, 387 ff.). Cic. *Off.* 3.47 and Suet *Aug.* 42 assume a large foreign element of servile origin in Rome in the late Republic and early Empire. Vell. Pat. 2.4.4 implies this was already true by the late second century BC.

13. See Rawson's (1986b) discussion and (1974: 279 n2), where she quotes from Last (1923: 231): 'The new ideals which had come in from the East where home life was hardly known, overlaid on the Roman reluctance to suppress the female sex, ended in the spread at Rome of a moral licence which finally destroyed its victims.'

14. Other examples cited by Rawson (1966: 79) are *CIL* VI 26755 (Daphne, sold before her first birthday); *CIL* VI 23151 (C. Nummius Mercurialis, freed by his tenth birthday); *CIL* VI 18886 (Gargonia Valentina, freed in a separate household by her eleventh birthday). Bradley's chapter on the slave family (1984) also shows the separation of slave mothers and children.

15. *Mil. G.* 697. Compare *CIL* VI 29116 to Aelia Helpis, *mamma* to the dedicator Ianuaria and her husband Ulpianus, both *vernae*, slaves born in the household (but see Chantraine (1967: 125-7) on the term).

16. E.g. *CIL* VI 26008. *CIL* VI 29191 was erected to M. Ulpius Felicissimus (three years) by his imperial *libertinus* father, his mother Flavia Phoebas and his *nutricii* M. Ulpius Primigenius and Capriola. *CIL* VI 12366 was dedicated to Cn. Arrius Agapetus — three years, 45 days — by his mother, father, *mamma* and *nutrix*.

17. As in *CIL* VI 26008, where the *libertina* Scetasia commemorates her *mamma* Musa before her mother Thais.

18. Just as élite half-brothers and sisters maintained close links in spite of being reared in separate households, e.g. Plut. *Brutus* 1-2; Cic. *Att.* 14.20.2; 15.11 (Brutus and the Iuniae); Cic. *Fam.* 5.2.6 (Mucia and Metellus Celer *pace* Wiseman (1971)).

19. See Flory (1975: 28-30) and *CIL* VI 21599, cited by Rawson (1966: 77), who suggests that the brother's and sister's status was determined by a change in the father's status between their births.

20. That is, current and former slaves; compare Weaver's (1972) observation that slaves tended to marry within that group — pp. 179-95 (Chapter 11).

21. Cf. the terms '*mamma*', '*tata*' and '*collacteus*', predominantly of lower-class usages. Consider *CIL* VI 36353 with *liberti mamma* and *tata*; *CIL* VI 14720 by a slave *mamma* to a slave child.

22. And see Flory 1975: 28-9 and n22 p. 50.

23. Sen. *de Matrimonio* 58 (frag. 13, Haase 1972: vol. 2) presents the continuation of the lineage as a commonplace justification of marriage which he refutes on philosophical grounds. This could be expressed, as in English, as concern for the survival of the family name.

24. See Chapter 4 for a summary of the terms of the laws. Csillag (1976) has a full account. Brunt (1971: 558-66) and Wallace-Hadrill (1981: 60-2) argue persuasively that the measures were not seriously directed at the peasantry or the free urban poor. Cf. Nörr (1981), des Bouvrie (1984)

25. See Geiger (1970). Saller (1984a: esp. 195) points out that the limitation of upper class families was probably intended to prevent excessive segmentation of estates. Cf. Musonius 15 and see Corbier (1985).

26. Cf. Ryder (1959: esp. 411-12) for the more prosperous social groups within a society limiting fertility, and Bogue (1969: esp. Tables 3-6, pp. 77-8) for the ranking of whole countries by wealth and fertility.

There is some evidence of a slow reduction in the negative relation between income and fertility, long taken as a commonplace by demographers, but the trend is barely discernible and, thus far, evident in metropolitan areas of highly industrialised countries. Compare the UN report *Recent Trends in Fertility in Industrialized Countries*, Population Studies no. 27 (NY 1958), Adelman (1963).

27. See Corbett (1930: 68-90); Crook (1967a: 103); (1986: 61); Watson (1967: 19-25). If the *paterfamilias'* wife were in his *manus*, she would be in a position of dependence comparable with that of her own children.

28. Eventually, a father who killed a grown child without calling a *consilium* was liable at law — *Dig.* 48.8.2 (Ulpian). From Constantine's time it became *parricidium* to kill one's child — *C. Th.* 9.13.1. See Thomas (1976: 414-18).

29. See Corbett (1930: 53-5); cf. *Dig.* 23.1.7 (Paul, giving his own view and citing Julianus); *Dig.* 23.1.12 (Ulpian); 23.2.2 (Paul).

30. See *FV* 116; Paul *Sent.* 5.6.15 (referring to a decision of Antoninus Pius); *CJ* 5.17.5, recording a decision of AD 294, citing an earlier one by the emperor Marcus.

31. This was a later, imperial development — *Dig.* 49.17.11 (Macer).

32. Cf. Rabello (1979). Daube (1969: 75-91) rather over-argues the extent to which the financial powers might have been tempered in practice.

33. In fact, the boy had died but his mother concealed this from her ailing husband until his own recovery — Plin. *Ep.* 3.16.

34. *Att.* 10.11.3; 10.6.2 (Quintus' 'softness'); 13.37.2 (on young Quintus' criticism of his uncle).

35. quibus incensus parens potuerit animum inducere, ut naturam ipsam vinceret, ut amorem illum penitus insitum eiceret [ex] animo, ut denique patrem esse sese oblivisceretur. (*Rosc. Am.* 53) and cf. *Dig.* 5.2.15 (Papinian).

36. *Att.* 6.2.2: ac mihi videtur matrem valde, ut debet, amare. Compare *Att.* 6.3.8.

37. As in the example of Brutus' marriage to Porcia against his mother's wishes — *Att.* 13.9.2; 22.4; young Quintus Cicero's support of Caesar — *Att.* 14.19.3. Compare Cicero's examples of 'bad' sons whose misguided political leanings were not to be held to their decent fathers' accounts — *Att.* 10.4.6.

38. Cic. *Att.* 15.11 and compare *ad Brutum* 1.18.1. From exile, Cicero could count on the support of his wife Terentia — Cic. *Fam.* 14.5 — and brother Quintus — *Q. fr.* 1.3.7 — as well as his brother-in-law and friend Atticus (e.g. *Att.* 3.9.3; 3.11.2) and son-in-law L. Calpurnius Piso Frugi — *post Red.* 7-8 (where Cicero lists the support and trials of various relations). When Favorinus and his followers visited an acquaintance whose wife had just given birth to a child, they found her mother in attendance — Aul. Gell. *NA* 12.1.5 ff. Seneca speaks of the support he gained in his candidacy for public office from his mother and aunt — *ad Helviam* 14.3; 19. Pliny *Ep.* 1.14.7 refers to the burden which a man's candidacy for office could impose on his wife's relations. Interestingly, I was unable to find an example of a parent being comforted by children for the loss of a spouse. Arria's married daughter and son-in-law took her

in when her husband Caecina Paetus was condemned, and Seneca speaks of the comfort Marcia should derive from her married children and grandchildren after the death of her (adult) son, but that is not quite the same.

39. See esp. his Table I, p.16, for the consequences of his method. This was to record the ages attained by half a 'cohort' who had all reached an earlier age — thus, of those who had lived to 15 at Lambaesis, half of the males subsequently survived to age 45, while half of the females survived to age 38.

40. Plut. *Tib. Gr.* 1. Only three survived to adulthood.

41. On the ground that the number of women commemorated was not representative, as can be illustrated by comparative figures — Hopkins (1966: 261-2).

42. Compare Burn 1953: 12-13; Weaver (1972: 105-7). Shaw (1987) argues that lower-class women in the Roman empire tended to marry relatively late — probably in their late teens and sometimes even the early twenties. The age of peasant girls at first marriage has been discussed by Brunt (1971: 136-40), den Boer (1973 and 1974) and Hopkins (1974). They raise different possibilities but there is not enough information to draw any firm conclusions.

43. On this, see Burn (1953: 11-13); Hopkins (1966) Figures 3 (p. 257) and 4 (p. 258).

44. Mothers of Coriolanus (Plut. *Cor.* 33-6), the Gracchi (Plut. *Tib. Gr.* 1; *C.Gr.* 19); Julius Caesar (Tac. *Dial.* 28) and Agricola (Tac. *Agric.* 4) respectively. See Chapter 5.

45. E.g. Goody (1973), especially the appendix pp. 16-20; Wrigley and Schofield (1981).

46. Notionally twelve for girls and fourteen for boys. Women then remained *in tutela* unless (after Augustan legislation probably dating from 18 BC) they had the 'right of children', *ius liberorum*, but this form of *tutela* was much less restrictive than *tutela impuberum* ('guardianship of young children'). Women *in tutela* actually administered their own property — Gaius 1.189-91. See Chapter 4

47. *Att.* 12.28; 30. His parents' divorce would have meant that he, like Augustus' daughter Julia, would not have been reared in his mothers' household in any case.

48. E.g. *CIL* VI 38638a by *parentes et mamma* to Galatia, or *CIL* VI 29634 to Zethus by his *tata* and *mamma*.

49. As in *CIL* VI 20938, by a grandmother and a *nutrix*.

50. E.g. *CIL* VI 5405 by Euhodus and Evander to their *nutricius* Ti. Claudius Epaphos; *CIL* VI 8925 by Alexander to a fellow imperial freedman, Pallas, his *nutritor*; and *CIL* VI 13221 to an *educator*. See Bradley (1985a) and Chapter 6.

51. Plut. *Cat. mai.* 20.5 and compare *CIL* VI 16057, to the slave child who was *collacteus* to the son of Rubellius Blandus. Nero's punishment of his nurse's son was listed by Suetonius with crimes against his 'connections' — Suet. *Nero.* 35.5. Cf Treggiari (1976; 103 and n50). See above all Bradley (1986).

52. Although his great grandchild would not, strictly speaking, have belonged to his lineage. Compare the provisions made by Cicero for his

grandson Lentulus, noted in Chapter 3. Again, we see that the emphasis on family did not coincide with the legal priority of descent through males.

53. Suet. *Gai.* 7. Augustus also had a statue of the boy in his bedroom.

54. See esp. Rawson (1986c) on the formal and informal status of *alumni*. George Eliot's short story 'Mr Gilfil's Romance' provides an entrancing parallel in the portrait of the girl Caterina taken up by Sir Christopher and Lady Cheverel:

> He loved children, and took at once to the little black-eyed monkey — his name for Caterina all through her short life. Neither he nor Lady Cheverel had any idea of adopting her as their daughter, and giving her their own rank in life. They were much too English and aristocratic to think of anything so romantic. No! the child would be brought up at Cheverel Manor as a protegée, to be ultimately useful, perhaps, in sorting worsteds, keeping accounts, reading aloud, and otherwise supplying the place of spectacles when her ladyship's eyes should wax dim — p. 152 Penguin edition (1980, Harmondsworth) of *Scenes of Clerical Life*, edited by D. Lodge.

Cf. Martial 5.37 and inscriptions such as *CIL* VI 11592 by Pedania Primigenia to four-and-a-half-year old Ampliata, her '*verna karissima*'. These were children born to slaves of the household.

55. Suet. *Gramm.* 21. He was eventually manumitted.

3

The Maternal Relationship and Roman Law

I argue in this work that the position of respect and authority of the Roman mother emanated in part from her effective power of disposition over her fortune, especially in the case of widows who assumed responsibility for a young family. Of course, this general argument needs some qualification. Most Roman families had little or no property to pass on and it is likely that children of the urban poor enjoyed the greater independence generally characteristic of those whose labour is their fortune. But the Roman social and legal system institutionalised the power of the older generation in all classes by *patria potestas* which, though seldom exercised to its full extent, guaranteed a position of respect to the *paterfamilias*. The position of the mother had no such legal reinforcement but she was ideally the object of respect and affection from her children throughout her life. Most of us like to think of sentiment and self-interest as distinct categories but they tend to overlap. There are few cultures in which a dependent poor relation is treated as respectfully as one of whom others entertain 'expectations'. However unconsciously, this was surely a component of that *pietas in matrem* stressed by the literature. Thus it is not surprising to find a wealthy widow like Brutus' mother Servilia being respectfuly heeded by her adult children (Cic. *Att.* 15.11).

Roman children normally expected to inherit and to attain juridic and economic independence on the death of their fathers. The material benefits they might look for from their mothers fell into three categories: testamentary inheritance of the mother's own property, inheritance from the father of the mother's dowry along with the rest of the paternal estate, and inheritance from the mother of goods left to her by her husband on the understanding that she would transmit them eventually to the children. None of these categories constituted a legal entitlement. At law Roman mothers had no obligation to leave their estates to their children nor did they have any automatic right to inherit from children who died intestate. In this chapter, I explore the relationship between the formal, written law, the praetorian code (*ius honorarium*) and the force of convention.

Law can be a rarefied system with little relation to everyday practice or commonly held beliefs about what is right. This is more likely to be the case in a system, like the Roman, in which the laws of an earlier day are held in reverence and there is great reluctance to amend or revoke them, so that they represent the values of a past age. It need not matter if people are able to manage their affairs without going to law, but the disparity can be exposed when conflict forces a recourse to the machinery of the law. This rarely happens in purely personal relations — Roman mothers did not, for example, bring actions against sons for visiting them infrequently — but when family feeling and property are associated, as in inheritance and dowry practices, the law can be forced gradually to keep pace with current notions of propriety. This is the sequence discernible in successive pronouncements on inheritance between mother and child in Roman law. Inheritance rules would clearly affect the wealthy more than others but it is probable that the same process was enacted on a lesser scale within the peasant and shop-owning classes. Although by our lights the operation of Roman law was status-conscious, it extended in principle to all Roman citizens, and therefore gives a general guide to social standards. Thus a *libertina* (freed slave) mother lacked complete freedom of testamentary disposition, and had to observe certain obligations to her former owner and his family, but these were eventually balanced against her children's claims to her estate in the later interpretation of Augustan laws encouraging maternity (Gai. 3.43-4).

Roman law was essentially casuistic. Not all cases mentioned in Justinian's *Digest* are necessarily historical but many which are attended with apparently authentic circumstantial detail indicate that significant legal decisions could be based on cases involving litigants of relatively modest means. The examples of this chapter are drawn largely from the literature of the élite, but it is reasonable to suppose that the attitudes to material obligation expressed in legal contexts reflect more general views within Roman society of the relationship between mothers and children. We examine in detail below the historical development of rights of intestate hereditary succession between mother and child and their significance. I look in addition at the areas in which a mother's effective powers exceeded her formal entitlement. This chapter is therefore an analysis of the Roman mother's powers, rights and material obligations within the family — both as defined at law and as conceded by custom.

The impressive authority of the Roman *paterfamilias* can distract attention from the reality. I am not suggesting that the authority of the mother was equivalent to *patria potestas*, ('paternal power') but it is important to look carefully at the force of convention, which apparently tempered the exercise of paternal authority and gave to the mother many effective rights which had little or no basis in formal law. The interplay between social and legal processes necessitates some technical discussion but I have kept this to the minimum required for illumination of the theme of maternal authority, since I have dealt in other works with detailed aspects of the legal position of Roman women.[1]

I have, for example, assumed the testamentary freedom of adult women *sui iuris* ('independent') as the background to the examples I cite, for I hope to demonstrate through them that by the late Republic social expectations were a more significant limitation on women's wills than the formal requirements. These were the permission of the *tutor* of the testatrix and the ritual sale (*coemptio*) which women had to enact before the testamentary procedures proper. Neglect of these formalities would cause the will to fail.[2] The system of *tutela* — often translated as 'guardianship' — applied traditionally to all women who were not in the power of a father or the control of a husband. It was originally a means of safeguarding the family property and a woman's *tutores* were likely to be her intestate heirs. By the late Republic, fewer married women followed the procedures which placed them and their property in their husbands' control. Instead, married women became *sui iuris* on their fathers' death and acquired a *tutor* or *tutores*, but even if these *tutores* were brothers and heirs of the woman *in tutela*, they acknowledged her duty to pass the bulk of her estate on to her children. *Libertinae*, freed slave women, passed into the *tutela* of their former owner (if the owner was male) who probably did exercise his right to monitor his erstwhile slaves' wills[3] but free-born women seem to have been able to dispose of their property as they wished, provided that they went through the proper forms.[4]

In principle, then, a Roman woman was always under some form of masculine control, even if independent of her husband and father. In this sense she resembled the women of classical Athens.[5] In practice, however, the term 'guardianship' was quite inapplicable to her. A Roman matron, whether legally in the power of her husband or father or *in tutela*, had a certain status of respectability as mistress of the household[6] which was enhanced if she became a mother and further elevated if she became a widowed mother. This hierarchy is reflected in changes introduced to the law over time. To trace such developments to their conclusion I must sometimes step outside the time frame of this work. Change was very gradual in Roman law, particularly family law. We sometimes find in Christian legislation the first formal acknowledgement of practices attested by authors of the first and second centuries BC.

The legal relationship between mothers and children

Lex duodecim tabularum ita stricto iure utebatur et praeponebat masculorum progeniem, et eos qui per feminini sexus necessitudinem sibi iunguntur adeo expellebat, ut ne quidem inter matrem et filium filiamve ultro citroque hereditatis capiendae ius daret, nisi quod praetores ex proximitate cognatorum eas personas ad successionem bonorum possessione unde cognati accommodata vocabant.

(*Inst.* 3.3. *pr*)

So rigorously did the law of the Twelve Tables observe the rigid rule of giving preference to issue by males and of rejecting those who were related to a person through the female line that there was no mutual right of taking each other's inheritance even between a mother and her son or daughter save in so far as the praetors would summon such persons to the succession, through the closeness of their cognatic relationship, by the possession of the estate styled 'as cognates'

(trans. from Thomas (1975))

This preamble to the revised version of the Hadrianic senatorial decree, *senatus consultum Tertullianum*, states clearly the traditional legal view of the relation between mother and child at Rome: legitimate children belonged to the descent group of their father. They inherited his gentile (family) name, his family rites and his property — even if the father died intestate. Such children were agnates of the father and of *his* paternal relations, and it was this agnatic link which had greatest legal significance (Paul *Sent.* 4.8; *Inst.* 3.3.3; *Dig.* 38. 7-9). The mother's 'blood' relationship was acknowledged, but given the general designation 'cognate' which covered purely formal *and* blood ties. It was always deemed the lesser for purposes of intestate hereditary succession. Thus a mother stood further from her children in the succession hierarchy than their paternal uncle or his children. This situation was altered if a woman entered her husband's (or father-in-law's) *manus* (literally, 'hand') on marriage by means of *usus, confarreatio* or *coemptio*:[7] she thereby virtually relinquished all claim to her patrimony and extinguished the ties with her natal family, who were henceforth only her *cognati/ae*. She then stood in line to succeed to her husband — on his intestate death — on equal terms with her children, who were also her agnates.

Until the mid-Republic, Roman women tended to take this step, but as the trend shifted it became increasingly common, then almost universal, for women to retain their natal status. Roman brides by the very late Republic generally remained *in patria potestate* ('in their father's power') or *sui iuris* ('independent') after marriage, depending on whether or not their fathers were alive. This meant that the situation was as described in the preamble to *Inst.* 3.3, and mothers and children had only a very distant claim on each others' estates on intestate death, since they belonged to distinct inheritance networks. The intestate heirs of such a woman were her brothers and sisters, or her brothers' children, not her own offspring.

This seemed shocking to the Byzantine compilators looking back on it, but, as so often, the stark description of the written law is only part of the story. The sentimental bonds between husband and wife and parents and children were strengthening from this late Republican period (Lucretius 3.894-6; Tac. *Ann.* 3.33.4; Val. Max. 5.7; Appian *BC* 4.3.12ff) and, to an extent, ties of property sealed this strong acceptance of the nuclear, conjugal unit as the primary focus of loyalty. In her 1976 study, 'The relationship of the married woman to her blood relations in Rome', Pomeroy argued that the legal status of the Roman matron went full circle over some four centuries to place her firmly in her husband's family. In this chapter I focus on the matron as a mother. I compare her links with siblings and husband in her own generation, and concentrate on her legal obligations to her children. My view is that it was the bond between mother and child, expressed particularly in inheritance, which occasioned change in the law. These changes themselves seem to reflect long-standing conventions of the responsibilities and privileges of the Roman mother.

The tendency for women to retain formal membership of their own natal families after marriage and the greater frequency of divorce from the second century BC did not prevent a growing feeling that a woman's 'natural heirs' were her children rather than her brothers' children no matter what form of marriage she had followed — and in spite of the fact that friction between husband and brother-in-law could dissolve the marriage bond.[8] We examine below the evidence for this development, but it is worth noting that such a trend could hardly have gained general currency without the compliance of patrilineal relations. The agnatic line of succession had been safeguarded in early Roman law by the institution of *tutela mulierum perpetua* (perpetual tutelage of women), whereby the intestate male heir(s) of a woman could oversee any major transfer of property from their inheritance network, since his/their permission (*auctoritas tutoris*) was required for her to promise dowry or pass into the *manus* of her husband (who thereby became owner of all she possessed) or to make a will (Ulpian *Tit.* 11.3 ff; Gai. 1.144; 192; Zannini 1976: I.72 ff; Crook 1986b: 84-5). These relatives — usually brothers — were termed agnatic *tutores* and were the intestate heirs of the woman *in tutela*.

Women of the late Republic who remained legally in their natal family were still governed by this system after marriage, and needed the permission of a *tutor* to institute their own children heirs. An agnatic *tutor* was therefore virtually cutting himself off from his 'rightful' inheritance — in traditional terms — by giving such authorisation. In fact, many women might by now have been *in tutela* of some man from outside the family (a *tutor extraneus*). The possibility had existed from at least the time of the Twelve Tables that a man could in his will name a *tutor* for the children in his *potestas* or a wife in his *manus* (*Tab.* V.3; Gai I. 144, 148). A 'testamentary' *tutor* (*tutor testamentarius*) had less authority at law than a so-called statutory *tutor* (*tutor legitimus*: such as an agnatic *tutor*) but his permission was still essential for the validation of a woman's testament. The increasing popularity of such *tutores* over agnatic *tutores* also suggests that family expectations were shifting, and the woman's natal relations were relinquishing the traditional custodial responsibility for her estate. A classic instance of this process is furnished by Cicero in *Verr.* II. i. 111, where the wealthy Sicilian Annaea instituted her daughter heir after consulation with her relations.[9] Cicero mentions the consultation to show that Verres' ruling on a similar case was not taken seriously as a precedent. The idea of men gathered in a family *consilium* to endorse the diversion of a substantial inheritance to the child of a female relation is not singled out for comment.

The widowed mother's life interest

Any attempt to discern patterns of succession within the Roman family soon uncovers the figure of the widow who inherits her husband's estate, or a large part of it, on the understanding that she will pass it on to their common children on her death — what might be termed a dowager's life interest in her deceased husband's holdings.

Two of the very few early examples of mothers' testamentary dispositions are provided by Polybius 31. 26ff in his account of Scipio Aemilianus' services to his family. Polybius reports Aemilianus' gracious gift to his married sisters of the estate bestowed upon him (alone) by their mother on her death in 159 or 158 BC (Polyb. 31.28. 7-9). The mother, Papiria, had long since been divorced from Aemilianus' father Aemilius Paulus (Macedonicus) and Aemilianus, like his full brother, had been adopted into another noble family. These steps, like the marriages of Papiria's daughters (which probably entailed transfer to the husbands' *manus*)[10] extinguished the legal bonds between mother and children, but Papiria seems to have come to some arrangement with her son to pass on her estate to her daughters after her death. Polybius represents it as an act of spontaneous magnanimity by Aemilianus, but the sequence of events suggests rather that he was behaving in accord with his mother's express wishes — though as a disinterested and responsible family member. If it had been a straightforward inheritance, she could have named both sons or all four of her children as her heirs, rather than her wealthiest child.

Scipio Aemilianus had already shown himself to be suited to

such a task on the death in 162 BC of his adoptive grandmother Aemilia, who had also instituted him heir. Together with the estate, he inherited the debt of his adoptive aunts' remaining dowry payments and he won great acclaim at Rome, Polybius tells us, by passing on this obligation in a lump sum before the husbands expected it. Given that the marriages had both taken place some years before — one almost twenty years earlier (Mommsen 1879: 489-91; Carcopino 1928: 47-83; Moir 1983) — it looks as if this dowry was in fact due to be paid on Aemilia's death, whenever that occurred, rather than at a specific time. Although it is never stated, the implication is that Aemilia had been *in manu* of her husband Scipio Africanus maior (Polyb. 31.26.3; Dixon 1985a: 157).

This kind of arrangement, whereby the widow was the husband's official heir and then passed on the joint parental estate to their children on her death, recurs in the literary and legal texts and might well have enhanced the authority a widowed mother wielded over her adult children. Aemilia probably had little to pass on from her own fortune[11] but in other cases the wealth from such a combination could be great. If the mother were her husband's principal beneficiary and a woman of substance in her own right — as was often the case in the élite of the late Republic — she would have control of great wealth, subject only to the conventions of proper transmission. Such an arrangement would necessarily be determined by testament: a wife *in manu mariti* ('in her husband's "hand" or control') would succeed on equal terms with her children (but in practice would probably have her dowry or its cash value restored to her as well)[12] if the rules of intestate succession applied.

The testamentary arrangements which conferred property on widows varied somewhat. Aemilia in effect had the use of part of her daughters' portion for life. Cicero tells us of the will of Fulcinius, a banker of Tarquinii who instituted his son heir but bequeathed to his wife Caesennia the usufruct or use of the whole estate. This meant that mother and son would share the income and administration of it for her lifetime. In this case she did not have the right of disposition, for the son's succession was specified (Cic. *Caec.* 11-12). It so happened that her son predeceased her but Cicero spelled out the idea behind the arrangement, that she should share the fortune with her son, who would inherit *her* estate in due course (*Caec.* 12; Frier 1985: 13-14).

Compare the case of Murdia, who was celebrated in a lengthy

epitaph by her oldest son. She had enjoyed a life interest in that son's patrimony. He was the son of her first marriage. He emphasised that in singling him out for a greater share of his estate she was not displaying favouritism over his half-brothers and sister but saw to it that he should take specific property because she was:

> mindful of my father's generosity and determined to render to me the fortune which she had accepted from my patrimony by her [first] husband's considered disposition with the intention that it should be restored to my ownership after she had kept it in custody and enjoyed its benefit.[13]

This arrangement had not been endangered by Murdia's remarriage, but step-parents were sometimes viewed as a threat to the rights of children of the first marriage. In Africa, the rhetorician and author Apuleius was accused of bewitching his older wife, Pudentilla. Although Apuleius claimed that Pudentilla's elder son had first suggested the match to *avoid* her property's loss to an unscrupulous second husband, Apuleius was subject to the same suspicion (*Apol.* 71-2).

Overwhelmingly in classical literature, stepmothers were regarded as evil and terrifying in a way not paralleled by the reputation of stepfathers. And yet some children might well have feared for their patrimony on the mother's remarriage. This was the sentiment behind the prosecution. Apuleius was at pains to insist that, far from endangering his stepsons' inheritance, he had agreed to a relatively modest dowry (*Apol.* 91) and had exerted himself to smooth over the differences between the two young men and their mother Pudentilla (*Apol.* 93). In this case, it was Pudentilla's personal fortune which was at stake rather than an estate she had received from her first husband to hold in trust, as it were. Technically, she was free to dispose of her holdings as she wished but Apuleius' wariness was probably induced not only by the influence of his opponents but by an apprehension that public opinion and the authorities would be inclined to side with the 'wronged heirs' in such a dispute. Valerius Maximus 7.7.4 recounts a similar case in which a woman, Septicia, who had quarrelled with her two sons, had disinherited them in favour of her second husband. As a result of their appeal, Augustus overturned the will on the ground that the marriage, between two elderly people, had not been properly constituted — not having been undertaken for the purpose of producing children — and gave the sons the right to inheritance *and* Septicia's dowry, which would normally have become the property of the husband on his wife's decease.[14]

Eventually it became the rule under the Christian emperors (in AD 392) that a woman with children who inherited a lifelong usufruct of his patrimony from her husband had to cede the property to his children if she remarried (*CJ* 5.10.1). Again the underlying idea seems to have been that she was the trustee of the children's estate rather than heir in her own right. It was not unknown for stepfathers to adopt a quasi-paternal role, but on the whole children tended to be relinquished by the woman when she remarried. Even with the change in marriage forms, the children of any legitimate marriage remained in the father's descent group and married women lived with their husbands for the duration of the union — which generally meant that a widow who remarried ceased to be directly involved in the daily expenses and administration of her children's upbringing.

That some widows at least were intended to hold part of the deceased husband's estate in trust for life — or until remarriage — is clear enough, although the firm examples are few and scattered. It is possible that some of the influential widowed mothers who figure in the biographies of great men derived their authority in part from this financial advantage. In practice, conventional expectation placed a strong onus on the mother, whether or not she had inherited from the husband, to favour her children in her own will (e.g. Val. Max. 7.7.4; 7.8.2) and the formal law came increasingly to enforce the principle that anything acquired from her first husband should not go to her second, but to her children from that first marriage. None the less, the power of disposition — however unlikely to be wielded capriciously — existed, and the fact that some husbands gave their wives such power is indicative of the esteem in which Roman matrons could be held. In most Greek states, *sons* would have been more likely to have been granted such a holding power over the estate on the understanding that they support their mother from it.[15] In the Roman case, the husband had no testamentary obligation to his wife and it must have been a token of personal confidence to entrust her with his estate.[16] The presumption of Roman practice, that the widow could be expected to maintain inherited capital for transmission to the next generation, suggests a greater general confidence in female administrative capability than was current in, say, classical Greece or Victorian England.

Maternal *officiositas*: testamentary conventions

In Chapter 2 we noted Cicero's insistence that the onus lay on Roscius' accusers to demonstrate what frightful sin he had committed to merit the exclusion from his father's will which they alleged against him. The formulation of the demand is melodramatic, but underlines the gravity with which Romans regarded exheredation.[17] The passage refers to a father's will. A Roman *paterfamilias* could have *sui heredes* — children or grandchildren in his *potestas*, ('power') or a wife or daughter-in-law in his *manus* ('hand' or 'control') — who had a definite claim on the estate[18] and must be expressly exheredated in his will if it was to be valid. This did *not* apply to mothers, who had no *sui heredes*, and therefore had no statutory obligation to explain or even to refer in their wills to the omission of certain parties (*Inst.* 2.13.7). This is not to say that mothers were in practice at liberty to leave their estates wherever they inclined: social pressure and the law gradually combined to lay down certain ground rules. Valerius Maximus makes it clear that any mother who did not give her children due consideration in her will was open to criticism. He tells us (7.8.2) of one women whose will was quite mad (*plenae furoris*) because she instituted only one of her two daughters heir, although both were equally respectable and she had no complaint or obligation which might have justified such a step. Even the grandchildren by the less favoured daughter received a small proportion of the substantial estate. He implies that the unfortunate daughter would have had a good case if she had wished to challenge the will, and sees her refusal to take it to court as further evidence of her filial piety and therefore of the injustice of her treatment. Valerius Maximus clearly felt that mere caprice and personal preference were insufficient grounds for excluding obvious heirs:

> moved by personal inclination rather than impelled by any specific wrongs or filial services of one daughter

> animi sui potius inclinatione provecta quam ullis alterius iniuriis aut officiis conmota

> (Val. Max. 7.8.2)

The inference that the exclusion might have been justified if the mother had suffered some wrong at the daughter's hands is not quite in accord with the decision of Augustus already noted in the case of Septicia's testament, which was declared void. The sons with whom she had quarrelled were awarded possession (Val. Max. 7.7.4).

Modern legal textbooks make much of the freedom of testamentary disposition in Roman law but the ancient sources suggest that conventional notions of rightful inheritance influenced judicial interpretation. Valerius Maximus, Pliny (*Ep.* 6.33) and Apuleius all convey the impression, for example, that stress on the influence of a designing stepmother or stepfather would arouse the prejudices of a praetor or *iudices* in one's favour. In pronouncing on whether an appropriate legal action lay to an aggrieved relation who wished to object to a will, the urban praetor had to justify his judgement in terms of existing legal means. There was no statutory sanction against an improper disregard of ties by a testator who observed the proper testamentary forms but by the late Republic praetors allowed a formal complaint against an undutiful will (*querela inofficiosi testamenti*). This legal remedy could be granted even where the testator had drawn up a valid will. It was rationalised by the legal fiction that in such a case disregard of propriety was tantamount to insanity (Watson 1971: 62-70), so that the will could be voided. Certainly the cases cited by Valerius Maximus 7.7-8 were based on the concept of undutifulness rather than technical failure of the will (Renier 1942: 82-106). This type of case developed into a more coherent legal process in the early Empire, but it had its origins in the Republic. Its chief application was to wills in which parents or children excluded each other, even — as in the case of an emancipated or adopted child or of mothers and children — where there was no clear right of succession on the rules of intestacy. This reflects the community feeling about the priority of certain relationships. The fact that no legal claim of undutifulness could be upheld against a spouse's will shows that the conjugal tie was not seen as imposing the strong mutual obligations implicit in the relationship between mother and child (Cf. Marcellus, *Dig.* 5.2.5.).

The inheritance tax introduced by Augustus was not applied to heirs to a paternal estate. The emperor Nerva later extended the exception to succession to maternal estates and a mother's succession to her children. Pliny the younger approved of this because, he said, people were more likely to resent government inroads on property inherited from close kin which they had always viewed as theirs by right (*Pan.* 37.2). This reasoning is reminiscent of the later argument of classical jurists such as Paul that *sui heredes* could be said to be coming into their own in succeeding to the estate of a deceased *paterfamilias* (*Dig.* 28.2.11, quoted in n18 to this chapter). The rights upheld in the exceptions are those between brothers and sisters (*Pan.* 39.1), parents and children, with deliberate — but not wholesale — relaxation of formal distinctions of status (*Pan.* 37.3) and kinship (37.6) in favour of the family ties acknowledged by common consent as imposing the strongest mutual rights and obligations.

The literary sources from the late Republic to the Flavian period make it apparent that children were expected to succeed to their mothers. In some cases at least, disappointed children appealed to the courts, with reasonable success. The developed law of the post-classical code — presumably based on decisions and 'opinions' from such cases — eventually spelled out the principle that children who did not receive one quarter of the maternal estate were entitled to bring a suit as long as they could establish that they had always behaved properly towards their mother (e.g. *C. Th.* 2.19.2, AD 321). This put children's rights to the maternal property (*bona materna*) almost on a par with their rights as *sui heredes* to the estate of a deceased *paterfamilias*. A maternal will which excluded children for no good reason was therefore *inofficiosum*. The imperial decision of AD 321 is in perfect accord with the assumption of Val. Max. 7.8.2, but the fact that the rescript was issued suggests that it required authoritative formulation.

The maternal bond was also accommodated in the rules governing succession on intestacy, but they had to be balanced against the statutory emphasis on the rights of *sui heredes* and agnatic relationships. Justinian's compiler remarks of the vaguely defined 'earlier' period that the praetor could award intestate succession between mother and child only under the rule of *unde cognati*, that is, the general category embracing any relations, blood and legal, whose claim was relatively weak (*Inst.* 3.2.3-3b; Ulpian, *Dig.* 37.8, esp. 1). Where a mother had not been in the *manus* of her children's father, their relationship was deemed more distant than that of the nearest agnates. This meant that a woman's brother or sister (her *consanguinei*) would have first claim on *her* estate and if one of her (fatherless) children died intestate the other children would have a claim prior to hers. Just as the importance of the mother-child bond was slowly acknowledged in cases involving undutiful wills, so it was granted recognition in cases of intestacy — but by a slow and partial historical process. Justinian's author tells us that Claudius had been the first to take pity on a mother deprived of propertied children. The wording of *Inst.* 3.3.1[19] suggests that he imposed a general ruling on the subject which was more carefully defined under Hadrian in a senatorial recommendation, the *senatus consultum Tertullianum*, to be followed in AD 178 by another, the *senatus consultum Orfitianum*, which granted a limited right of succession by children to the estate of a mother who died intestate.

The second-century rulings were tied to the Augustan grant of privileges (*ius liberorum*) to citizen mothers and only a free-born woman with three children or *libertina* mother with four had the benefit of this consolation for the loss of her children (*solatium liberorum amissorum*). The children had the right of maternal succession without such qualification. In both cases (i.e. mother-child or child-mother succession) the rights of closer agnates, as traditionally defined, superseded these newly elevated cognate relations. Thus a child, sibling or father of a deceased person would take the estate before her/his mother, but a mother would not take precedence over a paternal uncle. In the case of the children's succession to a mother's estate, the agnatic rules were more thoroughly undermined: her children took precedence even over her brothers and sisters. For a time, there was an inconsistency, and uncle and children probably shared the estate.[20] The Justinianic amendments went further towards honouring virtually all cognate ties, but it seems from the wording that even under the emperor Marcus, the mother's 'natural heirs' were emphatically her children rather than her brothers and sisters. The hereditary hierarchy to be extrapolated from these second century rulings is thus:

1. father/grandfather → children *in potestate* (or even emancipated)/wife *in manu*
   (and child → father, if the child had been emancipated)
2. brother → sister/sister → brother/sister → sister (except in the case of a deceased sister with children or grandchildren of her own)
OR: mother → child
3. child → mother

This was in contrast to the XII Tables system, still transmitted in the post-classical sources (e.g. *Dig.* 38.6-8; Gai. 3.1 ff), which was:

1. father/grandfather → children *in potestate*/wife *in manu*
2. brother/sister → brother/sister
3. to paternal uncle
4. to paternal uncle's children
5. to children of one's own brothers
6. if none of the above exist: to the *cognati*, such as mother-children/children-mother and so on through the maternal line, i.e. the mother's agnates

Such wills as we know of in the two centuries (and more) preceding this legislation suggest that the hierarchy had already existed long before in the popular mind: that the mother-child bond was seen as a primary one in terms of economic dutifulness and that this notional primacy had little to do with juridic definitions of the relationship. This can be seen not only from decisions and discussions about wills but occasionally with reference to the dowry. We have already noted that Papiria and Aemilia (maior) in the second century BC left their estates, in one way or another, to their children — though not to all children equally.

The best documented cases of maternal inheritance in the late Republic are those of Cicero's first wife, Terentia, and their daughter, Tullia. In 47 BC, when Cicero had fallen out with Terentia, but before their divorce, he expressed outrage at the terms of her new will, which he felt would endanger their daughter's economic security (*Att.* 11.16.5; 23.3). On being criticised two years later for his own will, Cicero countered that he had shown a finer sense of family duty than she had done, as if the duties of mother and father were analogous (*Att.* 12.18a). When Cicero and Terentia were divorced, they reached an agreement on the property which should be extracted from her dowry of thirty years before for their surviving child, Marcus. It seems from the correspondence that Marcus received the income from a block of flats as his allowance.[21] Tullia's death meant that there was no necessity to include her in wills or dotal settlements, but she had left an infant son. He was provided for by Cicero, after negotiations with the father, Dolabella, who retained 'custody' in modern terms (*Att.* 12.28.3; 30.1) and was apparently included in

Cicero's new will (*Att.* 12.18a.2). Tullia had almost certainly been a *filiafamilias* until her death, and incapable of owning or disposing of property in her own right: Cicero had made these dispositions on her behalf and they constituted succession by her child to property from her lineage.

In the case of Terentia's divorce, the terms of settlement might have been determined in principle during her father's lifetime, but she conducted the detailed negotiations with Atticus (acting for Cicero) and composed her own will in 47 BC — and possibly again in 45 BC, after the death of her daughter — according to her personal preference. There was evidently room for difference as to what constituted a just disposition — Cicero had thought her 47 BC will shocking (*Att.* 11.16.5) — but both sides apparently acknowledged the mother's duty to her children, regardless of whether she remained married to their father, and did not consider this duty discharged by the dotal settlement. A mother was expected to provide from the dowry for her children on divorce (even if there was no question of fault) *and* to include them in her testament on reasonable terms. It was on the definition of 'reasonable', not the basic question of obligation, that argument centred.

When Augustus voided the will of Septicia (Val. Max. 7.7.4) he not only awarded her estate to the sons she had tried to pass over, but gave them the dowry which would otherwise have passed automatically to her widower. He thus affirmed the right of legitimate issue to the *bona materna* and implied that the dowry only passed to the surviving husband so that he in his turn could transmit it down his line to their children (Val. Max. 7.7.4; cf. *CJ* 5.9.5 — AD 439). Thus, although this discussion concentrates on the practice and law concerning testamentary and intestate hereditary succession to the mother's property, it should be borne in mind that the dowry was also a form of mother-child succession, which does not always figure in the relevant texts.

The mother was apparently not expected to pass on her estate in strictly equal portions to all her surviving children. We have seen that Papiria named Scipio Aemilianus as sole heir, although she had four children, and that she probably intended him to pass the estate on to his two sisters, who were not as rich as he. The '*laudatio funebris Murdiae*' mentioned above praises Murdia for her impartial regard for the children of both her marriages. Yet further reading soon reveals that her *aequalitas*, or 'impartiality', is not all that we might imagine it to be. The sons were all instituted heirs, with the daughter being assigned a *legatum parti-tionis hereditatis* — that is, an equal share of the estate without the full status of heir.[22] We have seen that the son who erected the inscription was singled out for specific properties — not from unreasonable favouritism, but because they were due to him from his deceased father's estate.

In this way husband and wife could pass on some goods direct to their children and others to the surviving spouse on the under-standing that it would all eventually find its way to those chil-dren. Murdia had used property from her first husband which she passed on to her son, and her surviving husband would presumably pass on the dowry to *their* children on his death. Technically, his own children could only accept the inheritance with his authority and he remained its owner at law if they were *in patria potestate*; so in a sense even the direct inheritance was theirs only because he allowed it to be. The inscription is generally dated to the Augustan era by its orthography. The sentiments and practices it embodies fit well into the emerging pattern of maternal succession.

In a similar case mentiond by Pliny (*Ep*. 4.2), young Regulus had been instituted heir in his mother's will on condition that he be emancipated to take the inheritance in his own right, but there is no suggestion that this was normal practice. Indeed, Pliny implies that it reflects discredit on his enemy, Regulus senior, although this need not be seen as an objective judgement (cf. Plin. *Ep*. 8.18.4; Papinian, *Dig*. 35.1.70). It is possible that by this period some children *in potestate* had effective use of a *peculium*, a personal fund to which they could add property gained by inheritance on the understanding that it was, *stricto iure*, the property of the *paterfamilias*, but would be assigned to the appro-priate child in his will (cf. Rabello 1979: I. 207-8; Crook 1967a: 110). In general a woman who was survived by her husband and a child from that marriage had to rely on the husband's good faith to ensure that he pass on her property and her dowry to that child. Even the stipulation that the child first be emancipated to take the maternal estate presupposed the father's co-operation.

Pliny *Ep*. 7.24 provides us with an excellent insight into the concept of dutifulness. It concerns the dispositions of the near-octogenarian Ummidia Quadratilla, who died leaving an honourable will (*decessit honestissimo testamento*), despite the fears of her relations. Although given to a lavish personal style, this woman showed after her death that she had a proper appreciation of family feeling by leaving her grandson two-thirds of her estate and her granddaughter the remaining third, while the sycophantic legacy-hunters gained trifles. Pliny approved heartily (7.24.8), although his effusions suggest that she would have been entitled to leave her estate elsewhere. Yet Pliny, who praised the unexpected family piety of Ummidia Quadratilla and of Domitius Tullus (*Ep.* 8.18) and himself inherited estates from his mother and father alike (*Ep.* 2.15; 7.11.5), was instituted heir, together with several other 'outsiders' (*extranei*), by one Pomponia Galla, who passed over her adult son entirely. When appealed to by the son, Pliny agreed to consider the whole question. In general he favoured the observation of the testator's wishes (*Ep.* 5.7.2; 4.10.3), even in the case of slaves, who had no right at strict law to make testamentary dispositions (*Ep.* 8.16.1), but it emerges, especially from *Ep.* 8.18 and 7.24, that he felt strongly that family ties should, *ceteris paribus*, take precedence. In this case, there was a conflict which Pliny appears to have approached in a disinterested manner. He summoned two distinguished advisers and considered the son's case in council with them. They concluded that his mother had disinherited him for good reasons. In the end, the son managed to wrest a compromise from the heirs and gain rather more than a fourth part of the estate by a settlement out of court (Plin. *Ep.* 5.1).

The interesting thing is that Pliny's attitude and the private *consilium* reflect both the procedure and the assumptions of the *querela inofficiosi testamenti* which was then taking its classical form (Sherwin-White 1966: 313; 399) and which Valerius Maximus (7.8.2) had taken to apply in the case of the two daughters unjustly distinguished by their mother. Justinian's *Institutes* (2.13.7) spell out the formal position, that a mother or maternal grandfather need not disinherit children by name or formula, as a *paterfamilias* must do for his *sui heredes*, but Pliny twice employs the expression *exheredatus* ('disinherited') of Pomponia Galla's son, as if she had committed a positive action — contravened a rule — in failing to include her son in her will. The *principles* expressed in the developed law on undutiful maternal wills had been current long before (cf. Corbier 1985).

The statutory provisions on the *querela inofficiosi testamenti*, on second marriages and on intestate succession between mother and child, though formulated at different periods, demonstrate similar guiding principles. Children were taken to have a right — eventually — to the dowry given by the mother's family to the father, to the prenuptial gift (*donatio ante nuptias*) customary in the later Empire from the groom's family to the bride and to the estate acquired by the wife from her deceased husband by testament. This right was specifically protected against the encroachment of a stepfather or stepmother, but it was not usually realisable in the mother's lifetime unless she violated the rules on remarriage — again, a later provision, where the Christian emphasis stressed the importance of the widow's mourning period (*tempus lugendi*) which Augustus had tried to shorten (Cf. Humbert 1972: 378-87). The concept of *inofficiositas* was applied to the dispositions of mother and father alike. The jurists made a point of stressing the difference when defining the classes of heirs. Where a *paterfamilias* could have *sui heredes*, a mother's heirs were different, as were the children instituted heirs by a father who had emancipated them (Gai. 2.161) and we have seen that the freedom of a mother or maternal grandfather to institute or pass over children was reaffirmed in the *Institutes* 2.13.7. The general expectation was none the less that mothers, like fathers, would and ought to pass their estates on to children unless the children had behaved so disgracefully as to forfeit their birthright.

This notion is built into various headings of the codified imperial law: the most obvious is *de inofficioso testamento* (*C. Th.* 2.19.2; *Dig.* 5.2; Paul *Sent.* 4.5; *Inst.* 2.18 (*pr*); *CJ* 3.28.7). An eligible relation who claimed to have been passed over unjustly might be awarded the intestate portion by the court, but no claim could be brought by somebody who had received at least this amount (one-quarter of the disputed estate) by testament. The claim was pursued before the praetor, who could grant an action for possession of the estate (*bonorum possessio contra tabulas*). It could also be pursued by a mother excluded from her child's will (e.g. *C. Th.* 2.19.2). There was a similar action, developed later, for appeal against an 'undutiful dowry' (*C. Th.* 2.21). The burden of this title is actually similar to that of the titles on second marriages (*C. Th.* 3.8; *CJ* 5.9): that a widow not promise or give as dowry to her second husband an amount such that the mandatory three-twelfths of her estate due her children be put at risk. The provisions went further — as we have seen in the earlier discussion on dowry — and obliged the woman to pass on to her children at her death all property she had from their father, her former husband, whether acquired as *donatio ante nuptias* (a bridal gift), *donatio mortis causa* (a gift in anticipation of one's death) or by testament.

Yet, although children as a group had this claim on the mother's estate and to that part of the patrimony which she enjoyed for life, it was repeatedly stated that she had the right to distinguish between her children. Such distinction was assumed to be on proper moral grounds, but the burden of proof rested on the complaining child to demonstrate that she/he was *not* undutiful to the mother, while a mother passed over in a child's will was subject to investigation but not required to prove her merit in quite the same way. It is difficult to know how much to make of this: fathers could also distinguish between their children, although the moral pressure on them to include all of the children for a minimum share seems to have been greater, as is reflected in the rules of intestate succession granting equal rights to all children *in patria potestate* at the time of the testator's death.

There are instances of wills which award greater shares to the sons than to the daughters, although it is uncertain whether this is because daughters had already received dowry (cf. *Dig.* 37.7), because of the feeling that a senatorial male had greater expenses to meet[23] or because, as in the case of Scipio Aemilianus, the male was expected to carry out an executive function under the title of heir. In Murdia's will, the daughter received the same amount as her full brothers, but they were named heirs, which meant that they would have the task of dividing the estate, paying for the funeral and settling debts. Aemilianus actually passed on the whole of his mother's estate to his sisters (Polyb. 31.28.7-9).

In a very restricted sense mothers — and by extension grandmothers or maternal grandfathers (Plin. *Ep.* 7.24; Cic. *Att.* 7.18a.2) — were expected to 'do the right thing' by their progeny in general but this might not have involved the more demanding notion of impartiality applied to paternal wills. Even Ummidia Quadratilla's praiseworthy will assigned her granddaughter one-third and her grandson two-thirds. Perhaps this slight liberty was the one genuine effect of the legal dictum that mothers did not have either to institute or expressly exheredate children, as fathers did. Neither was quite as free to make dispositions outside the immediate family as legal theory would suggest and in general the force of custom was such that mothers and fathers alike were fairly unlikely to pass over children lightly. The law gradually enforced this convention, chiefly through praetorian intervention in the late Republic and early Empire. At the same time, the popular notion of succession between mother and child was incorporated in statutes governing intestate succession.

Spheres of maternal authority

At law, a Roman *paterfamilias* had the right of life and death over his children, the right to select their marriage partners and the right to administer his children's property and to appoint a *tutor* for this task in his testament. Mothers had none of these powers and responsibilities. That is, *stricto iure*. A closer examination reveals a numbr of exceptions and qualifications to this bare legal statement.

(i) Rights over progeny

The Roman *paterfamilias* had the *ius vitae necisque* over his legitimate children. The usual exercise of this would have been the decision to rear or to expose new-borns, although there are instances of fathers executing adult children for serious offences (such as adultery by daughters or treason by sons) — usually after a meeting of the family council.[24] Mothers had no such right. Marriage, whether or not involving transfer of the wife to the husband's power (*conventio in manum*), conferred rights in the woman's progeny on the father (or *his* father, if still alive). The mother might have had a right to sit in on family councils, but she had none *as* a mother to determine whether her child should live or die. The chief implication of this would be that she had no right to abort a legitimate child — or to use contraception, which might not have been seen as differing from abortion (Hopkins 1965b: 136-7). References by Seneca (*ad Helviam* 16.3), Favorinus (Aul. Gell. *NA* 12.1.8) and Juvenal (6.595-7) to the frivolous avoidance by society women of the dangers to health and beauty of pregnancy have been accepted at face value by scholars in the past (Nardi 1971: 199-201 n1). Abortion might have been the recourse of the adulterous upper-class matron, but it is moot whether she would have risked the indignation of a husband and his family by wilfully aborting *legitimate* issue without his permission. It is in the nature of the subject that we can never arrive at a firm conclusion. Cicero's allegation (*Clu.* 34) that a widow was bribed by the father of the husband's secondary heir to have an abortion is typical. It must have been based on self-interested gossip passed on by Cicero's client. Seneca (*ad Helviam.* 16.3) and others refer to abortion disapprovingly as the common practice of unnamed selfish society women. It is clear that abortion was viewed with distaste by moralists and unlikely to have been discussed openly by women with men. The generalisations are therefore very difficult to assess as evidence.

There was a tradition that the law of Romulus forbade abortion. Plutarch (*Rom.* 22.3) refers to the ancient rule that a woman who dispatched a husband's child with a poison or medicine could be divorced. Dionysius of Halicarnassus spoke of φθορὰ σώματος (2.25.6) as a marital offence. This could mean either adultery or abortion. Nero accused his estranged wife Octavia of having an abortion to conceal an adulterous affair (Tac. *Ann.* 14.63). The implication is that a wife procuring an abortion in secret would be seen as usurping the husband's right over his legitimate offspring *or* covering up adultery. It would be helpful to know whether husbands ever instructed their wives to abort children as a means of family limitation, but the sources, moralising and sensational, do not convey information of this kind. Whether women at Rome were ever charged with the offence as a crime is difficult to say.[25] A woman who killed her own children, once born, ought to have been subject to the usual rules of murder, unlike their father, but the evidence is sparse. The exposure of illegitimate infants would presumably have presented no problem since *spurii* were not *in patria potestate* and the mothers (or *their* fathers) had rights over them (Gai 1.64, 78; cf. Suet. *Aug.* 65 and Norden 1912: 27 on Apul. *Met.* 6.9). There were no legal strictures against abortion as such in our period. It was suspect because of its association with adultery and because it suggested female inroads on a male preserve — that of deciding the fate of legitimate issue (cf. Cic. *Clu.* 32).

(ii) Children's marriages

Children *in patria potestate* required the assent of the *paterfamilias* to make a valid marriage. The law makes no mention of the mother's permission until the *Codex Theodosianus* (9.24). Yet a glance at the literature soon dispels any impression that marriage was a purely paternal decision. Apart from the classic tale of Scipio Africanus maior being upbraided by his wife Aemilia for failing to consult her about the betrothal of their daughter Cornelia to Tiberius Gracchus,[26] which suggests that consultation with the mother was deemed reasonable, the letters of Cicero and Pliny convey the impression that a wide network of relations and friends was involved in arranging a match. Tullia's third marriage had such people as Servilia and Pontidia fielding candidates, and Cicero and Atticus considered the merits of them all. In the end, the choice of Tullia and Terentia prevailed (*Att.* 5.4.1; 6.1.10; *Fam.* 8.6; *Att.* 6.6.1; see Collins (1952)). Young Quintus Cicero offended both his parents, who were then divorced but apparently united in an unwelcome insistence that he should marry a particular lady (Cic. *Att.* 13.42.1). Pliny's advice was sought on the question of a husband for the niece of Iunius Mauricus (*Ep.* 1.14). Cicero speaks of the women of one family rejecting a suitor because of his relative lack of wealth (*Att.* 13.28).

All of this suggests that women in general played a part in arranging matches. Some mothers are represented as particularly active. Aemilia, daughter of Caecilia Metella and stepdaughter of Sulla, was divorced from her current husband and married off to Pompey to seal Sulla's recent political union with him at the instigation, so we are told, of Caecilia Metella (Plut. *Pomp.* 9). Servilia, mother of Brutus, appears to have had a hand in all her children's marriages and was incensed when Brutus divorced one wife and threw in his lot decisively with the Catonians by marrying Porcia (Africa 1978: 614; Syme 1939: 58, 69; *contra*, Hillard 1983). Sassia, who conceived an illicit passion for her stepson and nephew, forced her daughter to divorce him so that she could marry him herself, according to Cicero (*Clu.* 14). The Julio-Claudians abounded in dynastically minded mothers — such as Livia and Agrippina minor, who encouraged the intermarriage of their offspring with those of their imperial second husbands. Thus the right of a mother to determine a child's marriage was social rather than legal and a mature child might even successfully defy her wishes, but it is part of the overall authority of the Roman mother that she played an important part in such negotiations which was eventually recognised in the law although the father's authority remained virtually absolute in theory.[27]

(iii) Mother as tutor [28]

One of the most interesting developments in the rights of the Roman mother is her very gradual assumption of power to administer business for her children. Republican law had distinguished between the function of the *tutor impuberis*, who managed the affairs of a child below puberty too young to manage her/his own property, and of the person who brought the child up, who would commonly be a widowed mother with children rendered *sui iuris* at an early age by the death of their father. Such children seem generally to have lived with the mother unless she remarried. The power of the *curator*, initially an optional assistant at the transactions of those below 25 years but above puberty, gradually grew (de Zulueta 1953: II. 52-4) so that young people might be governed in their business affairs by a *tutor*, then advised by a *curator* and overseen throughout by the mother who lived with them.

Cic. *Verr.* II.i.105-6 furnishes an interesting picture of the division of function in the late Republic. The child Annia had been named heir in her father's will, although his estate had been sufficient to warrant inclusion in the first property class and therefore make him subject to the Voconian Law which forbade testators of that class to institute female heirs. The reversionary heir had appealed to Verres, as governor of Sicily, and Verres had approached the girl's mother with a view to making an agreement of some kind. She seems to have referred the matter to the girl's *tutores*, who decided cautiously that they could not risk such a proceeding — apparently fearful of the examination to which they would be subject when the girl Annia reached puberty. Here we have the difference set out for us: the mother was the one directly concerned with the girl's upbringing, but she had no power to release a capital sum to bribe Verres, who proceeded to enforce the Voconian provision.

Yet some mothers appear to have overseen their children's affairs conscientiously. Seneca praised his mother for her careful and disinterested administration of her fatherless children's fortunes.[29] The classical jurists, commenting on the operation of the *senatus consulta Tertullianum* and *Orfitianum*, repeatedly stated (e.g. Ulpian *Dig.* 38.17.2; *Inst.* 3.3) that it was a mother's duty to apply for a *tutor* for her pre-pubescent children. Failure to provide them with one deprived her of any right of intestate succession to their estates. Interestingly, Ulpian had dealt with the question 'What if the father had forbidden her to petition for a *tutor*, on the ground that he wished them to have their affairs managed by the mother?' To which the answer was, that she must none the less be excluded, since a mother could not exercise true *tutela* (*Dig.* 38.17.2.25). This is analogous to the later ruling, expressed with suspect syntax, that *tutela* was essentially a masculine affair.[30]

Perhaps, but the question was clearly arising as to whether a mother might not administer her own children's finances. As we have seen, some forms of husband-wife inheritance seem to have given her this right in practice — Aemilia's fifty talents and Murdia's unknown amount, both to be passed on to the children on the mother's death; and, in time, the ruling that all dowry and acquisitions from a particular husband must eventually be transmitted to his children (e.g. *C. Th.* 2.19-21; *CJ* 3.28-30).

By AD 390 the law bowed to this variously recognised idea and yet another antiquarian principles was laid aside: a mother who swore that she would not remarry was given the right to become *tutrix* of her children (*C. Th.* 3.17.4; *CJ* 5.35.2,3; Humbert 1972: 410-13). Again, it is noteworthy that the law took precautions against the possibility of inroads by a stepfather — the provision is reminiscent of the insistence in the titles 'On second marriages' (*De secundis nuptiis*) and 'On undutiful dowries' (*De inofficiosis dotibus*), that children must not be deprived of their birthright — a mother was apparently assumed to have the interests of her children at heart only if she was free of the influence of a wicked stepfather. In spite of the slight softening of the law on the question of gifts between parents and children, the Roman law generally retained its traditional suspicion of sentiment interfering with propriety in the matter of exchanges between spouses[31] and the suspicion was keenest when there were stepmothers or stepfathers who might scheme to divert estates from their proper recipients to themselves or their own children.

Conclusion

> In primitive societies, whether they have matrilineal or patrilineal institutions, it is normally recognised that the closest of all kinship bonds is that between mother and child.
>
> (A.R. Radcliffe-Brown 1950: 77)

This review of legal developments, extending at times beyond the usual second-century AD limit of this work, reveals a very gradual hardening of custom into law. The status of the mother, originally defined in terms of her agnatic relation to the children, was gradually recognised in its own right, both for purposes of intestate succession between mother and child and for claims of improper testation. This in spite of the fact that jurists continued to parrot the principle that mothers and those related through the maternal line had no specific obligation to include children and grandchildren in their wills. Convention insisted that the bond between mother and child was a fundamental one which had little to do with legal technicalities such as agnatic vs. cognate relationship. The dissolution of the marriage between parents did not exonerate mothers of the duty to provide for the children of that marriage from their own estates. We have seen that dowries formed part of the inheritance from mother to child, whether settled on (adult or young) children at the time of divorce or passed on with the estate of the widowed mother at her death or by the widower father as part of his estate on his death.

Other aspects of the mother's authority or rights over her children were determined by a similar admixture of convention and law. Neither seemed to award her any say in whether her children should live. That was a matter for the father's line, unless the children were unquestionably illegitimate — in which case, it was a matter for the mother's line, that is, her father, rather than her personally. That a married woman had no right to abortion is clear, although it is questionable whether legal remedies were employed, beyond the possibility of a plea of justifiable divorce by the husband.

In other respects the mother's authority seems to have been upheld by convention. Her right to participate in the choice of a child's marriage partner is taken for granted in the literary sources and eventually acknowledged in the legal texts of the later Empire. Her part in the administration of her child's finances seems to have been recognised at different levels, social and legal. It was by no means unusual for husbands to bequeath to their widows their whole estate or a sizeable portion of it on the understanding that they would manage and enjoy it for life, then pass it on to the common children of the marriage. Such an expectation could not originally have been enforced, but came gradually to be strengthened by legal judgements on the nature of the undutiful will and rulings on the rights of children subsequent to their mother's second marriage.

It is possible that wealthy Roman widows thus exercised particular authority over their children for an extended period, on the strength of their notional freedom to distinguish between them in the eventual disposition of the patrimony *and* the maternal estate. The estates of small children *sui iuris* were a different matter. Such children were financially independent of their widowed mother but would have lived with her, and the scant evidence suggests that she came to be seen — and to see herself — as the obvious person to administer their affairs in their best interests, although remarriage was apparently deemed to throw her disinterestedness into peril.

Notes

1. E.g. Dixon 1984a, 1984b, 1985a, 1985c and a monograph currently in progress on women and property (*Wealth and the Roman woman*).

2. Cic. *Top.* 18; *Fam.* 7.21 on the need for the *tutor*'s permission. After Augustus' legislation of 14 BC and AD 9, women with the right of children (*ius liberorum*) no longer required a *tutor* for any purpose. Vestals had always been exempt from *tutela* — Gai. 1.145. The requirement of the *coemptio* ceremony for women making wills was waived in the second century AD under the emperor Hadrian — Gai. 2.112; 118-22.

3. He was classified as a statutory *tutor*, a *tutor legitimus*, and had certain rights because of the social recognition of the bond between a former slave and owner — Gai. 1.192; 2.122; 3.43.

4. See (Dixon 1984a: 345-6) for a full exposition of this argument.

5. Athenian women were under κυρία, which is also described by most authors as guardianship. A Greek woman's κύριος could be her father, brother or husband. See Schaps 1979: Chapter 4, esp. pp. 48-9, 52-8.

6. Cf. Cornelius Nepos, *praef.* to *de Exc. Duc.*:

For what Roman would blush to take his wife to a dinner party? Or whose wife does not occupy the position of greatest honour in the home and join in social functions?

quem enim Romanorum pudet uxorem ducere in convivium? aut cuius non materfamilias primum locum tenet aedium atque in celebritate versatur?

Cornelius Nepos contrasts this with the Greek custom of his own day (*c.* 99-24 BC).

7. Corbett (1930: 71-90). *Coemptio* was probably the more common method by the late Republic. It involved a ritual sale of the woman (Gai. 1.113). The same ceremony was a prerequisite for free-born women other than Vestals making a will. *Usus* was the traditional mode whereby a woman who spent a whole year under her husband's roof entered his *manus* automatically. An absence of three consecutive nights within a year ensured against this consequence (Wolff 1939; Watson 1967: 19-23; 1976; 1979; Gai. 1.111). *Confarreatio* was an ancient religious ceremony which became very unusual by the early Principate (Tac. *Ann.* 4.16; Gai. 1.136)

and was probably confined to those families with an interest in holding certain priesthoods (Gai. 1.112; 136 — Krüger's reading).

8. Consider the conflict between Clodius and Lucullus (Plut. *Lucullus* 34; Dio 36.14) and the recurrent difficulties between Quintus Cicero and Atticus (esp. Cic. *Att* 1.17.1). On this, see Hallett (1984) 174-80, Dixon (1985b) 369-71.

9. 'In his nuper Annaca de multorum propinquorum sententia, pecuniosa mulier, quod censa non erat, testamento fecit heredem filiam.'

10. Both Aemiliae lived in the homes of their fathers-in-law. One, Aemilia Tertia, married an Aelius Tubero, and lived within an extended household — Plut. *Aem. P.* 5.6; Val. Max. 4.4.9. The other lived with her husband and Cato censor — and later, Cato censor's second wife and child — Plut. *Cat. mai.* 24.

11. Her brother had only a modest fortune (Polyb. 31.22; Cf Liv. *Per.* 46) and she had been married at a stringent time, soon after her father had fallen at Cannae.

12. Val. Max. 4.4.9 and Polyb. 18.35.6 suggest that this was usual by the second century BC. Cic. *Top.* 23 states that all property of a woman *in manu mariti* was classified as dowry — which seems to mean that it was liable to return on the dissolution of the marriage.

13. The son makes it clear that a monetary evaluation of the goods in question had been made and the mother consulted about the arrangement which constituted a charge on her good faith ('*fideicommissum*'). Lines 7-13 follow:

MIHI REVOCATA MEMORIA PATRIS EAQVE IN CONSI-
LIVM ET FIDE SVA AD | HIBITA AESTVMATIONE FACTA
CERTAS RES TESTAMENTO PRAELEGAVIT | NEQVE EA
MENTE QVO ME FRATRIBVS MEIS QVOM [E]ORVM
ALIQVA | CONTVMELIA PRAEFERRET SED MEMOR
LIBERALITATIS PATRIS MEI | REDDENDA MIHI STATVIT
QVAE IVDICIO VIRI SVI EX PATRIMONIO MEO | CEPIS-
SET VT EA VSSV SVO CVSTODITA PROPRIETATI MEAE
RESTI | TVERENTVR

CIL VI 10230 (*laudatio Murdiae*)

14. Cf. Plin. *Ep.* 6.33, in which Attia Viriola appealed against her exclusion from her father's will after his remarriage. Pliny tells us the hearing at the Centumviral Court was avidly followed by stepmothers and stepchildren eager to hear the decision (4: 'magna exspectatio patrum, magna filiarum, magna etiam novercarum').

15. Cf. Plutarch's observation that mothers favour sons because the sons will give them aid — *Coniug. Praecepta* 36 and see Lacey 1968: 117.

16. Cf. line 6 of the *laudatio Murdiae*:

VIRO CERTAM PECVNIAM LEGAVIT VT IVS DOTIS
HONORE IVDICI AVGERETVR

on Murdia's legacy to her second husband, or *magnus honos viri* of Fulcinius' dispositions to his widow Caesennia (Cic. *Caec.* 12).

17. '.. et id erat certi accusatoris officium, qui tanti sceleris argueret, explicare omnia vitia ac peccata fili, quibus incensus parens potuerit animum inducere, ut naturam ipsam vinceret ...' (Cic. *Rosc. Am.* 53. cited in Chapter 2, n35 and paraphrased very closely in the associated text).

18. Cf. Paul *in Dig.* 28.2.11:

Even during the father's lifetime they are deemed owners, in a certain sense ... and so on the death of the father they seem not to gain an inheritance so much as to take up the free administration of their property.

etiam vivo patre quodammodo domini existimantur ... itaque post mortem patris non hereditatem percipere videntur, sed magis liberam bonorum administrationem consequuntur.

19.
But this narrow view of the law was subsequently corrected and indeed the divine Claudius was the first to award the right of statutory inheritance to a mother as a consolation for the loss of her children.

sed hae iuris augustiae postea emendatae sunt et primus quidem divus Claudius matri ad solatium liberorum amissorum legitimam eorum detulit hereditatem.

20. Thomas (1976: 523-4) thinks this continued until AD 426 (*CJ* 6.55.11), when the *senatus consultum Tertullianum* was overruled.

21. Young Marcus' allowance from various rents (*merces insularum*) is alluded to in *Att.* 12.32.2; 28; 24. It appears from *Att.* 15.20.4 that it was made up at least in part from his mother's dowry (*dotalia praedia*).

22. AMOR | MATERNVS CARITATE AEQVALITATE PARTIVM CONSTAT.

(*CIL* VI 2 10230: 4-5)

— possibly to protect her from the provisions of the Voconian law of *c.* 169 BC which forbade testators of the top property class to institute women as *heirs* but did not prevent women from sharing a legacy equally with an heir. See e.g. Watson 1971: 29-31.

23. Compare the eventual concession of the Triumvirs (it is irrelevant to this discussion that it was never honoured) to award 10% of the estates of proscribed men to their sons, and 5% to daughters — Dio 47.14.1.

24. Cf. Val. Max. 5.8.1,2; *Tab.* IV.1; *Collatio* 4.8 (Papinian); Dion. Halic. 2.26 and see Rabello (1972) and Crook (1967b). Saller's forthcoming paper in *Continuity and Change* discusses between theory and practice.

25. Nardi apparently concluded that abortion was not treated as homicide, but I have been unable to secure the relevant paper: 'Credo Stoico e portata delle Leggi Cornelia e Pompeia sul omicidio, *Studi Grosso* I (1971) pp. 313-19.

26. The story was told also of the next generation, of the betrothal of Sempronia and Scipio Aemilianus (Liv. 38.57.7; Plut. *Tib. Gr.* 4.3 ff)

27. *C. Th.* 3.5.11 on the binding power of pre-nuptial gifts and 9.24 *pr.* on the definition of *raptus* as abduction/elopement without the consent of the *parents* represent an assumption of consent by both parents, although examples such as those cited in the text above show that mothers had long before been to the fore in matchmaking. Cf. Corbett (1930: 2-5) for the formal law.

28. The literature on the subject generally concerns Roman Egypt, and post-classical law. The most significant works are Kübler (1909-10), Frezza (1930-1) and Solazzi (1937).

29. Sen. *ad Helviam* 14.3: tu patrimonia nostra sic administrasti, ut tamquam in tuis laborares, tamquam in tuis abstineres.

30. — *CJ* 5.35.1: 'Tutelam administrare virile munus est, et ultra sexum femineae infirmitatis tale officium est' (AD 224). Solazzi (1930) rejected the second part of this as interpolated — correctly, I think, *pace* Beaucamp (1976: 448 ff). But the bare statement of the masculine character of *tutela* seems genuine. See Dixon (1984a: 358-60).

31. *Dig.* 24.1 and see Thayer (1929). *C. Th.* 2.24.2 makes the general point that it is not only illegal, but *contrary to good morals* for the property of any living person to be handed over to others, although a mother (or father) was — just — permitted to do it, as long as she continued to approve her division until her death. That is, the gift was not void in such a case.

4

The Official Encouragement of Maternity

Introduction: from general pride to state inducements

In Rome, as in many societies, motherhood had always established or enhanced a woman's status. Fertility was associated with the general good. Expressions such as *matrona* and *materfamilias*, denoting an honourable married woman, were derived from *mater* on the assumption that marriage and motherhood went together (Aul. Gell. *NA* 18.6.8-9; Cic. *Top.* 14). The ancient rites of the Lupercal involved flicking women with leather thongs to induce fertility (Plut. *Caes.* 61; Fowler 1899: 320). The censors traditionally enquired of married men whether they had married for the purpose of having children — *liberorum quaerendorum* (or *procreandorum*) *causa* (Aul. Gell. *NA.* 17.21.44; 4.3.2.; Dion. Halic. 2.25.7), a reflection of the community view of the function of marriage (e.g. Seneca *de Matrim.* 58; Plaut. *Mil. Gl.* 703-4). From time to time, censors had taken it upon themselves to pressure citizens to marry and have children (e.g. Plut. *Cam.* 2; Val. Max. 2.9.1; Plut. *Cat. mai.* 16; Cic. *Leg.* 3.7; Aul. Gell. *NA* 5.19.6).

There was therefore some precedent for the state to concern itself with private reproduction but Augustus was the first to legislate with a view to inducing Roman citizens to marry and produce several children.[1] The active official encouragement of parenthood thus dates from the beginnings of imperial rule. The transition is represented by the elevation of Venus Genetrix and by Augustus' restoration of the statue to Cornelia *mater Gracchorum* erected at public expense in the second century BC and encapsulating the traditional regard for mothers — particularly the mothers of outstanding male senatorials (Plin. *HN* 34.31; *CIL* VI 31610).

Augustus' encouragement of legitimate procreation took various forms. Of these, the Julian and Papian-Poppaean laws on marriage between the orders and on adultery have attracted the greatest scholarly attention.[2] Augustus and his literary supporters seem to have taken the view that civil war had in part been a punishment inflicted by the gods for the neglect of traditional religion and morals. Horace *Carm.* 3.6 presents this view. It is moot whether Augustus hoped by his legislation to replenish the Italian peasantry or simply the ruling class.[3] Quite apart from any specific aims, he hoped to inculcate a stronger sense of moral responsibility in his subjects and to make marriage and parenthood desirable.

He instituted a system of rewards and punishments. The childless and unmarried suffered limitations on their capacity to inherit or dispose of wealth. Free-born citizen parents with three children gained the *ius liberorum* ('right of children'), with resultant privileges for fathers in the timing of candidacy for office and financial autonomy for mothers. This was but one means he employed to achieve moral regeneration. He also set a conscious example through his own family. By public sculpture such as the frieze around the Altar of Augustan Peace, *Ara Pacis Augustae* (pictured in Plate 2 and see Kleiner 1978), and coinage, he stressed the dynastic significance and fertility of his line (Williams 1962). The bachelor poet Horace preached the virtues of ancestral family life. Venus Genetrix, founder of the Julian house to which Augustus belonged by adoption and maternal ('cognate') connection, was venerated as never before.

The stress on female chastity is evident in Augustus' legislation penalising adultery and fornication and in his severe punishment of daughter and grand-daughter alike for their alleged sexual transgressions (e.g. Suet. *Aug.* 65; Balsdon 1962: 82-7). Such stress tends to be associated with concern about paternity and descent through the male line, the traditional legal means of reckoning Roman inheritance. Women of the imperial family appeared on the coinage chiefly as personifications of virtues rather than as mothers (Grant 1954: 133-48), apart from the coins depicting Julia (the elder, Augustus' daughter) and her infant sons Gaius and Lucius (*RIC* I Augustus: 166/new ed. 404; *BMC Rep.* II 4648-9). On the whole parenthood and matrimony in general were advocated without any particular stress on motherhood as such but the seated figure variously interpreted as Italia or Terra Mater in the panel of the enclosure wall of the Ara Pacis

(Plate 1) could be seen as a public association of personal and national fertility (Kleiner 1978).

In view of the tendency we shall note elsewhere in literature from the late Republic on to idealise and sentimentalise conjugal and parental relations, it is interesting that there was so little stress in imperial propaganda on the intrinsic rewards of motherhood, as against the *ius liberorum*, 'right of children'. In the case of women this amounted to freedom from so-called lifelong tutelage (*tutela perpetua*) and possibly some sort of distinction in dress (Prop. 4.11.61; Camps 1965: 162 *ad loc.*; Jors 1882: 27). Mothers and father alike gained the right to inherit and bequeath property freely from the fact of parenthood.

In modern states such as Germany under the Third Reich and de Gaulle's France, where governments attempted to increase the birthrate, such honours were reinforced by an elevation of the emotional rewards of motherhood. This was not a feature of Augustan propaganda or of the conventional praise of ideal Roman mothers of the past (Quint. *Inst. Or.* 1.1.4-6; Cic. *Brutus* 211; Tac. *Dial.* 28-9; Hor. *Carm.* 3.6.38 ff). The virtuous mother won commendation from others and from her children (Sen. *ad Helviam*; Plin. *Ep.* 3.16; Marcus *Med.* 1.17.1; Tac. *Agric.* 4) for doing her duty. Self-fulfilment — the idea which has played such an important part in modern conditioning about motherhood — is barely discernible. Where maternal happiness is mentioned in the sources, it is associated with the tokens of respect from adult children (e.g. Sen. *ad Helviam* 15.1) rather than the delights of a small child's care and company.

The Roman emphasis was on the status which a mother gained, especially from distinguished sons. Seneca tell us that Augustus' sister Octavia spent her life in mourning after the death of her son Marcellus, who had been marked out for succession to the Principate (cf. Verg. *Aen.* 6.860-86; *RG* 21.1) and could not bear the sight of Livia, because the prospects of Livia's sons were enhanced by Marcellus' death (*Ad Marciam* 2.3-4). With all the distinctions she enjoyed, Octavia had set her heart on being the mother of a *princeps* (emperor). Within the ranks of the propertied classes in imperial times motherhood bestowed certain material and honorific advantages but the intrinsic satisfactions of motherhood which we now tend to emphasise (or react against) received little attention from the ancients.

Motherhood and the imperial family

In his funeral oration on his paternal aunt Julia, Julius Caesar praised her ancestory as deriving from kings on the maternal side and the goddess Venus in the paternal line (Suet. *Iul.* 6). In fact, Venus was not traditionally associated with the patrician state religion at Rome. She was primarily a rustic goddess with special responsibility for gardens (Varro *RR* 1.1.6; Macrobius *Sat.* 1.12.12). The earliest temple to Venus, near the Circus Maximus, dates to 295 BC and the first temple to Venus Verticordia (worshipped by patricians) was probably established around 215 BC,[4] at a time when the senatorial order was receptive to approved new deities (cf. Liv. 29.10.4-8). Her worship was gradually assimilated to the earlier, more plebeian ceremonies associated with Fortuna Virilis on the Kalends of April (*CIL* I: *Fasti Praenestini*; Ov. *Fasti*, 4.61; Fowler 1899: 67-9). On the eve of Pharsalus, Caesar vowed a temple to Venus Victrix (Appian *BC* 2.68). Yet the temple actually erected in the Forum Iulium was to Venus Genetrix, the founder of the Julian house and an appropriate deity to stand watch over the new forum (Plin. *HN* 36.103; Dio 43.22.2-3), which Octavian completed (*RG* 20.3). The goddess, whose significance appears to have been largely literary until then, henceforth assumed the proportions of a leading state deity. Augustus' temple to Mars Ultor in the Forum Augustum, dedicated in 2 BC some forty years after he had vowed it (Suet. *Aug.* 29; *RG* 21.1), included a statue of Venus (Ov. *Tristia* 2.295-6). The whole area constituted a monument to Augustus' *pietas* and a reminder of his own sublime association with the god Caesar and the goddess Venus. He was thereby not only fulfilling his mission as 'founder and restorer of all the temples', *templorum omnium conditor ac restitutor* (*RG* 19; cf. Liv. 4.20; Suet. *Aug.* 31; Hor. *Carm.* 3.6.2-4), but virtually elevating the family founder to the status of tutelary deity of the new state. The *Aeneid* reinforced the image of Venus as Genetrix, the 'Ancestress', the forceful mother pushing her son to his divine destiny and inextricably associating the fortunes of Rome and the Julian house.

Augustus stressed the importance of marriage and family life as a moral and sentimental ideal. Apart from legislative measures, he used the example of the imperial house. Just as he led the way for other aristocrats in encouraging (re-)building, particularly of temples (Suet. *Aug.* 29.4-5), and generally wearing cloth spun by the women of his household (Suet. *Aug.* 73), so he displayed the fertility of his house. The Ara Pacis relief shows the various members of his family over three generations at a state religious ceremony, namely the dedication of the altar (Kleiner 1978). The small children appear with the consular sons-in-law and adopted sons. When patrician families showed reluctance to offer their daughters as priestesses of Vesta, Augustus insisted that he would have surrendered one of his own granddaughters if any had been of a suitable age (Suet. *Aug.* 31.3). Once, at some public games, in response to a demonstration of knights against his laws penalising the unmarried and childless, Augustus made a point of holding and displaying his great-grandchildren in the imperial box.[5] Indeed, we are told that he often appeared at the games with Livia and his '*liberi*' (Suet. *Aug.* 45), a term which probably covered the three generations in his *potestas*.[6] Livia dedicated to Capitoline Venus a statue of a son of Agrippina and Germanicus who had died as a child and was known to be a particular pet of Augustus (Suet. *Gai.* 7). She also established a temple to Concordia, (conjugal) harmony (Flory 1984). Family sentiment and conscious standing-setting went hand in hand.

Other members of the imperial family also served as models of conjugal and parental behaviour, thus reinforcing and glamorising the ideals of their contemporaries. The 'princes' Germanicus and Drusus (maior) made a point of travelling on state and military business with their Julian wives — Agrippina, Augustus' granddaughter, and Antonia minor, his niece — and even their children. This was not traditional, as the consular Severus Caecina pointed out in a senatorial debate in AD 21 occasioned by the corrupt and presumptuous behaviour of some provincial governors' wives (Tac. *Ann.* 3.33-4). Tiberius' son Drusus put forward the clinching argument of the debate, that the divine Augustus had travelled on state business with Livia and that he himself would have been reluctant to travel as far afield as he had done had military duties imposed separation from his wife.[7]

Inscriptional evidence confirms the impression that it was common for provincial governors to travel *en famille* to their posts in this period (Raepsaet-Charlier 1982). The imperial family reflected this trend, but sometimes exaggerated its 'togetherness' for propaganda purposes. The young Gaius (Caligula) was popularly but erroneously supposed to have been born in military camp. Suetonius records a couplet about him beginning:

in castris natus, patriis nutritus in armis
born in the camp, reared in the midst of the ancestral arms
(*or* of his father's weaponry)

Gaius' mother Agrippina did give birth in a variety of places. Pliny the elder had apparently observed altars in Gallia Lugdunensis inscribed OB AGRIPPINAE PVERPERIVM ('for Agrippina's delivery'), and the child Gaius *was* a mascot of his father's armies, but an apparently genuine letter from Augustus to Agrippina, quoted by Suetonius, suggests that he spent his early infancy in Rome and was dispatched by his great-grandfather to his parents in Gaul at the age of two (Suet. *Gai.* 8).

The imperial family continued, on the whole, to set an example of conspicuous enjoyment of conjugal and family life. The reality sometimes fell short of this ideal. Nero's filial piety and Caracalla's brotherly love were scarcely exemplary, but one of the first actions of Nero's accession was the institution of the password '*optima mater*' 'excellent mother' (Suet. *Nero* 9), and the coin issues of 54-5 A.D. linking Nero and his mother,[8] while a coin representing Caracalla and Geta sacrificing at an altar before their father Septimus Severus — or possibly Concordia (brotherly harmony in this case) — preceded fratricide (*RIC* Caracalla: 452). The *concordia* of the imperial house, however notional, was important to uphold as a reassurance of the stability of the ruling regime and as a standard to which subjects were to aspire.

Children repeatedly figured in this parade. Augustus' conspicuous caressing of his great-grandchildren to reproach the dissident bachelors was of a piece with Germanicus' exploitation of his troops' fondness for the child Gaius when mutiny threatened on Augustus' death (Suet. *Aug.* 34; *Gai.* 9; Tac. *Ann.* 1.41). Claudius as *princeps* was in the habit of holding up the young Britannicus at public games or military reviews, for the acclamation of the commons and troops (Suet. *Claud.* 27). This official insistence on family probably reflected the new sentimental celebration of family life which we have noted in late Republican art and literature (Manson 1983; Luc. 3.894-6; Cic. *Fam.* 14.1.4; *Att.* 1.18.1 and cf. *CIL* VI 1527 and *CE* 59). The well-publicised adherence of successive imperial ruling houses to such ideals was itself a call for emulation which reinforced the legal sanctions: marriage and parenthood were virtues to be applauded and rewarded. The frieze of the Ara Pacis enclosure combines the official, formal element with an appeal to family sentiment reminiscent of modern photographs of royal families in popular magazines. For a state monument, the poses are strikingly naturalistic (see Plate 2). The children represent the stability of the ruling house: the boys are *principes*-in-training, while the girls are potential mothers of princes.

The charm of this part of the frieze lies in the casually affectionate hand-holding and head-patting of the children. It is a more intimate portrayal of that CONCORDIA which was to figure increasingly on coinage. Kleiner (1977: 177-9) argues that it had an impact on funereal sculpture of the time, particularly in the inclusion of young children in family groups, which suggests that this public celebration of family togetherness *did* impress Augustus' subjects. Surviving statue bases indicate that the imperial children appeared in some of the statues erected in public places throughout the empire (Hanson and Johnson 1946) and on coins issued at Rome and other imperial mints (Manson 1975), so the Ara Pacis was probably not the sole attempt to interest subjects in the imperial family as a whole in Augustan times.

Although as we see below imperial children appear on occasional coin issues, the Augustan tendency to include young children in official sculpture groups was not imitated by his successors. Even Marcus, the most prolific Roman emperor, is represented in surviving sculpture with his wife, but not his children. Septimius Severus, who had his wife and young sons depicted on coinage (e.g. *RIC* 540), was himself portrayed only with his wife in sculpture, such as the panel from the Arch of the Argentarii AD 204. In the second century, married couples stood for the harmony of the ruling family, and groupings of mother and children for continuity. The chief celebration of motherhood — or of mothers — as such was primarily dynastic. Maternal ancestry — and in the case of Tiberius and Nero, a mother's remarriage — was significant for some Julio-Claudian *principes*. Distinctions granted a mother could serve as a reminder of an emperor's own claim to rule. Tiberius was thought to resent his mother's political presumption (Suet. *Tib.* 50-1; Tac. *Ann.* 3.64, Dio. 58.2), and to have fumed at a senatorial decree which honoured him as son of Livia and Augustus,[9] yet she was granted certain honours, particularly on her recovery from illness in old age. The coin issue of SALVS AVGVSTA probably commemorated this.[10] His veto of his mother's posthumous deification was attributed by hostile sources to his malice but accords with his usual attitude to excessive honours for the imperial family.[11]

On his accession, Gaius made a point of restoring the members of his family to favour, giving an honoured burial at last to the remains of his mother Agrippina and his brothers Nero and Drusus. The month of September was renamed 'Germanicus' after his popular father, and his grandmother Antonia granted the same titles Livia Augusta had accumulated in her lifetime (Suet. *Gai.* 15). He instituted annual memorial games in his mother's honour in which a canopied wagon (*carpentum*) paraded ceremonially. This is the subject of the lovely *sestertius* issue minted at Rome some time during his reign (*RIC* 42/new ed. 55). Agrippina's bust appears on the obverse with the legend:

AGRIPPINA M F MAT C CAESARIS AVGVSTI
(Agrippina, daughter of Marcus, mother of Gaius Caesar Augustus)

The reverse shows a *carpentum* and the legend:

S P Q R MEMORIAE AGRIPPINAE
(The senate and the Roman people, to the memory of Agrippina)

Gaius went further than Augustus or Tiberius in the depiction of women on the coinage. His three sisters appeared as full-figure representations of *Securitas*, *Concordia* and *Fortuna* on the reverse of his *sestertius* issue of AD 37-8 (Rome, *RIC* 26/new ed. 33). They were actually named in the legend. Even Augustus' daughter Julia, portrayed as a young mother with her two sons, had not enjoyed such distinction. The honours probably inspired or reinforced suspicions of incest between Gaius and his sisters (cf. Suet. *Gai.* 24). By comparison, the gestures of respect to his deceased relations were more conventional marks of piety, which exploited his parents' popularity, the sympathy aroused by Tiberius' persecution of his mother and brothers and the quality of his descent. His grandmother Antonia, daughter of Octavia and Marcus Antonius, and his mother, granddaughter of Augustus, were reminders of his Julian claim, as well as earnests of his *pietas*.

The emperor Claudius was unmistakably elevated by the

praetorian guardsmen. There could be no pretence of a regular succession and senatorial endorsement of the *fait accompli* was a sham (Suet. *Claud.* 10). Yet he, too, emphasised his ancestry through the maternal side and Antonia, who had been honoured by Gaius as an imperial grandmother, was now celebrated by her emperor son. He issued a *dupondius* depicting her on the obverse with the legend:

ANTONIA AVGVSTA

the title she had been granted during Gaius' rule (*RIC* 82/new ed. 104). This filial display is unlikely to have stemmed from fond memories of the dead Antonia, for she had made no secret of her contempt for her son's disabilities.[12] Like others in the imperial family, she must have assumed that they would disqualify him for the Principate and imagined that she would not enjoy the greatest maternal honour — that of being known as mother of the emperor. Claudius dutifully instituted annual memorial ceremonies in honour of both his parents, Antonia and Drusus (Suet. *Claud.* 11).

His grandmother Livia had also treated him with scorn (Suet. *Claud.* 3.2). She, too, was honoured by Claudius, who initiated the deification which her son Tiberius had denied to her memory. He took other steps to ensure that her distinctions should approach those still granted the deified Augustus by upgrading her memorial celebrations (Suet. *Claud.* 11.2) and depicting Augustus and Livia on almost equal terms on commemorative coin issues (*RIC* Claudius: 86/new ed. 101). It is significant that Claudius was not a direct descendant of Augustus, but of M. Antonius, whose memory he also honoured (Suet. *Claud.* 11.3. See the Julio-Claudian family tree in Appendix 2).

Agrippina's daughter of the same name achieved unprecedented honours. In her brother's reign, she had, as we have seen, been depicted and named on a *sestertius* issue (*RIC* Gaius: 26/new ed. 33) with her two sisters Drusilla and Julia. Ambitious for her son, she married her paternal uncle Claudius after Messalina's downfall and persuaded him in AD 50 to adopt her son by Domitius Ahenobarbus. Known henceforth by the Claudian *cognomen* 'Nero', he soon eclipsed his younger stepbrother, Britannicus, and was marked as heir by the title *'princeps iuventutis'* ('prince of youth'), conferred in AD 51. *Denarii* were struck to mark this, with a bust of Nero on the obverse (*RIC* 95, 96, 97, 99).

One of these (*RIC* 100) also portrayed Agrippina on the reverse, with the legend 'to Agrippina the Augusta':

AGRIPPINAE AVGVSTAE

Livia had been granted the title of 'Augusta' on her husband's death. It had also been granted posthumously to Antonia, as grandmother of the emperor Gaius. Agrippina now gained this honour as a relatively young woman, while her husband, the Emperor, was still alive. It marked the adoption of Nero by Claudius.[13] On Nero's accession in AD 54, she appeared on successive coin issues (*RIC* Nero: 9, 10, 11/new ed. 1, 6-7, 3). All celebrated Nero's claim in terms of his Julian and Claudian forebears, presumably to overcome any disfavour at his preferment over Claudius' natural son Britannicus. Thus the obverse of an *aureus* minted at Rome AD 54 shows the facing heads of Nero and his mother with the legend:

AGRIPP AVG DIVI CLAVD NERONIS CAES MATER
('Agrippina Augusta, wife of the divine Claudius, mother of Nero Caesar')

while the reverse bears the legend:

NERONI CLAVD DIVI F CAES AVG GERM IMP TR P
('To Nero Caesar Augustus Germanicus Imperator, tribune of the *plebs*, son of the divine Claudius')
                        (*RIC* Nero: 9/new ed. 1 and 2)

Like Tiberius, Nero owed his position as emperor to his mother's marriage and political manoeuvres. On coming to power, he heaped a number of honours on Agrippina (Suet. *Nero* 9) in recognition of her role in securing the rule for him and as a way of stressing the quality of his own ancestry, particularly through the maternal line. He and his mother appeared together on coin issues early in his reign but as her power declined she became less prominent on them.[14] The process is discussed in some detail in Chapter 7 below, but even after Agrippina's expulsion from the palace, there was no public acknowledgement of the rift until Nero had her killed on a pretext of treason (Suet. *Nero* 34; Tac. *Ann.* 14.1-10). If the chronology of Dio's excerptors is to be trusted, Nero gave a huge public festival in her honour as late as AD 59 (Dio 62.17 = Xiph. 156.6 ff).

Vespasian was known to revere the memory of the maternal grandmother, Tertulla, who had reared him for part of his childhood (Suet. *Vesp.* 2). Like many another emperor — and the Gracchi, whose mother had always been held up for praise — he had his ambitions fired by the taunts of a forceful and sarcastic mother, Vespasia Polla (Suet. *Vesp.* 2) but she does not seem to have been venerated by Vespasian himself or by senatorial vote. It was his wife Domitilla, already dead on Vespasian's succession, who was honoured by Titus as divine imperial mother, as in the *denarius* issues at Rome AD 80-1 (*RIC* Titus: 69-73). In this case, perhaps, it was piety alone rather than the relatively humble lineage which was being shown off.

The imperial women of the second century BC feature less in the literary sources than their predecessors, but they do appear on coins and in inscriptions. There is a marked tendency to associate these ladies with the virtues the ruling regime wished to stress, with no lingering reservations about representing young, living women on the coinage (Grant 1954: 138-9; Giacosa 1977: 23 ff). These women who figure so little in the formal history of the period make up for it in their appearance on the coins of the realm. We see, too, the familiar official emphasis on conjugal and familial solidarity. Plotina accompanied Trajan on military excursions and this habit was maintained by successive empresses. Emperors tended to revere their parents or adopted parents and their children on coin issues and public sculpture. Trajan's niece Matidia had her portrait on a coin during his lifetime, linking her with her recently deceased and deified mother Marciana (*RIC* 759) and representing her full length on the reverse with her two daughters under the legend:

PIETAS AVGVST

(cf. *RIC* Trajan: 760-1). A series of similar coins (e.g. *RIC* 1041, Plate 5(b)) was issued by Hadrian celebrating his wife Sabina, daughter of Matidia, who had probably been one of the children on the earlier celebration of PIETAS AVGVST[A] (cf. Manson 1975). Hadrian further stressed his link with the established imperial house in AD 134-8 by an *aureus* to his deified adoptive parents, with facing portraits of Trajan and Plotina (*RIC* 232 A and B). That is, Hadrian was urging his connection by marriage and adoption with his predecessor. He hammered home the continuity with iconographic echoes of earlier issues (cf. *RIC* 29-34). Unlike Titus, he showed no interest in celebrating his real mother, who was irrelevant to his claim.

The association of the imperial women with PIETAS and FORTVNA AVG. also set a standard for later issues, where other female deities or virtues continued to be paired with the imperial women. In the meantime, the younger Faustina, daughter of the emperor Pius and wife of the future emperor, Marcus Aurelius (her cousin), was granted the title Augusta on the birth of her first child in AD 146. One *aureus* minted some time between AD 147-61 had her portrait on the obverse, while the reverse carried the figure of Venus Genetrix, presumably in tribute to her welcome fertility (*RIC* Pius: 511-12). Other examples of such pairings are of Marcus Aurelius' daughter Lucilla with PIETAS (*RIC* Marcus: 774) and his daughter-in-law Crispina with PVDICITIA and HILARITAS (*RIC* Commodus: 285, 668). They were being honoured not as mothers but as wives and daughters of emperors. In a sense the succession lay with the imperial women, for an emperor's wife might produce a male heir and, if not, an emperor's daughter could become the means of adopting a son-in-law as successor, to maintain the imperial line in the coming generation. This consideration lay behind the celebration of the women.

In the light of the fatal conflict between their sons in later life, there is a certain irony in the optimism of the *aureus* of AD 198 issued under Septimius Severus, showing the draped bust of his wife Julia Domna on the obverse and the confronted busts of Caracalla and Geta on the reverse with the legend AETERNIT[AS] IMPERII ('eternal nature of the imperial regime': *RIC* 540) This, like the full-length portrait of the elder Matidia (*RIC* Trajan: 759) and the Augustan issue depicting Julia with Gaius and Lucius (*RIC* 166/new ed. 404), thus honoured the young woman as a mother and her children as heirs to the throne. Julia Domna appeared again, now as the mother of the Emperor, on a *sestertius* minted at Rome AD 211-17 in Caracalla's reign, with the legend IVLIA PIA FELIX AVG., while the reverse held a portrait of Vesta seated (*RIC* 593). She was notable for acquiring the titles MATER SENATVS ET PATRIAE ('mother of the senate and fatherland') as well as MATER CASTRORUM ('mother of the camp').[15]

Julia Domna's sister Julia Maesa was largely responsible both for the elevation of the emperor Elagabalus, her grandson, in AD

218 and for his murder in AD 222. As emperor, Elagabalus honoured her (e.g. *RIC* 414; *RIC* 263, pictured below, Plate 5(d)) and her daughter Julia Soaemias (*RIC* 243), his mother. This could have been in part to stress the connection, through the mother of Caracalla, with the previous regime but it was primarily a gesture of appreciation for the part played by the two women in his acquisition of power and their influence during his reign. His three wives were also featured on the coinage, but more fleetingly, simply to advertise the imperial house in a general way.[16] Julia Maesa continued to enjoy publicity on the coinage of her other grandson, Alexander Severus, until her death in AD 225, when she was honoured on the coins as Diva Maesa (*RIC* 712-14), while her daughter, Julia Mamaea, was celebrated as Augusta (e.g. *RIC* 343). These mothers, like wives of the emperors, were associated in the usual fashion with deities and virtues, but no particular reference was made to their motherhood as such on the coinage. Slogans such as CONCORDIA AVGG ('harmony of the Augusti') focused on the (mythical) harmony of imperial marriages, which was not explicitly related to the hope of stable succession.

The women of the imperial family, then, continued to appear on the coinage, often in association with virtues, particularly womanly virtues such as PUDICITIA ('modesty') and with goddesses like Vesta, Venus and Juno. Their function was in part to emphasise that all was well in the palace and the succession secure. In this sense it resembles modern publicity about the Prince and Princess of Wales and their progeny, with the significant difference that the Roman imperial family was the *political* centre of the Empire. The consequences of disputes between family members were potentially serious and warfare was likely if the succession were not firmly established. It was in this context that women appeared on the coinage. The birth of an heir might occasion a special issue featuring the mother, as in the case of Faustina the younger (*RIC* Pius: 1386), or an imperial princess might be honoured when her sons were marked out as imperial heirs, as in the case of Augustus' daughter Julia (*RIC* Augustus: 166/new ed. 404), or simply as a reminder that there were sons to carry on the imperial tradition, as with Julia Domna (*RIC* Septimius Severus: 540). Matidia, niece of the childless Trajan, appeared with her young daughters (*RIC* Trajan: 760-1), one of whom (as wife of Hadrian) constituted the link with the next regime. The function of these women was dynastic rather than exemplary. They were not intended to inspire other women to become mothers but to assure subjects that the imperial regime would continue, just as posthumous portraits of newly elevated emperors' mothers served as reminders of their claim to the throne.

The official promotion of parenthood

We have seen that Augustus consciously insisted on an exemplary standard of old-fashioned virtue from the women of his family (if not from himself), a role which was taken up by his grandchildren and other relations such as his niece Antonia in his lifetime. The influence of the Ara Pacis representations of the different generations on funereal group sculpture of the time has, as we have seen, been persuasively argued by Kleiner (1977: 178-9), but the example of fertility within the imperial family did *not* inspire widespread imitation. The main thrust of the Augustan effort to promote marriage and parenthood was enshrined, not in example or pictorial propaganda, but in the legislation offering rewards to the married and penalties for the unmarried and childless — the *caelibes* and *orbi*.

The legislative packages, sometimes known loosely as the Augustan marriage laws, have engrossed and baffled scholars for generations. The content, purpose and effects of the laws continue to be debated by legal and social historians. The account which follows is necessarily simplified and concentrates on the significance of the measures for Roman women and reproduction — that is, motherhood and its official encouragement. Propertius' reference 2.7 to a *lex sublata* has been taken by many to suggest that Augustus (then still Octavian) first attempted to introduce legislation reforming Roman sexual and marriage habits in 28 BC (cf. Hor. 3.24 and Williams 1962, Hallett 1973, Besnier 1979, on the poems), but Badian's (1985) discussion of the issue throws serious doubt on the possibility. It is generally agreed that there were two successive bills, one introduced *c*. 18 BC by Augustus himself ('the Julian law on marriage between the orders' and/or 'on the suppression of adultery'), the second actually emanating from him but sponsored by the consuls of AD 9 — who, as the Roman wits noted, were both bachelors (Dio 56.10.3) — and bearing their names, that is, the *lex Papia Poppaea*. This raises certain difficulties which do not affect this discussion (Csillag 1976: 29-35).

We know that the legislation was unpopular with the upper classes and that Augustus was obliged to modify its provisions and defer its effects in response to public demonstrations and remonstrances. Ancient accounts are confused[17] and modern discussions, though prolific, hardly more illuminating.[18] In broad terms, the legislation penalised men who remained unmarried after the age of twenty-five and women who were not married — or had been divorced or widowed, but did not have any children — between the ages of twenty and fifty. The main imposition was that they were ineligible to receive legacies and their capacity to make valid wills was limited. The production of one child removed the most severe disabilities, but the greatest rewards were reserved for those who gained the full *ius liberorum*. For the free-born, this usually meant three legitimate children.[19] The *ius liberorum* gave men priority in ascending the ladder of office: it liberated women, as we have seen, from the formal necessity of 'perpetual tutelage' (*tutela mulierum perpetua*: Gai. 1.145, 194).

This summary — like the ancient accounts — undoubtedly telescopes the provisions of successive acts and generally simplifies the conditions. Amendments, exceptions, refinements and special conditions accrued and are sometimes scattered through the surviving legal complications.[20] The principle that marriage and child-rearing should be enforced fell out of favour in the later Empire and was not included as such in the Christian compilations, which makes it difficult to resurrect the terms of the original legislation. The historians' and biographers' incidental references form the basis of modern reconstruction of the laws on marriage and the family. The rules on adultery have fared better, since they were strengthened by the Christians. Chapters in the *Digest* are devoted to the so-called *L. Iulia de adulteriis coercendis*[21] and, for various reasons, these rulings have preoccupied commentators since their inception.[22] These have some bearing on a consideration of attitudes to maternity, since *adulterium* was defined in terms of the status of the woman involved,[23] presumably on the usual patrilineal assumption underlying such dual sexual standards, that the chastity of the woman is the guarantee of a child's paternity.

Augustus' concern that marriages should be contracted between the 'proper' social groups and that property should be passed down within families is evident from the fragmentary remains of the laws. This, and the stress on female chastity, were traditional moral concerns with some history of state intervention in the form of legislation. The *lex Furia testamentaria* of *c*. 204 *BC*, the *lex Voconia* of *c*. 169 *BC* and the *lex Falcidia* of *c*. 40 *BC* limiting legacies, together with the occasional public punishment of female moral transgressions, fall into this category.[24] Yet in spite of his attempts to argue for ancient precedent,[25] Augustus was innovatory in his wholesale invasion of the private sphere. His insistence on the punishment of adultery (or of its toleration by a husband) as a criminal offence, like his insistence that equestrians and senators marry (preferably within their own class), and produce children, was built on existing moral standards but changed their character with his system of legal sanctions (Tac. *Ann.* 3.24; cf. Williams 1962: 35; Brunt 1971: 561). This went much further than the occasional censorial *nota* for violation of the marriage bond or the stock census question about marrying for the purpose of creating children.[26]

It has recently been argued (Wallace-Hadrill 1981: esp. 58-9) that Augustus must have aimed his legislation solely at the upper class, since most of the penalties were inapplicable to those of meagre income or no political aspirations.[27] From this, the argument proceeds to the view that the legislation was formed primarily to preserve property within the leading families (Wallace-Hadrill 1981: 59, 62 ff). Brunt concludes (1971: 564-5) that, although there were no systematic incentives for the poorer classes to reproduce, probably because of the limitations of the treasury, Augustus did wish the whole Italian populace to be replenished, and rewarded even freed slaves in some measure for having children.[28] There might well have been some vague idea of supplying the army with Italian stock (Prop. 2.7.14; Dio 56.2), but the incentives adopted were hardly likely to achieve it. Augustus distributed intermittent largess to the populace, extending it to free-born *minores* — probably, but not necessarily, boys only (Suet. *Aug.* 41) and whenever he toured the city voting-districts he would offer a cash sum to those who could present a free-born Roman child, male or female (Suet. *Aug.* 46). People vary in their perception of what constitutes an adequate incentive for procreation, especially in relation to social groups other than their own. Augustus might have entertained unrealistic views of lower-class motivation but he can scarcely have imagined that such haphazard rewards as he furnished for the prolific poor would induce the Italian peasantry or proletariat to rear more children. The later alimentary schemes of emperors and some private citizens suggest a more consistent encouragement of the poor to rear children they might otherwise have exposed.[29]

In his praise of Trajan, Pliny implied that imperial beneficence was the only incentive which could really assist the poor in this way.[30] Trajan's alimentary schemes were a new departure — even if they had been instituted or envisaged by Nerva.[31] They differed from Julius Caesar's settlement of fathers-of-three on Campanian plots (Suet. *Iul.* 20) and from the system of grain distributions to poor citizens rationalised under Caesar and Augustus. The scheme of Trajan approaches the modern idea of a child endowment or family allowance to help poor families feed their offspring. Pliny's letters (1.8; 7.18; 10.8) bear witness to imperial attempts to encourage members of the upper class to foster similar schemes throughout Italy. Even so, the schemes as a whole were never undertaken on such a massive scale that they could have affected the overall population of the country (Duncan-Jones 1974: 317-18), in spite of Trajan's emphasis on the revival of Italy with coin legends like ITAL[IA] REST[ITVTA] (*RIC* 470, 472-3) and perhaps ALIM[ENTA] ITAL[IAE] (*RIC* 459-60).

Duncan-Jones (1974: 319) argues that the Antonine foundations were less ambitious and 'probably meant only some additional recipients of the corn-dole at Rome' but this is difficult to test from the available evidence — chiefly references in the unreliable *Historia Augusta*, with occasional corroboration from inscriptions and coin issues. Antoninus Pius established the '*puellae Faustinianae*' (literally 'Faustinian girls') on the death of his wife Faustina the elder (SHA *Pius* 8.1; *RIC* Pius: 398-9). Marcus Aurelius founded one scheme to commemorate the wedding of his daughter Lucilla and Lucius Verus (SHA *Marcus* 7.7-8) and another as a memorial to his dead wife, Faustina the younger (SHA *Marcus* 26.6), who in her lifetime, as heir to her great-aunt Matidia, was directed to make annual payments to a group of poor children named by Matidia in her will (Fronto *ad Amicos* 1.14 = Naber p. 183).

Coin issues celebrating Matidia the elder and her daughter Sabina echo the style of Trajan's alimentary issues. A typical example is *RIC* Trajan: 759, which has Matidia's bust on the obverse and depicts her full figure on the reverse with her hands on the heads of her small daughters, Sabina and Matidia the younger, with the legend PIETAS AVGVST[A]. The force of PIETAS here seems to be in the celebration of motherhood and the virtues of family life. The memorial issues (e.g. *RIC* Trajan:

— but probably issued by Hadrian — 751-7) could be associated with an alimentary scheme. So could *RIC* 760, issued in Matidia's lifetime, in which a woman is depicted on the obverse with two small children. Matidia's daughter Sabina, married to Hadrian, figures in similar issues, such as *RIC* Hadrian: 1041 (Plates 5(a) and (b)). These might simply celebrate the range of feminine virtues personified on the reverse, but the recurrence of two small children on the coins of a childless empress could refer to alimentary schemes or beneficence directed specifically at children.

Whatever the practical measures being taken and their efficacy, the imperial house of the second century appears to have made the children of Italy its notional concern and to have emphasised this aspect of its benevolence in official publicity. Modern politicians notoriously kiss babies and modern royal houses lend their names to schemes promoting youthful talent on the same assumption, that their public images will benefit from conspicuous gestures of faith in the coming generation. I believe the ancient practice also exploited a general sentimental interest in children as such (cf. Manson 1975). The imperial women were particularly associated with the schemes — as benefactresses rather than as mothers who would inspire their subjects by their example.

Later emperors did not display the same zeal as Augustus in promoting marital fidelity and legitimate reproduction, although chastity and fecundity continued to be viewed as desirable feminine qualities within the palace and throughout the Empire. The Augustan legislation on marriage and procreation remained in force and the associated penalties and privileges were incorporated in later rulings. We saw, for example, in the preceding chapter that women with the *ius liberorum* enjoyed better rights of intestate succession to their own children's estates (*Inst.* 3.3 *pr.*). After Hadrianic rulings simplifying the cumbersome testamentary procedure women had had to adopt in the past, a testatrix with the full *ius liberorum* (who therefore had no *tutor*) could make a will by the same process as a man (Gai. 2.112).

We have seen that motherhood in itself conferred certain rights on a woman under the Augustan provisions penalising the childless. Thus a widow with one child was able to accept a testamentary inheritance from her husband and was not obliged to remarry in order to retain this fairly basic status. She was also capable of accepting legacies from friends (Ulpian *Tit.* 14-18).

The full privileges of the *ius liberorum*, however, were reserved for those women who produced three legitimate children (four in the case of freedwomen). These consisted of freedom from the provisions of the *l. Voconia* limiting female inheritance and dispensation from *tutela* (Gai. 1.194; Dio 56.10.2). It is moot whether the *l. Voconia* or the institution of *tutela* had been a serious bar to freeborn women even before the Augustan legislation. There were many ways in which the *l. Voconia* could be circumvented (Daube 1964; Dixon 1985c) and even by the late Republic women of substance like Cicero's wife Terentia freely disposed of property and drew up wills in accordance with their own wishes, treating the permission of their *tutores* as a formal requirement which was theirs for the asking.[32] In the event that a *tutor* did not comply with a woman's wishes, she could appeal to the praetor, who could compel him to give his formal assent (Gai. 1.190). The praetor was unwilling to do this in the case of a 'statutory *tutor*', *tutor legitimus* (Gai. 1.192; cf. 2.122), a category which included agnatic relations, a father who had emancipated his daughter and become her *tutor* or the former owner of a female slave (Gai. 1.157; 175). The emperor Claudius abolished the category of agnatic *tutores* (Gai. 1.157; 171), so from that time *tutela* was a serious limitation only for women in the *tutela* of their former owners or their fathers. It has been argued (Brunt 1971: 563; cf. Hopkins 1978: 163-8) that there was little chance of a freedwoman actually producing after manumission the number of children required for the *ius liberorum* and subsequent release from *tutela*. Given that the number of emancipated daughters is unlikely to have been great at any time, it seems to me that the privilege was all but unattainable by the body of women (*libertinae*) to whom it might have made a significant difference. For free-born women, to whom *tutela* had been a formal requirement no more onerous than the need to collect witnesses to a signature, the grant of *ius liberorum* was probably honorific rather than a practical advantage.

This is confirmed by reference to the women of Augustus' family. Livia and Octavia were early granted freedom from *tutela* as a mark of prestige (Dio 55.2, 49.38.1), putting them almost on the level of the Vestals, who had hitherto been the only (Roman) women citizens to enjoy the privilege (Gai. 1.145). When Augustus later introduced legislation instituting the *ius liberorum*, he granted it *ex officio* to all the Vestals, so that no ordinary woman could claim rights in excess of these prestigious priestesses (Dio

56.10.2). In their case, the *ius* had no practical significance, since they had always enjoyed full financial autonomy and exemption from the application of the *l. Voconia*.

Sijpesteijn (1965) has demonstrated that the women of Roman Egypt who claimed the *ius liberorum* seem to have done so for reasons of status. Those of Greek background continued to conduct transactions with the aid of a male κύριος in traditional fashion. He also uncovered examples of women with the requisite number of children who had not claimed the *ius*, while those who enjoyed it did not always meet the conditions and seem to have secured it through influence. In spite of Trajan's — or possibly Nerva's — disclaimer that he rarely conferred the full *ius liberorum* on the childless (Plin. *Ep*. 10.95.1; cf. 2.13.8 and Sherwin-White 1966: 178 *ad loc.*) we know that Pliny, Suetonius and Martial all enjoyed it (Plin. *Ep*. 10.2.1; 10.94-5; Martial 2.92.1-3; cf. Daube 1976 and Statius *Silvae* 4.8 20-27), as did women of the imperial family such as Livia, who had not produced the requisite number of children. The way in which the grant was viewed is indicated, for example, by Propertius' characterisation of his noble contemporary Cornelia (4.11.61-2) and by inscriptions such as *CIL* VI 1877 (AD 73) in which a woman is commended for the *ius* in the same spirit in which the dedicator mentions her son's equestrian status:

> ... C CORNELIO PERSICO F HABENTI EQVVM PVBLICVM | CORNELIAE ZOSIMAE MATRI EIVS HABENTI IVS QVAT | TVOR LIBERORVM BENEFICIO CAESARIS ... (lines 5-7)

> To my son Gaius Cornelius Persicus of equestrian standing and to his mother Cornelia Zosima, who enjoyed the right of four children by the grace of Caesar

The words 'BENEFICIO CAESARIS' suggest that the *ius* in this case was specially granted by the emperor. In *CIL* VI 10246, one Septimia Dionisias refers to herself as *ius liberorum habens*. It was a badge of honour, like an imperial office.

In a sense, the *ius liberorum* and the celebration of imperial mothers simply extended a traditional Roman regard for motherhood. The temple of Fortuna Virilis, frequented by plebeian women, was supposed to be a memorial to the intercession of Volumnia and her daughter-in-law with her son Coriolanus when he marched on Rome (Plut. *Cor.* 37). Cornelia, who had fuelled her sons' political aspirations, was commemorated on her death as 'mother of the Gracchi' (*CIL* VI 31610), the title she had coveted (Plut. *Tib. Gr.* 8.1), which was inscribed on the base of her statue by an admiring populace (Plut. *Gai. Gr.* 4). It was restored by Augustus for the porticus Liviae (Plin. *HN* 34.31). Julia's depiction on the coinage with the infants Gaius and Lucius *c.* 17-13 BC (*RIC*: Augustus 166/new ed. 404) and the funereal reliefs portraying children and parents from the later Augustan era (Kleiner 1977: 64, 179-80 and Illustrations 64-6, 71, 81, 84, 90, 92) could be seen as a continuation or development of those notable early examples. In the fourth century AD, one Anicia Faltonia was praised for her exemplary antique virtue and her status as child and mother of consuls (*CIL* VI 1755). The moral is that maternity, chastity and nobility were always the qualities in women which were celebrated by their families and by the state.

For free-born women, the *ius liberorum* was an additional mark of honour for display to peers and to posterity, not to be compared with the testamentary advantages already gained by the mother of one child. To men, the *ius liberorum* made a real difference to progress in a senatorial or equestrian career. The significant rewards for large families were for fathers, apparently on the assumption that decisions about family size were made by men. Although childbirth depictions show the midwife lifting up the new-born (cf. Plate 7) and Soranus' advice about the new baby's fitness (*Gyn.* II.VI [xxvi]: 10) assumes that the doctor could influence his choice, the law and custom gave the *paterfamilias* the right to decide whether a child should be reared or exposed (cf. Suet. *Gai.* 5.1).

Propertied men were the prime targets of Augustan measures to promote larger families and opposition to his programme was mounted by men of this class (Dio 56.1-10; Suet. *Aug.* 34). There were no female demonstrations as there had been in the past over the retention of the *lex Oppia* (in 195 *BC*: Liv. 34.1 ff) or against the tax imposed by the triumvirs on the wealthiest women related to the proscribed (Appian *BC* 4.32-3). Augustus' legislation seems to have been loosely based on certain demographic, moral and possibly racial assumptions which are difficult to test. Popular and scholarly ideas about the decline of Roman morality and the family (cf. Csillag 1976: 66) have often stemmed from conclusions about the Augustan programme and the picture of Roman society drawn for us by contemporary satirists and moralists. Ancients and moderns alike have been quick to blame women for most of the undesirable trends, but there is no ancient testimony to female resistance to marriage. Pliny's portrait of the girl Minicia Marcella (*Ep.* 5.16) echoes traditional tombstone laments in pitying her for dying unmarried (cf. Lattimore 1942: 194), on the assumption that marriage was the universal female ambition.

Objections to compulsory marriage came from men but the reason for their protests is not clear. Anti-marriage/anti-wife sentiments had long constituted a popular joke-form in Roman society but can hardly be taken as serious reflections of social behaviour. The numerous quotations amassed by Marquardt (1886 I: 71-4) on the theme are chiefly attributable to married men. Seneca's Theophrastian philosophical arguments against marriage (Haase 1872-4: frag 13) should be set against his well-known devotion to his young wife and the manner of his death (Tac. *Ann.* 15.62-3).

More serious, perhaps, is the suggestion that some men permanently refrained from marrying. This is a fairly unusual phenomenon. The best documented occurrence is in the English landed gentry of the 18th and 19th centuries (cf. Stone 1977: 47, Graph 3; Hollingsworth 1964, Graph 11). Brunt also adduces the example of the Venetian nobility of the 17th century (1971: 140; cf. Davis 1962: 69). In both instances, noble families came to an end because children did not marry for fear of impoverishing the family estates. In England, even some 'elder sons' refrained from marriage, perhaps influenced by the bachelor mentality which ranged beyond those who had first adopted it as a matter of necessity or prudence. It is very difficult at any historical period — and equally so for contemporary actors and observers — to distinguish externally determined demographic developments from the moral 'superstructure' which they generate. In the late 19th century, moralists repeatedly sought to discern the flaws in Australian maidenhood which would explain why so many young women remained unmarried. Recent examination of census figures suggests that the answer was to be found in the imbalance of men and women within the endogamous groups, broken down by age and regional distribution (Quiggin 1986; Table 2, 'Conjugal condition', *Censuses of Victoria 1861-1901*).

Equally, while Augustus was railing at the selfishness of bachelors, he might well have been addressing men who had nobody to marry.[33] This could explain why some men tried to evade his strictures by affiancing themselves to children and why, in spite of his dislike of social miscegenation, Augustus allowed free-born men below senatorial rank to marry *libertinae* (cf. Paul, *Dig.* 23.2.44). Perhaps it was less acceptable for women to marry into a lower social group than their own.[34] This tendency was reinforced by penalties for free-born women who cohabited with slaves. No such penalties applied to men and concubinage — a marriage-like relationship between people of unequal station — received some acknowledgement in Augustan legislation.[35] Like the insistence on rapid remarriage of childless widows and divorcees during their reproductive years (Humbert 1972: 146-70), this suggests that marriageable women were, as Dio claimed, a scarce commodity (Dio 54.16.2). Brunt accepts that this was probably the case, but he argues, from the enactment of further legislation with the same aim after a lapse of some 26 years (Dio 56.2.2; 56.4.3), that initial imbalance could not alone explain persistent failure to marry. He reasons that if the first legislation had been successful the sex ratios should have evened out (1971: 561). The implication is that upper-class Roman men did avoid marriage and legitimate procreation and that imperial legislation failed to curb this tendency.

A significant difference between the 17th century Venetians or 18th-19th century Englishmen and the Romans of Augustus' day was the attitude to family size after marriage. Those English and Venetian noblemen who did marry had large families, apparently careless of their inability to provide them with adequate fortunes. Romans, once married, had to be persuaded to have families of such a size. It is not clear whether abortion, *coitus interruptus*, abstinence or infant exposure was the favoured method (Hopkins 1965b; Nardi 1971. Compare Pomeroy 1983, Hopkins 1983: 225-6 and Polgar 1972 on infanticide in general), but the ancient sources are in accord in their assumption that the number of children in a family was determined by choice.[36] Hopkins' statement (1983: 95), 'Some upper class women had children; others restricted their fertility' — apparently based on *Nux* 23 and Sen. *ad Helviam* 16.3 — assumes that women had the power to determine family size, but the evidence for respectable matrons aborting legitimate issue without the knowledge of their husbands is very weak. Hopkins has demonstrated elsewhere (1965b) that contraceptive and abortive techniques were known in Rome in the late Republic and early Empire but many of the techniques were misguided and no clear pattern of their use emerges from the patchy sources. Some of the techniques, like abortion, could have been employed secretly by married women, but the ancient sources tend to assume that only adulteresses resorted to clandestine abortion. Classical scholars have seized upon the few texts on the subject as evidence of the decadence of upper-class women. Nardi (1971: 200-3) cites authors from 1743 to 1966 on the subject, and the collection makes fascinating reading but is not informative about the ancient situation (indeed, one gains the impression that many of these gentlemen were unaware that abortion was practised in their own societies).

Seneca (*ad Helviam* 16.3) praised his mother at the expense of other, unnamed women who extinguished the new life quickening within them; Ovid (*Amores* 2.14) mused pompously on 'Corinna's' abortion of an illegitimate child; Juvenal (6.592-9) implied that rich women were able to avoid childbirth and breast-feeding and associated abortion with adultery. In Aulus Gellius' representation of Favorinus' speech in favour of breast-feeding, the philosopher likens a mother who refuses her child the breast to one who aborts a foetus (*NA* 12.1.8-9). All of these are very general, moralising references which reveal only the public male attitude to abortion. It is worth noting in passing that Favorinus, who assumes female vanity as the reason for abortion, makes a similar assumption about maternal breast-feeding, while the grandmother of the new baby in question — whose knowledge of the subject is presumably less theoretical — is concerned for her daughter's health and that of the new child. Like Juvenal, Nero associated abortion and adultery in his trumped-up charges against his first wife Octavia (Tac. *Ann.* 14.63). For an adulterous woman, abortion might have been an obvious solution to an incriminating pregnancy. The alternative was to risk disgrace with the public repudiation by the husband of an illegitimate child (cf. Suet. *Claud.* 27). Abortion of a legitimate child without the knowledge of the father would have been a serious undertaking. Cicero's argument, *Clu.* 32; 34 and 125, assumes that a widow or divorcée who took it upon herself to abort progeny from the marriage would have been regarded by Roman men as depriving the husband or his line of what was rightfully theirs (cf. Tryphoninus at *Dig.* 48.19.39). This suggests that abortion *during* a marriage would have been regarded at least with suspicion, not because of any strong belief in the sanctity or humanity of the foetus, but because such decisions rested properly with the father, who had rights in the child after birth.[37] Abortion was probably one of the grave offences for which a wife could be divorced in archaic Rome (Plut. *Rom.* 22.3).

The power of life and death (*ius vitae necisque*) which the Roman *paterfamilias* held was not to be despised at any period of history. It was rare for men to exercise their technical right to kill adult children but the right of the father (or the *dominus*) to expose a new-born infant or to acknowledge it and by implication pronounce his intention of rearing it (*tollere liberos*) was a standard proceeding. Claudius exercised his right to expose the child born to his first wife Plautia Urgulanilla five months after he had divorced her for adultery (Suet. *Claud.* 27). Cicero's daughter Tullia appears to have gone to the home of her divorced husband's adoptive father for the confinement which in the event caused her death.[38] If her husband's rights — or, more accurately, the rights of the *paterfamilias* — were so observed after the dissolution of a marriage, we should be wary of unsubstantiated and unspecific charges that they were commonly disregarded during the marriage. It is not impossible that some society beauties resented pregnancy as a disfigurement outweighing the distinction and material advantages of motherhood. It is, however, quite unlikely that any woman who felt like this would openly give it out as her reason for performing an act of dubious acceptability and even legality on her own initiative and without her husband's agreement. The sources of the moralists must have been gossip. It might be as well to show caution in dealing with the evidence of ancient authors and generalising about the behaviour of respectable matrons.

The position of a courtesan or any woman involved in a sexual relationship with a man with whom she had no *conubium* (legal right of marriage) was otherwise. If she were widowed or unmarried, she could decide to abort or expose a child of the union — although her father or patron might claim rights.[39] In the case of legitimate issue, the 'father' or potential father was the primary target of imperial legislation and propaganda alike, on the assumption that he controlled sexuality *and* made the decisions about rearing children within the marriage.

Again, examples can be adduced from later history of noble houses which mysteriously limited their progeny to avoid the erosion of estates by inheritance and dowry and the expenses, as parents thought of them, of rearing children. Stone's summary of this phenomenon (1977: 41) in early modern Europe may be applicable here:

It is significant that the first groups in Europe to practise contraception within marriage were the aristocracy and the urban élite, who did not depend upon their children for labour in the fields or shop, or for support in their old age, and who were the first to experience the rising costs of education and marriage. They were, therefore, the class with the most to gain and the least to lose by restricting births.

Certainly the expenses of a senatorial son's career could be considerable — as were a daughter's dowry and obligations to a son-in-law, who could also claim the right to canvassing (Plin. *Ep.* 1.14.7). Children were proverbially deemed a burden.[40] It may seem odd to us, in view of the great wealth of the Roman upper class, but it is plain from their own testimony that they felt several children to be financially crippling. Suetonius' example of Hortensius Hortalus' relative impoverishment was apparently taken seriously. His patriotic decision to rear four children endangered his senatorial status.[41]

Not everybody necessarily limited his family from choice. With the best will in the world, many people were simply unable to produce many children or to rear them to adulthood.[42] The two brothers Cicero produced three children between them. Of these children, young Quintus perished unmarried in the civil war of 43 BC, while his cousin Tullia died leaving only one child behind her after three marriages and as many miscarriages. Neither Augustus nor Livia had produced the quota necessary for the full *ius liberorum* grant. In terms of the Augustan legislation, they would strictly have been qualified to make wills and inherit from each other, but not to take legacies. They were unable to produce a common child and few of their numerous grandchildren outlived them (Tac. *Ann.* 1.3; Suet. *Aug.* 62-4). Claudius and Tiberius were the only Julio-Claudian *principes* to produce legitimate sons — and there can hardly be any doubt as to the strong desire of the others to achieve that end. Pliny, too, was clearly disappointed that he had not achieved paternity from any of his marriages and, in his petition for the grant of the *ius liberorum*, gave assurances of his sincere attempts to comply with the imperial wishes on the subject (Plin. *Ep.* 10.2; and compare the families traced by Corbier 1985: 518-20). If the Augustan laws failed in their aim, there are many possible explanations apart from wilful avoidance of marriage in order to attract the attentions of *captatores* (legacy hunters), which the satirists (cf. Juv. 2.6.38-40) are so eager to stress.

The numerous applications of the Augustan laws on marriage and the family, as well as the amendments,[43] show that successive Principates attempted to enforce the idea that people of means should marry and refurbish the population of the Empire, particularly of Italy and particularly of the urban upper class. The original legislation had introduced the possibility of prosecution by a 'disinterested' third party for adultery or *lenocinium* (complaisance). The economic incentive for this ensured that the provisions on adultery would take prominence in the public eye.[44]

Conclusion

Motherhood as such, then, was rewarded by general prestige and a sense of virtuous fulfilment, much as it had always been, but enhanced by 'official' imperial approval and the release from certain testamentary limitations. This took the specific form of the *ius liberorum*, which carried privileges such as liberation from *tutela*, possibly some distinction in dress and, more concretely, the ability to take legacies even beyond the limit imposed by the *lex Voconia*, and, in the second century, a limited right to succeed to one's own children in the event of their death intestate (*Inst.* 3.3). It is, however, probable that as time passed this privilege was granted honorifically.

In more general terms, the imperial houses publicly celebrated their women as mothers — especially after their death — of reigning emperors or new mothers of heirs. In other words, the women of the ruling houses served as reminders of dynastic continuity and of an emperor's *pietas*. Tiberius' refusal to allow Livia Augusta posthumous deification did not prevent her many admirers in the senate from referring informally to her as *mater patriae*.[45] Expressions like this, or MATER SENATVS, MATER CASTRORVM[46] both reflected and elevated the general regard for motherhood.

The effect — and, indeed, the aim — of Augustus' legislation to promote marriage and the family is still debated. The general view is that he did not substantially increase the birthrate of the senatorial and equestrian class.[47] It is even more difficult to determine whether adultery became less common. Certainly it continued to be reported and prosecuted, and, of course, denounced and discussed by self-righteous historians and poets alike. At the same time, the *ideals* of conjugal love and (nuclear) family life seem to have been adopted within the upper classes, possibly in response to imperial exhortation and — very occasionally — example, but essentially as the continuation of existing traditions extolling motherhood and matronly chastity.

Motherhood now had the official seal of approval, as it were, but it is moot whether any senatorial woman of the first two centuries AD outside the imperial family enjoyed the respect the widowed Cornelia (*mater Gracchorum*) had commanded in her bereft old age (Plut. *Gai. Gr.* 19). Hundreds of inscriptions in *CIL* VI are dedicated to mothers but there is no way of relating them to imperial policy by content or dating. For most women, motherhood probably remained a significant aspiration and experience regardless of whether it was enforced by the *ius liberorum*.

Notes

1. In spite of the tradition that the laws of Romulus had prohibited the exposure of healthy male citizen babies (and first-born daughters — Dion. Halic. 2.15), there is no evidence of systematic incentives for rearing children. Compare Astin (1967: 322ff.), Brunt (1971: 559) and now des Bouvrie (1984).

2. The laws themselves are reconstructed from ancient references such as *RG* 6; 8.5; Hor. *Carm.* 4.5.21-4; Ov. *Fasti* 2.139; Dio 54.16; Suet. *Aug.* 34; Ulpian XI.20: *Dig.* 23.2, e.g. 19; 44-6. These sources have been collected by Rotondi (1922: 445-6) and Riccobono (1945: I.166 ff). Jörs' (1882) analysis of the legislation is still helpful.

3. The demographic purpose of the legislation is discussed by Field (1945), Brunt (1971: 154, 565-6); Csillag (1976: 45). Humbert (1972) does not consider the question, even in his discussion pp. 170-8 of the efficacy of the laws. Wallace-Hadrill (1981: esp. 58-9) insists that the laws were directed at the well-to-do. Nörr (1977; 1981) accepts a general demographic aim but agrees that the laws had little effect on the poor.

4. Val. Max. 8.15.12; Plin. *HN* 7.120. Tradition actually assigns this to a Vestal scandal of 114 BC, to which Ovid alludes indirectly *Fasti* 4.160.

5. Suet. *Aug.* 34, which appears to telescope incidents recounted by Dio 56.1-10, set in AD 9, before the second round of 'marriage laws'. Both authors refer to a demonstration at the games.

6. By adoption, Augustus was *paterfamilias* of his sons-in-law, grandsons and their children. See the use of '*filii*', *RG* 14.

7. Drusus made a few additional remarks about his own marriage. For, as he said, the imperial princes all too frequently had to attend the far reaches of the Empire. How often had the divine Augustus

been accompanied on his travels to West and East by Livia! He himself had been to Illyricum and if he were called upon he would go to other countries, but not always in a settled frame of mind if he were parted from his wife, who was very dear to him and the mother of their many children.

addidit pauca Drusus de matrimonio suo: nam principibus adeunda saepius longinqua imperii. quoties divum Augustum in Occidentem atque Orientem meavisse comite Livia! se quoque in Illyricum profectum et, si ita conducat, alias ad gentis iturum, haud semper aequo animo si ab uxore carissima et tot communium liberorum parente divelleretur.

(Tac. *Ann.* 3.34)

8. E.g. *aureus* minted at Rome AD 54 — with portraits facing on the obverse with the legend:

AGRIPP AVG DIVI CLAVD NERONIS CAES MATER

Agrippina Augusta, wife of the divine Claudius, mother of Nero Caesar (*RIC* Nero: 9/new ed. 1 and 2), or the *denarius* minted at Rome AD 54, the portraits of Nero and his mother both side-on, with the same legend on the reverse (*RIC* Nero: 10/new ed. 7). Note that references to the coins of Mattingly/Sydenham's *Roman Imperial Coinage* are given by issuing emperor and number, followed where applicable by the reference to the *1984* edition of vol. 1 by Sutherland.

9. In contrast to coin issues in which Gaius and Nero, as *principes*, celebrated their mothers. Compare the obverse of Gaius' *sestertius* issue *RIC* 42/ new ed. 55:

AGRIPPINA M F MAT C CAESARIS AVGVSTI

Agrippina, daughter of Marcus, mother of C. Caesar Augustus, or Nero's (*RIC* 9/new ed. 1 and 2 (obverse)) *aureus* and (*RIC* 10/new ed. 7 (reverse)) *denarius* legends, cited in the previous note.

10. It is more doubtful that the *dupondii* issued under Tiberius AD 22-3 as PIETAS and IVSTITIA personifications were, as Giacosa assumes (1977: 34), intended to portray the young Livia. On this see Grant (1954: 134 ff) on *RIC* Tiberius: 22/new ed. 46. I am, however, satisfied that the dupondius issued at Rome AD 22 with the legend SALVS AVGVSTA (*RIC* 23/new ed. 47) was intended to represent the Emperor's mother. Compare Tac. *Ann.* 3.64.

11. On the veto of Livia's deification: Dio 58.2; Suet. *Tib.* 51. On Tiberius' general conservatism about honours: Tac. *Ann.* 4.8 ff; 4.15.

12. Suet. *Claud.* 3.2:

His mother Antonia used to call him a human freak, only begun by nature and not properly finished; and if she was accusing anyone of stupidity she would say he was sillier than her son Claudius.

mater Antonia portentum eum hominis dictitabat, nec absolutum a natura, sed tantum incohatum; ac si quem socordiae argueret, stultiorem aiebat filio suo Claudio.

13. Tac. *Ann.* 12.26. Other honours accorded her during Claudius' lifetime included naming a colony (modern Cologne) after her — Tac. *Ann.* 12.27. Tacitus disapproved of the fact that Caractacus, as a defeated enemy, should have addressed himself as much to the Emperor's wife as to the Emperor himself (*Ann.* 12.37.6), but as Furneaux (1907: II. 107) points out, she was the first Empress who could boast of her own descent from Augustus. Before Nero's accession, she was marked out for her own distinction, not only for being mother of the imperial heir. In *RIC* Claudius: 92 (an *aureus* coined at Rome. Compare new ed. 80) and 54 (an Eastern Mediterranean *cistephoros* issue), she appears in association with Claudius and with her title of 'Augusta'.

14. Contrast the obverse of the *aureus* and *denarius* on which Nero and his mother face inwards towards each other (*RIC* Nero: 9/new ed. 1 and 2) with those in which the Emperor's profile is superimposed on that of his mother (*RIC* 10/new ed. 6 and 7).

15. E.g. *CIL* VI 1035 (= 31232) to Julia Domna (as Julia Augusta). An earlier incision was overlaid with the words ET SENATVS ET PATRIAE, so that line 4 reads:

IVLIAE AVG MATRI AVG N ET CASTRORVM ET SENATVS ET PATRIAE
'To Julia Augusta, mother of the Augustus and of the camp and the senate and the fatherland'

Compare *CIL* VI 1048. Instinsky (1942: esp. 203-5) plots the use and significance of titles such as 'mother of the camp' and 'mother of the senate'. Compare Dio 58.2 and Tac. *Ann.* 1.14 on Livia, who was informally given such titles by the senate but denied their official use by her son Tiberius.

16. E.g. *RIC* 211 (Julia Paula); *RIC* 390 (Aquilia Severa); *RIC* 399 (Annia Faustina). It is ironic, in view of the brevity of the marriages, that all of these issues celebrate CONCORDIA on the reverse.

17. E.g. Suet. *Aug.* 34; Tac. *Ann.* 3. 24-8; *RG* 6; Dio 54.16; 56. 1-10; Gai. 2.111, 286; *CJ*.8. 57-8; *Dig.* 48.5; 35.1. 60-1. See note 2 above.

18. See again the references listed in note 3 above for the purpose of the legislation. Other works include Astolfi (1970), R.I. Frank (1976), Nörr (1977), Besnier (1979), Cairns (1979), Raditsa (1980), Galinsky (1981), Williams (1962). Raditsa has a useful review of the scholarship and some interesting remarks on the cleavage between social and legal historians (esp. pp. 280-1). Besnier conveniently draws the bibliography together at n1, p. 192. Other recent works include Nörr (1981), Wallace-Hadrill (1981) and des Bouvrie (1984). There is also an extensive literature on the nature of the courts which tried the adultery cases, e.g. Garnsey (1967), Bauman (1968), Thomas (1970). It will be apparent that the works about the legislation greatly exceed the remaining fragments of the laws. It has almost become an exercise in academic masochism to wade throughout the accretion of scholarly speculation before daring to add one's own inconclusive

reflections on the subject, but the topic remains a classical growth area.

19. On the *ius liberorum* generally, see Suet. *Galba* 14.3; Gai 1.194; 3.44 ff; Plin. *Ep.* 2.13.8; 10.2.1; 10. 94-5; Juv. *Sat.* 9. 72-85; Aul. Gell. *NA* 2.15; Tac. *Ann.* 2.51; 15.19; Dio 53.13.2; *Lex Malacitana* 56 (vol. 2 no. 23 *FIRA*) and Sherwin-White (1966: 558) on Plin. *Ep.* 10.2. See also Steinwenter (1893), Kübler (1910), Sijpesteijn (1965). Most of these authors concentrate on the privileges conferred on men by the *ius*.

20. *Inst.* 4.18.4 and see the collection of references in Riccobono (1945: 168). Cf. Gai. 3.44-53 for the complex implications of the *lex papia* provisions for inheritance of *libertinae* (freedwomen) and female patrons (*patronae*).

21. = *Dig.* 48.5; *CJ* 9.9 and *ADA*: 113 ff. On the tension between the Augustan legislation and Christian ideals (especially with relation to the remarriage of widows), see Humbert (1972: 360-87).

22. E.g. *Dig.* 25.7.1.2 (Ulpian, his second book on the law); *Dig.* 48.5.9 (Marcianus); and see Corbett (1930: 139 ff) and Mommsen (1899: 691).

23. *Dig.* 48.5.6 (Papinian); 48.5.35 (Modestinus); and see Csillag (1976) n718. Modestinus (*Dig.* 50.16.101) made the point that the Augustan law had used '*adulterium*' (adultery) of wives and widows. '*stuprum*' (fornication) was later deemed more appropriate for errant widows. Cf. *Inst.* 4.18.4.

24. See e.g. Gai. 2.226-7, 254; Plin. *Pan.* 42; *Dig.* 35.2 (inheritance); Liv. 8.22.3; 10.31.9; 25.2.9 ('*stuprum*' judged by aediles).

25. Cf. Dio 56.6.4 ff; Suet. *Aug.* 89; Liv. *Per.* 59; *RG* 8.5:

legibus novis me auctore latis multa exempla maiorum exo-
lescentia iam ex nostro saeculo reduxi.

By initiating new legislation I revived many traditional examples which had fallen into disuse in our day.

Suet. *Aug.* 34 echoes this official view.

26. Married men were formally asked by the censors to swear that they had married for the purpose of producing (legitimate) children: Cic. *Leg.* 3.7; Dion. Halic. 2.25.7; Aul. Gell. *NA* 4.3.2. Compare Nörr 1977: 310-11; 1981: 358.

27. This is substantially correct. Compare Dio 56.1.2; Tac. *Ann.* 2.51; *Gnomon Id.* 29 ff (83 ff); Aul. Gell. *NA* 2.15 and Brunt 1971: 561-2.

28. Dio 56.7.6 and see Gai 3.40 ff on compromises between patronal rights and the *ius liberorum*.

29. An alimentary scheme of a kind was established at Atina in Nero's day — *ILS* 977. On the aims of such schemes, see Duncan-Jones (1964).

30. Plin. *Pan.* 26.5. As Wallace-Hadrill points out (1981: 59), this shows Pliny's awareness that the incentives attached to inheritance and a public career applied only to the prosperous.

31. As Plin. *Ep.* 7.18 and 10.8 (esp. 1) imply. On official schemes under Trajan, see *RIC* 459, 460, 461, 470, 471, 473, 474; *CIL* XI 4351; *ILS* 6509, 6675 and see Veyne (1957-8).

32. Cic. *Fam.* 14.1.5; *Att.* 2.4.5; 2.15.4. See further the examples of

Dixon 1984a: 347. Inscriptions confirm the implication of Cic. *Mur.* 27, that some adult women had freedmen *tutores* who acted as agents rather than monitors. Cf. *CIL* VI 2650; *CIL* VI 7468; *CIL* VI 29398. Compare the remarks of Gai. 1.190.

33. Dio 56.7.2; Liv. *Per.* 59; Suet. *Aug.* 34 and see Brunt 1971: 151 ff, esp. 155: '... the fundamental reason why many did not take wives or rear children was their simple inability to do so ...' Cf. Dio 54.16. 1-2.

34. *Ingenuae* were prepared to marry imperial *libertini* and slaves, who constituted a special status group. See, for example, Weaver (1972: 141-2).

35. Cf. *Dig* 48.5.35 (34) Modestinus. See Csillag (1976: 143-6) for a discussion of the views about whether the Augustan legislation explicitly excepted concubinage. Csillag's own views on the prevalence and function of concubinage should be tempered by a reading of Rawson (1974) who has demonstrated that concubinage existed almost exclusively between partners whose unequal status barred them from *iustae nuptiae*.

36. The subject is bedevilled by moralising. The childless Pliny and Seneca spoke as if their peers limited families from greed and personal vanity, e.g. Plin. *Ep.* 4.15.3 and Sen. *ad Helviam* 16.3. Musonius Rufus (frag. 15 Lutz) and Tac. *Ann.* 3.25 predictably took the view that limitation of fertility was motivated by unworthy materialistic aims. As evidence for either low fertility or its motivation such comments are almost valueless but the assumption that family size was the result of choice is consistent. The few ancient references to infant exposure take it for granted (Hopkins 1983: 225-6) but most of the modern discussion is about Greek practice. See most recently D. Engels (1980), Harris (1982), Golden (1981), Patterson (1985). General studies of exposure and infanticide include Polgar (1972), Langer (1974), and Dickemann (1979).

37. Compare *Dig.* 47.11.4 (Marcianus):

The divine Severus and Caracalla decreed that a woman who procured an abortion should be sent into exile for a fixed term by the official for it would seem unworthy that she should have deprived her husband of children without incurring a penalty.

Divus Severus et Antoninus rescripserunt eam, quae data opera abegit, a praeside in temporale exilium dandam: indignum enim videri potest impune eam maritum liberis fraudasse.

38. Plut. *Cic.* 41.7: Tullia gave birth in the home of Dolabella's adoptive father in January 45 BC. She died in February at Cicero's Tuscan villa. Cicero fled the place, passing through Astura from which he wrote *Att.* 12.13. Compare Oppianicus' aunt who had agreed to stay on with her mother-in-law until she had given birth to the child she was expecting when her husband died — *Clu.* 33.

39. Note that certain (unrespectable) categories of women were excluded from charges of *stuprum* (criminal fornication) — *Dig.* 25.7.1-2 (Ulpian); Paul *Sent.* 2.26.11; *Dig.* 48.5.11 (Papinian). On the 'rights' of the father of a woman caught in the act of adultery, see *Dig.* 48.5.23 (22) (Papinian) and consider Augustus' exposure of his illegitimate great-grandchild (Suet. *Aug.* 65). Norden (1912: 127) points out that Venus

assumes the role of the pregnant Psyche's father in ill-treating her (Apul. *Met.* 6.9). The successive amendments designed to balance the Augustan marriage laws against the venerable claims of patrons are interesting. If patrons could traditionally demand that *liberti* swear not to have (legitimate) children — *Dig.* 37.14.6.4 (Paul) — they probably took an even more proprietorial attitude to the children of the *libertae* in their *tutela* (Gai. 1.192; 3.42 ff). On the whole, the assumption seems to have been that patrons, as intestate heirs of their former slaves, were more inclined to limit their fertility than to resent exposure and abortion.

40. Aul. Gell. *NA* 2.23.21 and cf. Duncan-Jones (1974: 318-9). Imperial sources tend to labour the theme that *orbitas* (childlessness) was a social advantage, e.g. Sen. *ad Marciam* 19.2; Tac. *Ann.* 15.19; Plin. *HN* 14.5.

41. Suet. *Tib.* 47; Tac. *Ann.* 2.37. His grandfather's famous fish-ponds and estates must have been severely eroded — perhaps by confiscation. The famous orator's wealth had been well known and his daughter was still one of the wealthiest women in Rome after Philippi (Appian *BC* 4.32). See Geiger (1970) on the identification of this impoverished descendant of a famous family.

42. See e.g. Humbert (1972: 142 ff). Brunt (1971: 141-2) points out that some noble families 'disappeared' only in the sense that they became poorer and therefore obscure. Cf. Hopkins (1983: 60-76).

43. See e.g. Suet. *Claud.* 19; 23; *Nero* 10; *Galba* 14.3; Plin. *Ep.* 2.13.8; 10.95; *Dig.* 4.4.2 (Ulpian); *Dig.* 38.1.37 (Paul); *Dig.* 23.2.19 (a *constitutio* of Severus on the *l. Iulia*); *FV* 216; Ulpian *Tit.* 29; *CIL* II 1964 (= *lex Malecitana*); *Inst.* 3.3.2; Ulpian *Tit.* 3.1. See Csillag 1976: 201 ff and esp. n185: Nörr (1977: 314). The application of the laws was formally in the hands of the senate at least until Nero's principate — Tac. *Ann.* 15.19 — but, like the official introduction of the *lex Papia-Poppaea*, was very much in conformity with the wishes of the ruler.

44. See e.g. Tac. *Ann.* 4.42; Dio 67.12; Plin. *Ep.* 6.31. 4-6; *Dig.* 3.2.2.3 (Ulpian) and the whole of 48.5. We have more information about Augustan provisions on adultery. On the eradication of the marriage rules, see *Inst.* 3.3.4 where Justinian expressly rejects the notion of reward for the number of children born to a woman on the ground that it is not her fault if she produces fewer than the quota imposed by his predecessors:

quid enim peccavit, si non plures sed paucos peperit?

and compare *C. Th.* 8.17.1.

45. Or possibly *parens patriae*: see Dio *Per.* 58.2 (Xiph. 142-3). Because, says Xiphilinus (/?Dio), she had interceded to save the lives of some, had reared the children of others and contributed to the dowries of some senators' daughters. Compare Tac. *Ann.* 1.14.

46. E.g. *CIL* VI 226u and compare *CIL* VI 1035 (= 31232); 36932s; 31335; 31332; 1063 etc. Again, see Instinsky (1942) on Julia Domna.

47. E.g. Csillag (1976: 70 ff); Humbert (1972: 142 ff); Brunt (1971: 154 ff and Appendix 9).

5

The Roman Mother and the Young Child

Come baby, start to acknowledge your mother with
your smile, for she had endured ten long, tedious
months of waiting

Incipe, parve puer, risu cognoscere matrem
(matri longa decem tulerunt fastidia menses)
(Vergil. *Ec.* 4. 60-61)

Where are the children? Sources and concepts

Plutarch tell us (*Numa* 12) that Numa Pompilius had strictly
rationed the mourning of infants in archaic Rome (cf. *FIRA* I:12),
and it is notable that small children are of little account in many
cultures, perhaps because their chances of survival have been too
low to permit a great emotional investment.[1] This kind of reasoning has been attacked[2] and it is true that Roman parents did
sometimes erect costly tombstones for very small children, but it
cannot be denied that children are under-represented in
sepulchral inscriptions as a whole (Hopkins 1983: 225; Burn
1953: 4; cf. Stone 1977: 69ff and George 1930: App. 1). The strictures on formal mourning have parallels in other cultures[3] and
while formal commemoration and feelings are not necessarily to
be equated, it gives us some idea of the relatively low social value
Romans placed on small children. Cicero (*Tusc. Disp.* 1.93) tells
us that those who lamented untimely death in general terms bore
easily the loss of a small child and did not even mourn babies.

Children as such are not well represented in the ancient
sources, and small children are almost absent. Manson (1983:

104

151-3) points out that there was no specific word for 'baby' in Latin. He plots the development of different expressions from the early first century BC, to demonstrate his thesis that this period saw a heightened tenderness in family life and a new interest in the small child as a person. This accords with my own view of the development of sentimental ideals of conjugal and familial happiness during this period. Yet even so, the period of *infantia* — which Quintilian seems to use to cover the whole period up to seven years, when most educators recommend the beginning of formal learning (*Inst. Or.* 1.1.15-26; cf. Neraudau 1979) — is not well represented in literature after that period. The satires and comedies, which generally supply more information about social life than the 'higher' genres of epic and history, are meagre in their yield on children. Subjects such as sex, legacy-hunting or food are better documented. Children — more even than women or slaves — are an assumed part of the social backdrop. Where they are mentioned, the language is vague and it is difficult to distinguish the stages of childhood by the terms used (cf. Neraudau 1979; Slusanski 1974; Gray-Fow 1985).

In our own culture the sentimental appeal of infants is bound up with the image of the nurturing and protective mother: advertisements for babies' toiletries invariably include a smiling mother in physical contact with the child. This stress on the physical and emotional bond between mother and baby may simply be an outgrowth of our predominantly middle class ethic, since in our society mothers have to perform such functions (Minturn and Lambert 1964), in the absence of servants or female helpers from the extended family who share them still in the Third World.

In the Greek-speaking parts of the contemporary Mediterranean, it was common to find the motif of the mother nursing her baby. This occurred in funereal art and in representations of deities — it is not always possible to be sure of the difference (Price 1978: 67-8). There are examples of such statuary in Italy, and Price (1978: 166) insists that they manifest an ancient Mediterranean-wide religion rather than Greek influence. She includes them in her study, however, because they became assimilated with the cult of Greek goddesses, and the examples she gives (such as her Plate 17) have a very Greek appearance. This is also the case with the seated Etruscan mother and child usually identified as Mater Matuta, now in Florence (Latte 1960: Plate 2). The objects uncovered in connection with this cult also include small statues of swaddled babies. The motifs do not appear in pictorial Italian art, and are very likely to be offerings for a safe delivery at childbirth.[4]

Children sometimes appeared in Roman funereal art, but not usually in conjunction with a mother. Sarcophagi on which the stages of a youth's or man's life are depicted often include his birth or his being raised up immediately after birth by a midwife, while the mother sits in the confinement chair (see Plate 7). There are examples of mothers, seated, holding a baby or small child, but they are not an identifiable genre.[5] In the panoramic scenes of life's stages, the mother is present at or just after the birth. Subsequent scenes usually depict the small boy playing, attended by a crouching nurse or other servant, then at school with a male teacher, then in a chariot. The mother reappears, if at all, as a mourner at his death-bed. Mothers are usually distinguishable from servants because they are seated — midwives crouch, and *nutrices* stand. There are exceptions, but that is the convention. It might represent the reality, where the servants brought the young child to a seated mistress. Interestingly, that is the convention recorded in photographs of the nineteenth-century upper-class household in Europe, where it reflected the role played by mother and servant in a child's life.

This differs from modern artistic convention. Although some people make home movies of childbirths we do not commonly depict it in our decorative art. The nursing Madonna is a long-standing motif, and the young mother and child has become, if anything, more popular in the last century and a half, with the rise in the cult of the family.[6] It would be interesting to know whether childbirth scenes depicted on memorials to midwives and as part of the dead person's life were produced by men who had witnessed such scenes or were done to a pattern, perhaps with the aid of models. We have some literary references to the ritual following childbirth: Octavian's father was absent from the Senate during the vital debate on the Catilinarian conspiracy because of his wife's confinement (Suet. *Aug.* 94.5). Even if that is too good to be true, it shows that fathers were expected to absent themselves from public business for the occasion, but does not tell us whether they were actually present at the birth. Aulus Gellius provides us with an account of a visit. Some admirers of Favorinus, hearing that a friend's wife had just given birth to a son, went to visit her and congratulate the father. They went to his house and embraced him and asked details of the labour. It had been protracted, and the newly delivered young mother was asleep, so they could not see her. Her mother was also present and clearly in charge of the practicalities, for she had already decided to engage wet-nurses to spare her weakened daughter the strain of breast-feeding (*NA* 12.1.1-5). The congratulation of Nero's parents after his birth and polite queries about the baby's name are reported as routine social niceties (Suet. *Nero* 6).

The art and literature, then, gives us a glimpse of the circumstances of childbirth and the social ritual surrounding it. The mother's role in the years following that event is more difficult to reconstruct. It is curious that the art evidence is so unhelpful, given the literary references to the pleasures of family life. They do not seem to have been reinforced in depictions of the family. Sarcophagi and stelae were more likely to depict a married couple than the group of parents and children. Where 'children' were included in pictures, they were usually shown as adults.[7]

Under Augustus, there was an emphasis on the virtues of marriage and procreation. This was combined with propaganda stressing the stability of the succession, as in the Ara Pacis enclosure frieze displaying the generations of the imperial family, and numerous portraits of the imperial princes, such as Gaius and Lucius, which were distributed about the empire.[8] Kleiner (1977: 178-9; 1978) has shown the special influence of the Ara Pacis sculpture on private funereal sculpture, which set a fashion of family groups, including young children, which lapsed again after Augustus' demise. The mother-and-child type did not appear as part of this trend, officially or privately. Augustus made a point of restoring a statue of Cornelia with the inscribed base 'to the mother of the Gracchi', yet the statue itself was of Cornelia alone, not of her with her sons, at any age (Plin. *HN* 34.31; *CIL* VI 31610).

Children themselves tended to be included in art, apart from mythical representations, to fulfil a specific function, such as advertising the Julio-Claudian line or illustrating Trajan's munificence on the Arch of Trajan at Benevento or that of Marcus Aurelius on the triumphal arch later incorporated in the Arch of Constantine (Plates 3 and 4). These yield some idea of how children might conduct themselves on important public occasions, but throw little light on detailed questions of the relative roles of mothers and fathers — save that fathers seem more likely to hoist small children on to their shoulders.

Children appear in the wall-paintings of Pompeii and Herculaneum performing light auxiliary tasks — bearing a small container, or attending to an adult's shoes. The references in literature to the child *in gremio matris*, 'in its mother's lap' (Tac. *Dial.* 28), or on the tombstones to the child *ab ubere raptus*, 'snatched from the breast' (*CIL* VI. 2390), are not parallelled in art. Apart from the frieze of Italia (or Terra Mater) on the Ara Pacis enclosure (Plate 1), children small enough to be found in laps or at bosoms are scarce. The children who appear on private funereal sculpture[9] are formally posed and as expressionless as the staidest Edwardian family photograph. They tell us that the essential family was often defined as the nuclear unit, but little more. We get no sense of a special relationship between children and their mothers. Even mothers who died in childbirth or with their children seem not to have been regularly represented with them on funeral monuments.

On the whole, then, the evidence from art tells us little about the relationship of the mother with the young child. Both children and mothers are dealt with by two special categories of writer: the medical and the rhetorical. Soranus is known to have been popular and influential in Rome in his day (*c.* AD 98-138), so his writings on pregnancy, childbirth and breast-feeding might be taken as relevant. They are, however, prescriptive and might not represent everyday practice. Art confirms the assumption that midwives rather than doctors usually delivered babies and there is no reason to believe that they sought advice from books rather than the traditional method of training and transmitting information. Soranus also advocates maternal breast-feeding, which might have been unusual in the propertied classes. Even the fashionable women who could afford a doctor like Soranus might have employed midwives and taken advice from them and their own mothers. We have already seen one example of such a woman whose mother appeared to be directing proceedings. It is difficult to tell whether Soranus' detailed advice about the diet and care of the young child was taken as seriously as Spock's detailed diagnostic information is taken by modern parents. Étienne has concluded that even the ancient medical writers paid scant attention to the welfare of the small child. This could be because that was considered the province of women — midwives, mothers and nurses — and not worthy of the attention of professional doctors (Étienne 1973: esp. 43).

In approaching a subject so sketchily treated by the sources it is particularly difficult to chart change over time and to assess the relation of moralising prescriptions to practice. The young child was of interest to ancient authors chiefly as a potential orator. Quintilian's *Institutio Oratoria* and Tacitus' *Dialogus* devote some attention to the small boy because of the belief that oratory has its foundations in early linguistic and moral development. In the course of such a discussion, they reveal some interesting opinions about children and the maternal role.

Dismayed at the decadence of modern youth, the orator Vipstanus Messalla looked back in AD 74 to the virtues of a lost age (of unspecified date):

> For in the early days every child born of a good mother was reared not in the dismal room of a mercenary nurse, but in the lap of its own mother, enfolded in her care. Such a woman took particular pride in being described as looking after her home and devoting herself to her children.

> nam pridem suus cuique filius, ex casta parente natus, non in cellula emptae nutricis, sed gremio ac sinu matris edu-cabatur, cuius praecipua laus erat tueri domum et inservire liberis.

> (*Dial.* 28)

There might have been some germ of truth in this romantic vision of the pure Roman past when mothers looked after their own children and houses, although the praise lavished on out-standing examples of motherly virtue suggests that it had ceased to be usual in the senatorial class even from the late Republic. It is important, though, to note that *inservire liberis* probably did not equate with the menial and custodial aspects of child care required of modern mothers. The famous mothers mentioned in Roman literature are not characterised by their physical attentions to infants or loving ministration to childish demands so much as by inculcation of the traditional virtues. Indeed, one of the criticisms of the modern style offered up in *Dialogus* was that the servants tended to indulge young children and 'spoil' them, with the result that they grew up frivolous and selfish, in contrast to the paradigm of maternal vigilance encapsulated in Cornelia, Aurelia and Atia, whose *disciplina ac severitas* had trained leaders for the state — the Gracchi brothers, Caesar and Augustus — with the ability to concentrate on a set goal. For all his emphasis on the foundations of eloquence, Vipstanus Messalla was mind-ful, too, of the moral aspect. He noted that guidance had once

extended even to childish play. The mother's role was emphasised, but mother surrogates as such were not despised, if they
were of the right type (*Dial.* 28. 5-6).

Quintilian's concern was more clearly linguistic — education
of the orator could not begin too early, he argued, and the
babbling of foreign slaves was a poor substitute for pure Latin.
He did not disdain the notion of a paid nurse or *paedagogus*, but
insisted that such servants should speak well (*ante omnia ne sit
vitiosus sermo nutricibus*) — on the assumption that they would
have most to do with young children:

> These nurses are the first people the child will listen to, it is
> their words the child will attempt to form by imitation and
> we are naturally most firmly influenced by the things we
> have learned when our minds were unformed.

> has primum audiet puer, harum verba effingere imitando
> conabitur, et natura tenacissimi sumus eorum quae rudibus
> animis percepimus.

> (*Inst. Or.* 1.1.5)

He stressed the desirability of cultivated parents, making it clear
that mothers were included in this: those very mothers, known
for their elegant prose style or their eloquence, whom Cicero had
praised in the *Brutus* (set 48-47 BC p. 210-12: Cornelia and
Laelia).[10]

All three authors assumed the importance of early influences;
all three stressed the mother's role in differing ways. She was a
cultivated model of speech, much as the father was — indeed,
Cicero's point is only partly that a mother may transmit style:
most of the women he cites are themselves examples of learning
from eloquent fathers (the Liciniae and Hortensia, for example).
Both authors list women in the sense of '*even* the mothers ...'
rather than on the assumption that they are the key figures of
infant learning.

These fairly dogmatic statements about the mother and infant
generally reveal surprisingly few specifically maternal relations
(with the self-evident exception of the *mater nutrix*, the 'nursing
mother'). Cicero and Quintilian, intent on the need to learn the
rudiments of good speech in the home, include the mother as a
formative influence but not the major or only one. Vipstanus
Messalla, in the *Dialogus*, deplores the disappearance of maternal

attention to (presumably young) children and equates the change with a relaxation of discipline, although both parents are seen as responsible for this decline. The implication of the texts is that upper-class women in general did not involve themselves very closely with the physical care of small children. This does not really seem to have been expected of them, although an overseer role in their moral education was vaguely hoped for and, if given, praised extravagantly.

In general, the role of the upper-class mother seems not to have been very clearly distinguished from that of the father. There is, for example, little suggestion that mothers were more indulgent and fathers more severe with children, or even that mothers had closer, more frequent contact with small children. In an elaborate architectural analogy, Plautus (*Most.* 118-21) represents both parents as 'building' the child. Although Quintilian says that one would normally expect a small child to be attached to the women he saw most frequently, it emerges (*Inst. Or.* 6 *pr.* 8-12) that Quintilian was directly involved in his son's upbringing. A similar impression is conveyed by Aulus Gellius' regretful admission (*NA pr.* 23) that he could give to his writing only the time he had to spare from his primary duty of administering his patrimony and bringing up his children. Cicero's close monitoring of his son's education into adulthood (*Att.* 6.1.12) then appears as the later version of a continuous paternal obligation.

Ariès (1962) argued that the concept of childhood as a separate stage of life is a modern development. Certainly children were prized in part because they continued the family line and the death of a child, when mourned, was regretted because the parent could not have the satisfaction of knowing that his rites would one day be performed by the child. There are, however, some indications that children were valued as such by Roman parents, at least from the first century BC, although little evidence shows this to have been a particularly maternal feeling. Quintilian speaks of the deaths of his young wife and each of his sons with equal regret and specifies the characteristics of the dead children in such a way as to leave no doubt of his interest in them as individuals. There are instances of parents erecting tombstones to small children and dwelling on their personal qualities, as in *CIL* VI. 34421, which celebrates the charm and chatter of the three-year-old Anteis Chrysostom. Most inscriptions are briefer, but this is also true of dedications to husbands and wives.

111

Manson (1983: 154) points out that affectionate adjectives such as *dulcis, suavis* and *mellitus* appeared in the language of family life in the first century BC in literature, then became commonplace in later sepulchral inscriptions. We are told (Suet. *Gai.* 7) that Augustus and Livia greatly regretted the loss of one particularly endearing grandson in his childhood. Livia placed a statue of him, as Cupid, in a temple on the Capitol, while Augustus kept another in his own bedroom which he kissed on entering.

Some few literary allusions to small children actually celebrate their childish features as part of their charm. Lucretius paints the idyllic picture of the young father whose 'sweet' children run to kiss him (3.895-6). The image too, of the infant Torquatus in Catullus' *Epithalamion* shows an appreciation of typically babyish behaviour similar to that of modern literature or photography:

> I hope that there will be a tiny Torquatus in his mother's lap, stretching out his tender hands towards his father and smiling with half-open baby lip.

> Torquatus volo parvulus
> matris e gremio suae
> porrigens teneras manus
> dulce rideat ad patrem
> semihiante labello.

> (61.209-13)

Martial's epigram about a slave-girl who died before her sixth birthday mentions her childish speech and playfulness:

> May she play freely about her elderly patrons and may she prattle my name in her lisping talk.

> Inter tam veteres ludat lasciva patronos
> et nomen blaeso garriat ore meum.

> (5.34:7-8)

Such examples demonstrate that individual Romans became attached to particular children. Some actually kept small children virtually as pets, *delicia*, for the entertainment value of their pert ways and unformed speech (Slater 1974). Even this dubious taste, probably linked with sexual exploitation, was not incompatible with affection and reveals a recognition of childhood as a distinct stage of life. Romans were touched by characteristically childish features — affectionateness, smallness, impulsiveness, lisping — and celebrated their charm explicitly. This appreciation co-existed with more formal praise of their adult-like virtues such as industry and *pietas*, which Quintilian attributes to his ten-year-old son and Pliny to the twelve-year-old Minicia Marcella.[11] This dual appreciation of children, as potential adults and as childlike, would seem to go against Ariès' view.

It cannot, however, be overlooked that there was a strong tendency to treat the deaths of small children as less distressing. People might not be entirely rational in their emotional investments, but expectations do affect mourning. In our own culture, aged parents and grandparents are not lamented in the same way as those who die young. Lattimore notes that in Greek and Latin epitaphs alike, children do not express loss at the death of parents, while parents regularly register their sense of loss at the death of adult children.[12]

Cicero's comment, that people do not in fact mourn small children extravagantly (*Tusc. Disp.* 1.93), is one of the few preserved observations of practice. Seneca wrote a reproachful letter to a friend who was taking the death of his small son too hard:

> I have sent you a letter which I wrote to Marullus because he had lost an infant son and was said to be indulging his grief...

> epistulam, quam scripsi Marullo, cum filium parvulum amisisset et diceretur molliter ferre, misi tibi...
>
> (*Ep. Mor.* 99.1)

Cicero himself spoke quite casually about the poor prospects of his own grandchild, born prematurely.[13]

The hasty cremation of Oppianicus' young son is treated as suspicious in the *pro Cluentio*, but might not have been unusual. Cicero describes the child as being disposed of before his mother could mourn him, because she was elsewhere when he died suddenly in his father's company. Cicero represents her as hurrying there and conducting the obsequies over the vaulted remains (*Clu.* 27-28). This account is so clearly tailored to a forensic purpose that it is difficult to determine what is genuinely sinister or even unusual in the sequence of events. Who knows but that the mother, Papia, received reproachful letters afterwards for her excessive behaviour? In general, it can only be observed that, while there was always an underlying notion that babies and small children were not entitled to full mourning ritual, some parents and others found their deaths very painful — sometimes, no doubt, because this meant the loss of support in old age and the hope of pious burial, but sometimes unquestionably because they missed the dead child as a person. The whole relationship between the rules and practice of formal 'mourning', the personal sense of loss and the degree of attachment to the live child is complex. It is not susceptible to objective analysis and must, in the end, remain speculative.[14]

Children, then, were under-represented in art, literature and even tombstones in ancient Rome. As a group they were considered less important than the modern child, but there is evidence of a change in attitude by the late Republic. Though still not seen as entitled to various forms of social recognition, particularly at death, they were to an extent appreciated for their specifically childish qualities and individual parents could be passionately fond even of very young children.

This apparent development of interest in children did not coincide, as in recent European history, with more demanding standards of child care. There is no reason to believe that children were better watched or better fed by Soranus' time than they had been in Plautus' day. Nor does the development seem to have carried with it a stress on the mother's role. Prescriptive literature acknowledged the mother's part in a son's general education, but she was not expected to play a major role in young children's upbringing.

Child development and the Roman character

Children, in their first days, have the greater benefit of good mothers, not only because they suck their milk, but in a sort, their manners also, by being continually with them, and receiving their first impressions from them. But afterwards, when they come to riper years, good fathers are more behoveful for their forming in virtue and good manners, by their greater wisdom and authority: and ofttimes also, by correcting the fruits of their mother's indulgence by severity.

They are a blessing great, but dangerous ... Above all

other, how great and many are their spiritual dangers, both
for nourishing and increasing the corruption which they
bring into the world with them.

J. Robinson *Of children and their education* (1628)

Our souls contain within them innate seeds of the virtues. If
they were allowed to develop, nature herself would carry
them through to a flourishing existence, but as it is, as soon
as we are brought forth into the world and raised up at
birth, straightway we are caught up in a never-ending whorl
of evil practice and the worst possible principles, so that we
seem to have drunk in error virtually with our nurse's milk.
Indeed, by the time we are passed on in due course to our
parents, then handed over to our teachers, we are so
immersed in different kinds of error that truth gives way to
specious rationalisation and nature herself to the views of
the world.

sunt enim ingeniis nostris semina innata virtutum; quae si
adolescere liceret, ipsa nos ad beatam vitam natura
perduceret; nunc autem, simul atque editi in lucem et
suscepti sumus, in omni continuo pravitate et in summa
opinionum perversitate versamur, ut paene cum lacte
nutricis errorem suxisse videamur; quum vero parentibus
redditi, dein magistris traditi sumus, tum ita variis
imbuimur erroribus, ut vanitati veritas et opinioni con-
firmatae natura ipsa cedat.

(Cic. *Tusc. Disp.* 3.1.2)

Modern interest in young children and stress on early training
or influences seems to coincide historically with the development
of Protestantism. It has been plausibly connected by historians of
the family with the emphasis on original sin and on the role of the
parents, especially the father, in early discipline (Stone 1977: 162-
7; Morgan 1966). Since the late nineteenth century, there has
been a stronger emphasis on the importance of the mother to the
infant and the connection between training in infancy and adult
development (e.g. Kuhn 1947; Reiger 1981).

In the prescriptive literature of this last century, it is not so
much the mother's ethical teaching as her *presence* which has
increasingly been stressed. Her chief function is seen to be the
provision of high-quality physical and emotional care, as defined
by professional experts. Moral education has sometimes been

vaguely associated with these — for example, the idea that children fed when hungry (demand, as opposed to schedule feeding) will be 'spoilt', or that 'latchkey' or 'eight-hour' adolescents with mothers in the paid work-force necessarily become juvenile delinquents. In general, though, the underlying assumption is that a sound provision of the requisite needs — affection, hygiene, nutritious food and the constant maternal presence — will result in the proper personality. Formal learning, such as reading and mathematics, has largely been relegated to the school, although there is a recent trend even to add early teaching of these to the mother's tasks.

This century has produced a bewildering volume of literature on the subject of proper infant care and theories of child development which have influenced the behaviour of teachers and parents. Freud's writings would be read by few of them but have had a great impact through intermediaries on Western attitudes to children. Infantile sexuality is no longer viewed as a contradiction in terms and the Oedipus complex is regularly spoken of as a universal phenomenon, notwithstanding some criticism, chiefly from anthropologists and feminists.[15]

It was, however, left to others — most notably the British psychiatrist Bowlby (esp. 1952; 1958; 1969: I) and the American paediatrician Spock (1946, reprinted regularly with revisions ever since) — to process Freudian ideas for the masses. Their emphasis on the mother's role was really a development from Freud rather than a strictly Freudian notion. Freud himself, reared in the nineteenth-century Viennese bourgeoisie, spoke (rather as Romans like Seneca and Quintilian did) of the infant's attachment 'in the first instance to all those who look after it, but these soon give place to its parents' (1910: 47). He clearly had in mind a household with servants and leisured parents. His insistence on the importance of infant experience as the origin of adult psychopathology was easily merged by the later writers with the assumption that the mother *ought* to attend the young child; for 'all those who look after' the baby had disappeared from all but the most élite households of England and the United States by 1946, and the father was out of the house for much of the day.

Bowlby's studies of children in hospitals and orphanages resulted in the theory that all children needed to form an 'attachment' to a mother or mother-like figure in the first two years if they were to develop morally and emotionally as adults. 'Maternal deprivation' could result, he said, in severe adult disorders. Roman upper-class children do not seem to have spent their early years in close contact with the mother. They might have had an intimate association with a nurse or other attendant which would suit Bowlby's model, but his general finding was that a great number of attendants made attachment very unlikely and Bradley's work (1985a; 1986) suggests that élite Roman children were often in this position in their early years. It is tempting to draw parallels with British children of the ruling class in the nineteenth century, since that social group consciously identified with the avowed goals of Roman imperialism and the ideal Roman character. It could be argued that such an upbringing produced a distant personality type which put duty to family and country before personal preference and emotion, the type of personality best suited to gain and administer an empire and to marry and procreate according to reason rather than inclination.

This would accord with Fromm's sociological law (1941. Cf. Reisman/Glazer/Denney 1953) that the 'social character' of a given group — that is, the normative personality — would arise from the function which the group was expected to perform: leadership, child-rearing, menial work or whatever. Many studies of national character or cultural personality undertaken since the 1940s have attempted to link child-rearing techniques and the stock personality type of a given society (e.g. Benedict 1946; Gorer 1948; Mead 1954; Muensterberger 1951), although authors, when taxed with this, have denied drawing causal connections between the two. Their denial seems at odds with much of the literature. Bateson (1949) virtually argued that relations between parents and children prepare the younger generation for their role in society as a whole. Certainly, historical works on the Protestant work ethic link it fairly directly with allegedly Protestant approaches to the treatment and training of children (Fromm 1941; Morgan 1966).

There is a superficial appeal in trying to establish connections for the Roman ruling class. The stress on restraint evident particularly in letters written on bereavement (the so-called *consolationes* such as Cic. *fam.* 4.5. and Seneca *Ep. Mor.* 99), the emphasis on *dignitas* in historical biographies and *pietas* in tombstones, the preference for duty over romantic love evidenced by Aeneas and the Flavian prince Titus (and transgressed by Marcus Antonius, who persisted in his relationship with Cleopatra and severed his Roman marriage, with Octavian's sister Octavia) — all demonstrate the value placed, however notionally, on restraint, not to say coldness, and identification with the corporate rather than individual good. Specific connections between such ideals and childhood training are very difficult to produce, but the ancient sources themselves assume that there *was* an ideal Roman character and that early training and parental example were important elements in its formation. The connection appears in the stock literary lament for the decline of ancestral virtue which accompanied the shift from the austere rural milieu of old to the enervating luxury of city life. Consider Horace's idyllic picture of the past in *Carm.* 3.6. 37-41:

> Quite different were the young men born of peasant-soldier stock, trained to turn clods of earth with a Sabine hoe, and to haul kindling at the bidding of a stern mother

> sed rusticorum mascula militum
> proles, Sabellis docta ligonibus
>   versare glebas et severae
>   matris ad arbitrium recisos
> portare fustis ...

— where maternal harshness, hard work and desirable prowess are linked.

Juvenal's *Sat.* 14 argues that children might reasonably blame their parents for the shameful immorality they display in neglecting proper ties and amassing wealth without any scruple about the method — in a word, by setting a bad example. In the same spirit evident in Cato censor's legendary punishment of the senator for kissing his wife in their daughter's presence (Plut. *Cat. mai* 17.7), Juvenal insists (ironically) on propriety before young children:

> A child is entitled to the greatest respect, if you have some shocking scheme in hand. Don't look down on his years: your baby should deter you from your sinful intent.

> maxima debetur puero reverentia, siquid
> turpe paras, nec tu pueri contempseris annos,
> sed peccaturo obstet tibi filius infans.

> (14.47-9)

Plate 1. A relief panel from the Ara Pacis enclosure sometimes identified as Italia or Terra Mater, a symbol of fertility. DAI Neg. No. 32-1744.

Plate 2. Part of the sacrifice frieze on the Ara Pacis enclosure, showing the adults and children of Augustus' family, advertising the fertility and stability of his regime. DAI Neg. No. 72-2403.

Plate 3. A relief from the passageway of the Arch of Trajan at Benevento showing Trajan distributing largess to poor children. Alinari No. 11496.

Plate 4. One of the Aurelian panels on the north side of the Arch of Constantine, showing the Emperor Marcus benefiting the children of the poor. Alinari No. 2541.

Plate 5. Coin issues showing the Empress Sabina as Pietas; Julia
Domna, wife of Septimius Severus and her sister, Julia Maesa.
(*RIC*: Hadrian 1041) ANU 69.02; (*RIC*: Septimius Severus 555)
U/Q 91; (*RIC*: Elagabalus 263) U/Q 93.

Plate 6. Terracotta relief of a child-birth scene from Ostia,
Museo Ostiense Inv. 5204.

Plate 7. Fragment from a sarcophagus showing a baby immediately after birth and as a youth or child. DAI Neg. No. 42-101.

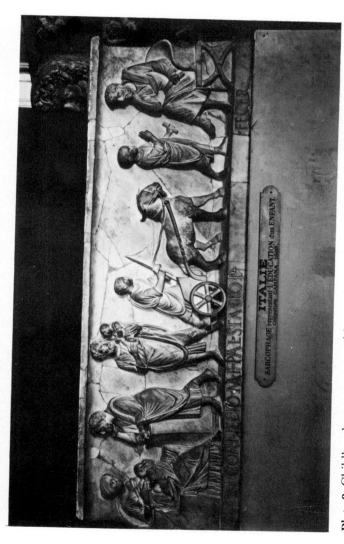

Plate 8. Childhood stages on a marble sarcophagus from Trier. Marburg Archiv No. 180249.

Plate 9. Part of a funerary altar to the nurse Severina, showing her with a swaddled baby. Rheinisches Bildarchiv, Köln 120 328.

Plate 10. Baby's feeding bottle, either for use in weaning or for a child whose mother had died. U/Q Classics Inv. 73/6.

In *Dialogus* 28, where Vipstanus Messalla harks back to a time when mothers monitored their children's upbringing and the young were protected by a vigilant relation from exposure to indecency or inferior Latin, the connection between the form of child-rearing and the production of the desired character is explicit. Favorinus' ideas, as passed on by Aulus Gellius, are far removed from modern ones in the assumption, for example, that the breast-milk of a mercenary nurse might of itself transmit extraneous moral traits (*NA* 12.1.17; cf. Robinson, quoted above). He accords, however, with modern schools of thought in his belief that the physical intimacy between mother and child reinforces existing pre-dispositions and forms the basis of an abiding, lifelong attachment:

> For when the removal of a baby from sight has been accomplished, the strength — so well acknowledged — of maternal love wanes perceptibly and gradually ... Moreover, the feeling of the baby itself, the love, the sense of familiarity, is directed solely towards the woman who nurtures the infant. Just as happens in the case of children exposed at birth, the child eventually has no special feeling or longing for the mother who bore it.

> nam ubi infantis aliorsum dati facta ex oculis amolitiost, vigor ille maternae flagrantiae sensim atque paulatim restinguitur, ... ipsius quoque infantis adfectio animi, amoris, consuetudinis in ea sola, unde alitur, occupatur et proinde, ut in expositis usu venit, matris, quae genuit, neque sensum ullum neque desiderium capit.

> (*NA* 12.1.22-3)

It is characteristic of modern research that little attention has been accorded the development of maternal feelings, but in practice hospitals and nursing homes have for some time taken babies at birth from mothers who planned to adopt them out, to prevent the development of the bond which might endanger prior arrangements or make a necessary parting unduly painful. Bowlby's theory of attachment — that is, the attachment of the infant to the mother or mother substitute — extensively tested and elaborated since its initial expression, is based on the same premise as Favorinus', that the person who feeds and handles an infant regularly arouses the child's strongest feelings.

The testimony of the ancient sources reveals that Roman aristocrats from the late Republic on used wet-nurses to feed and tend small children. The role of the mother, though stressed by some of the moralists, was therefore necessarily different from that performed in our own culture, where the mother's relation to the infant is deemed central. It remains to examine the detailed similarities and differences.

In cellula emptae nutricis: nurses and mothers

The nurse has throughout history been the target of comics and moralists.[16] The denunciation extends to the mother who, in passing the baby over to a nurse, neglects her own duty.[17] Yet the only certain statements we can make about wet-nursing in wealthy circles in Rome are that it was the norm (Bradley 1986), and that it was routinely denounced. The details of such denunctions vary slightly, but it emerges clearly that traditional virtue was associated with greater maternal involvement in the early years of a child's life and that the milk, the morals and the Latin of the common run of nurse were suspect.

There might have been some germ of truth in Vipstanus Messalla's romantic vision of a pure Roman past, when mothers spent more time with their own children and houses (Tac. *Dial.* 28.4). Yet the similar tone of Cicero's *Brutus* 210-11, in which certain women are praised for their elegant speech, suggests the same pattern of nurses, *paedagogi* and parents in the young child's life by the late Republic — and compare:

to have drunk in error with the nurse's milk

cum lacte nutricis errorem suxisse
(Cic. *Tusc. Disp.* 3.1.2, quoted above at length)

It was probably unusual even then for a senatorial mother to supervise her son's education as closely as Messalla claims that Atia and Aurelia had done. It is improbable that she breast-fed her own children.

Authors such as Tacitus (through Vipstanus Messalla) were not advocating the type of physical ministration to infants currently performed by mothers. Such work is characterised as servile or low. Nor is there advocacy of maternal patience, affection and understanding such as modern mothers are adjured to supply. Rather, the emphasis is on discipline and moral vigilance. The mother should ideally provide the child with ethical, and perhaps linguistic, standards. Indeed, the *Dialogus* author, critical, as we have seen, of the indulgence displayed by modern parents and servants to children, praises the vigilance of the famous historical mothers as the basis of their sons' single-mindedness and skill as orators. This is contrasted with contemporary youthful frivolity and the unwillingness of parents or teachers to check it. The stress on maternal attention is not exclusive, in the twentieth-century style. The author sees both parents as forming the child (*ipsi parentes*: 29) and commends the earlier custom of assigning a respectable older relative to supervise the child's behaviour even at play. The constrast is with the modern habit of assigning a new-born baby to slaves of foreign extraction who do not moderate their speech or behaviour before their young master. It is the nature of the attendants rather than the idea of people other than the mother caring for the child which is attacked (*Dial.* 28-9).

The *Dialogus* passage appears to owe its inspiration to the *Brutus*, where the speaker notes the importance of the domestic example, as well as later instruction, to the budding orator:

> It is very important whom each child hears every day at home, with whom he speaks from childhood and the type of speech employed by fathers, *paedagogi* and even mothers.

> sed magni interest quos quisque audiat cotidie domi, quibuscum loquatur a puero quem ad modum patres, paedagogi, matres etiam loquantur.
>
> (Cic. *Brutus* 210)

The list of eloquent women which follows includes Cornelia, who is credited with influencing her sons' oratory:

> Her children, it seems, were reared not so much in their mother's lap as in her speech.

> apparet filios non tam gremio educatos quam in sermone matris

but this is not to be confused with the modern stress on the mother's role in early language development, which is posited on the assumption that the mother is the constant and most important companion of the young child. Rather, the mother is the afterthought of the list — '*even* the mothers' (*matres etiam*) might affect such learning. Most of the women cited in the list at *Brutus* 211 are said to have inherited or learned their eloquence from their fathers.

We have already noted Quintilian's assumption (*Inst. Or. 6 pr.* 8) that the nurse is the person with whom the small child will have greatest contact and that the list of those who loomed large in his own five-year-old son's life included nurses, the grandmother and other unspecified people, presumably servants. Elsewhere, advice about the nurses is followed by:

> But I would like the parents to be as cultivated as possible. And I do not just mean the fathers ...

> In parentibus vero quam plurimum esse eruditionis optaverim. nec de patribus tantum loquor ...
> (*Inst. Or.* 1.1.6)

Again, the mothers are an afterthought. There follows the now-familiar catalogue of famous eloquent women: Cornelia, Laelia, Hortensia. Even those parents who are not learned should pay great attention to teaching their children (1.1. 6-7). Critical of a friend's reported grief at the death of an infant son, Seneca says scornfully:

> You have undoubtedly made great advances in philosophy, if you yearn with your stout spirit for a child so far better known to his nurse than his father.

> sine dubio multum philosophia profecit, si puerum nutrici adhuc quam patri notiorem animo forti desideras.
> (Sen. *Ep. Mor.* 99.14)

The advice of Favorinus (Aul. Gell. *NA* 12.1) and of Soranus is of a rather different character. Both advocate maternal breast-feeding. The advocacy seems to have been a commonplace, but its form suggests that the practice was not the norm, at least in the wealthier echelons of society. Thus, Tacitus' approval of the Germanic custom of suckling children at the maternal breast implies criticism of his social peers at Rome:

Each child is nurtured by its own mother's breasts. *They* are not handed over to slaves and nurses.

sua quemque mater uberibus alit, nec ancillis ac nutricibus delegantur.

(*Germania* 20)

Juvenal suggests, however accurately, that rich women were able to escape the rigours of breast-feeding as of childbirth:

Yet at least these [poor] women undergo the peril of child-birth and, pressed by hardship, endure all the trials of breast-feeding, but gilded beds seldom see labour.

hae tamen et partus subeunt discrimen et omnis
nutricis tolerant fortuna urguente labores,
sed iacet aurato vix ulla puerpera lecto.

(Juv. *Sat.* 6. 592-4)

Soranus advocated the mother's feeding her own baby if she was healthy, but proceeded to give detailed instructions not only on the choice of a wet-nurse but on her diet, proper comportment and exercise (*Gyn* II.xi (31) 18 [260]). If he had seriously regarded the mother as the norm, most of these sections should have been directed to the mother, or mother *and* nurse.

Consider the funereal inscription:

To Graxia Alexandria, an outstanding example of womanly virtue, who actually reared her children with her own breasts'
OR who *also* reared her own children ...

GRAXIAE ALEXANDRIAE
INSIGNIS EXEMPLI
AC PVDICITIAE
QVAE ETIAM FILIOS SVOS
PROPRIIS VBERIBVS EDVCAVIT ...

(*CIL* VI 19128)

The name Graxia Alexandra suggests freedwoman status, but her husband was an imperial freedman and the inscription is on a marble sarcophagus.[18] This makes it difficult to know whether the inscription testifies to the rarity of maternal feeding in the servile or lower orders (Bradley 1986: 201-2). There are general indications in the inscriptions that children at different social levels might be reared or fostered by people other than their parents (Treggiari 1976: 88; Rawson 1986c; Bradley 1986: 208-10). *Nutrices* were probably paid nurses, while *mammae* and *tatae* seem to have been foster-parents, sometimes of a higher social group than their foster-children, though not necessarily. The inscriptions are discussed in some detail in the following chapter.

It is difficult to assess the sort of relationship which a *nutrix* would have with her charge in later life. Her early attendance and possible influence take on a proverbial form, as in Cicero's point (*Tusc. Disp.* 3.1.2) that bad habits are learned almost from birth. This closely parallels Juvenal's assertion that immorality is learned by children from an early age through the example of parents — though his metaphor for denoting early childhood is:

> This is the lesson children learn from their aged dry-nurses before they can walk ...

> hoc monstrant vetulae pueris reptantibus assae ...
>
> (*Sat.* 14.208)

Such expressions correspond to our own 'drink in with our mother's milk' or 'learned at his mother's knee', where the symbol of that stage of early life is invariably maternal.

Favorinus' suspicion of nurses is founded in part on the diversion of affection from the parents — its natural object — to a stranger. He argues that the close relationship with the nurse will be the intense one, and even later displays of love to the parents will be an acquired politeness rather than the spontaneous love it would have been if the mother had breast-fed her child:

> And what is more, once the foundations of natural feeling have been entirely eradicated, any sign of affection which children reared in this way might show their father or mother is primarily an acquired piece of etiquette, not natural love.

> Ac propterea oblitteratis et abolitis nativae pietatis elementis, quiquid ita educati liberi amare patrem atque matrem videntur, magnam fere pàrtem non naturalis ille amor est, sed civilis et opinabilis.
>
> (*NA* 12.1.23)

This is perhaps the nearest we have to evidence of the effect on family relationships of the practice of wet-nursing. Yet it is rather theoretical, for Favorinus does not deny that children reared by nurses show affection for their parents. He simply insists that such affection is not as deep-seated as it appears to be.

The argument accords reasonably with modern research, though that is based on quite different assumptions. Favorinus' insistence on grouping both parents rather than concentrating on the mother is a significant difference. Recent writing on the connection between wet-nursing in early modern European history and relations between parents and children is based more often on the custom of sending the children away to the nurse's peasant residence for two to three years.[19] The Roman examples[20] assume that the nurse was usually brought into the child's home on salary or was part of the child's *familia*. This is evident from such statements as:

> Especially if the woman you procure for the provision of milk is a slave or of servile stock and — as is often the case — of a foreign and barbarous nationality ...

> praesertim si ista, quam ad praebendum lactem adhibebitis aut serva aut servilis est et, ut plerumque solet, externae et barbarae nationis est ...
>
> (*NA* 12.1.17)

and

> Nowadays, a baby is handed over to some wretched Greek maidservant ...

> at nunc natus infans delegatur Graeculae alicui ancillae ...
>
> (*Dial.* 29.1)

There are indications that *vernae* might be sent away to nurse[21] but it does not appear to have been usual for the owner's children.

There was another side to the nurse's image. A certain tenderness was assumed in such passages as Lucretius 5. 228-30, on the contrast between the independence of animal young and the needs of human infants, where he refers to the 'beguiling, broken talk of the tender nurse' (*almae nutricis blanda atque infracta loquela*). This presents a rather charming picture, thrown out incidentally, of the nurse's 'baby talk'. Like Fronto's simile of the typical dry-nurse, *assa nutrix* (later designated as '*stulta*'), who prefers her charge to remain childish (*Ep. ad Ant. Imp.* 1.5 = Naber p. 102), it is the kind of picture we associate with mothers.

Both Nonius (II. *De Propr. Serm.* 57 M) and the scholiast on Juvenal 14.208 define an *assa nutrix* as a nurse who does not provide milk, but attends the child constantly in its early years.[22] In the stock references to nurses' characteristics, it is not always clear whether the nurse is a wet-nurse, but the definition of *assa nutrix*, like the use of the term *mater nutrix*[23] to denote a 'nursing mother', suggests that the usual association of *nutrix* was with breast-feeding and any other kind of nurse would be specified by an additional modifier. Possibly the unqualified noun could also denote a wet-nurse retained as the child's attendant for some time after breast-feeding ceased. Cicero refers to the nurse's role in weaning[24] and Fronto to the part played by the nurse in tending the imperial children through illness (*Ep. ad Ant. Imp.* 1.2.6 = Naber p. 94). If the nurse was a member of the *familia*, she might well have been a presence, though no longer the principle one, throughout the childhood of her charge.

Bowlby concluded from his observation of modern hospitals, orphanages and other institutions that fragmented care of infants, with constant personnel changes, affected a child's development adversely.[25] In theory, the attendance of the same *nutrix* or set of *nutrices* should have satisfied his criteria. It is important, though, to note how closely such theories are tied to the experience and cultural values of the various authorities on child-rearing through the ages. Conditions which Bowlby claims are essential for the development of proper social behaviour cannot have been met in all periods of history and throughout all social classes; yet the kind of childhood environment described by authors such as deMause (1974), Badinter (1980: 73-139) and Shorter (1975: 204-62) did not produce whole societies of psychopaths. The idea of a single, constant attendant for every small child is recent and tied to specific economic and architectural developments.[26] Even the children of the imperial family at Rome were left unattended sometimes,[27] although they are not, perhaps, to be upheld as models of stable personalities and social responsibility.

Children reared by social inferiors might become attached to them, but also develop an awareness of their social difference as they get older and understand that it is the parents' social group to which they themselves belong. Gathorne-Hardy (1972: 78) points out that the British nanny who worked with upper-class children often fostered the social sense which led to her own denigration in the children's eyes. In the twentieth century, the 'nanny' has become a literary *topos*, a stock figure of affectionate ridicule in novels about the English upper class. The highly sentimental view of the relationship with the nanny and the associated picture of the nanny's power within the family in novels like Nancy Mitford's *The Blessing* or Evelyn Waugh's *Brideshead Revisited* can be directly related to the scarcity of nannies since the First World War (Gathorne-Hardy 1972: 78; Gibbs 1960: 96). Relatively few nannies ever worked for the upper classes, in any case. In her study of nursemaids to middle-class Victorian families, McBride (1978) has demonstrated that the children's nurse was typically a young, untrained drudge who was unlikely to remain in the same situation for long.

Caution must be exercised in assessing literature on children's nurses in any period. On the one hand, it is likely to be tinged with parental resentment of the diversion of the child's affections to an outsider, and class suspicion of the competence and different social habits of the servants, slaves or peasants to whom the wealthy entrust their young. On the other hand, it is as important to avoid the contrary error of assuming a close tie of mutual life-long affection between nurse and nurseling without sufficient grounds.[28]

Given the nature of Roman society, it is not surprising that the primary bond demonstrable between nurses and their aristocratic charges in later life has the appearance of patronage. This would have applied both in the literal sense, in the case of a *liberta* nurse, or in the wider sense of 'patronage' for a relationship between the two people of disparate social groups in which each owed the other certain offices.[29] The nature of these obligations can be reconstructed from inscriptional and literary sources. Greater detail is adduced in the chapter following, but the ageing nurse's role is glimpsed in the reassurances given by Poppaea's nurse in Seneca's *Octavia* 740 ff, or those offered Nero by his nurse on the occasion of Galba's revolt (Suet. *Nero* 42). (It should be noted in passing that reassurances were based on false premises in both cases.) Suetonius also tells us that Nero harshly punished the son of a nurse in Egypt — but the fact that the man was a *procurator* and presumed on his relationship, as well as Suetonius' classification of Nero's discipline as an injury against intimates and connections, suggests that the relationship between nurse and nurseling had lifelong implications in the network of reciprocal obligation.[30] This is confirmed by gifts and legacies to nurses and their burial by the families they had served.[31] Such relationships might have been tinged with affection. This could, for example, be the implication of Plin. *Ep.* 6.3.2[32] or *Ep.* 5.16.3,[33] but we should not read too much into such statements. They might indicate no more than a dutiful acknowledgement of service.

As we have seen, it was considered highly desirable in principle for a mother to breast-feed her own baby, but seems not to have been usual practice in the propertied classes. There are references to the relevance of the mother's health as a factor in deciding to engage a wet-nurse,[34] but this might have been a polite pretence. It is clear from the abundance of literary references that the nurse's presence was taken for granted as part of the normal background of childhood. Her tasks almost certainly included feeding children, tending them in illness and keeping them clean.[35] In a society with great distinctions of wealth and function like the Roman, such work would necessarily have been thought demeaning. The relationship between nurse and nurseling might have become more distant socially as the child became more aware of these factors, but there was room in the early years for the development of close ties with the nurse and others associated with her.

Bradley's (1986) study throws welcome light on the status of nurses at Rome. It would be helpful to have more information on the families of nurses and their association with the nurse and her charge, but it is difficult to form a precise picture from existing sources of the detailed domestic setting. Inscriptions from the vicinity of Rome demonstrate that *nutrices* regularly had marriage or *contubernium* relationships.[36] Wet-nurses were by definition mothers and the bond between the nurseling and the nurse's own child was recognised in Roman society, not least by the term *conlacteus.* Although Pliny refers to slave quarters built at a sufficient distance from his country villa to shield guests from the noise of the slave children,[37] the courtyard houses of Ostia and Pompeii give no ground for any belief that Roman children were regularly separated from the life of the household. It is possible that the nurse's child moved into the household with her (or was already there, in the case of a slave nurse) and became a companion for a time of her charge. We know that upper-class infants were regularly assigned child slaves of their own who grew up with them (Bradley 1985a), so the large Roman household could have contained a free and easy nursery element, loosely supervised by the permissive servants so criticised by ancient moralists and educators. It was not necessarily a grim training-ground for aristocratic coldness.

There is really no evidence to support the idea that wet-nursing and relegation of child care to servants interfered with the development of relationships between Roman children and their parents. There have been a number of studies, autobiographies and retrospective analyses of Victorian and Edwardian upper-class English training which stressed the distance of the mother, the severity of the nannies or the sexual problems caused by associating warmth and physical intimacy with women of the lower classes (Gathorne-Hardy 1972: 90-104). Yet many of the retrospective laments in autobiographies published in the early twentieth century emerged from an awareness of a different style of family life available in the bourgeoisie and changing expectations even within the élite group. As we have seen, Roman ideals of conjugal and familial satisfaction seem to have grown stronger from the late Republic, but there is no evidence of discontent with parents for failing to live up to expectations. It is true that very young children of the Roman upper class saw little of their mothers by the standards of some modern societies, and the distinctions we expect between the maternal and paternal role in the early years were somewhat blurred. Even maternal supervision of children's training seems to have been stronger once they had passed beyond early childhood. Where we tend to see that part of the life cycle as at home with Mother, then at school with Teacher, Romans saw it as spent with nurses, then with teachers and parents.

In gremio matris educatus: the mother's role

His mother was Julia Procilla, a woman of rare virtue. Reared in her lap and tender affections, he passed his childhood and youth in the full training of an honourable education.

mater Iulia Procilla fuit, rarae castitatis, in huius sinu indulgentiaque educatus per omnem honestarum artium cultum pueritiam adulescentiamque transegit.

(Tac. *Agric.* 4)

It is possible, then, to piece together from stray references to nurses some of the tasks which the Roman mother — particularly the upper-class mother — did *not* do. It is more difficult to determine what she *did* do for her young children, but it is not quite hopeless.

Although the formula occurs more commonly of a nurse or *mamma*, there are tombstones in which a child — presumably a very young one — is referred to as 'snatched from the mother's breast':

: DIS MANIB
C PAPIRI IANVARI
HIC SVM MATRIS AB VBERE RAPTVS:

(*CIL* VI 23790)

The infant Tiberius, being smuggled out of Naples during the civil war, set up a dangerous wail on being taken first from his nurse's breast, then from his mother's arms, by friends anxious to relieve them of the burden:

... vagitu suo paene bis prodidit, semel cum a nutricis ubere, iterum cum a sinu matris raptim auferretur ...

(Suet. *Tib.* 6)

Even the aristocratic child, then, was familiar with the maternal breast as a place of solace, if not of sustenance.

The persistent references to children being reared *in gremio matris* or *in sinu matris*, ('in the mother's lap' or 'at her bosom')[38] however metaphorical, also suggest a typical intimacy and affection between the mother and the young child. This impression is strengthened by references to the greater grief characteristically displayed by mothers, although most of the literary references fail to indicate the stage of life of the deceased child.[39] Parents sometimes erected inscriptions to young children but figures are misleading, because the age might not always have been specified and a parent could set up a dedication to him or herself, including the children in the formula ET SVIS.[40]

In appreciating the distinction between ancient and modern notions of the proper and usual relationship between mother and infant, it is important to acknowledge élite women's tasks. Even in households with ample slaves to perform the menial functions, aristocratic women appear to have attended sick-beds.[41] It is worth noting that genteel Victorian ladies performed many distasteful offices for the sick. Certainly the wives of Domitius Tullus and Caecina Paetus faithfully supplied comfort at the sick-bed — to an almost superhuman degree, in Arria's case. Yet we learn that Quintilian and Minicius Fundanus attended their dying children's sick-beds.[42] Perhaps we must not see this, either, as an exclusively maternal or female function.

There are some senses in which the stereotypes and ideals of the Roman mother resemble those of our own culture. We have already noted Seneca's observation (*Dial.* 1.2.5) that mothers, unlike fathers, tend to be over-protective and wish to save their children pain — although one finds it difficult to imagine Cornelia or Livia fitting this model. Generally, such juxtapositions of maternal indulgence and paternal severity are to be found in the comedies, where the debt to Greek originals makes their application to Roman cases suspect.[43] The *indulgentia* of Agricola's mother, Iulia Procilla, is noted — but was apparently compatible with checking her son's pursuit of philosophy, a motherly notion she shared with Agrippina the younger (Tac. *Agric.* 4.4; Suet. *Nero* 52).

In general, though, the parallel is weak. The proverbial references to mothers are as disciplinarians. Cicero speaks of children being severely punished by mothers or teachers for any breach of mourning (*Tusc. Disp.* 3.64) and Horace (*Epist.* 1.1. 21-2) speaks of time dragging for the children of widows, subject to maternal authority. In lamenting the lack of attention paid by modern mothers to their young offspring, Messalla (Tac. *Dial.* 28) was regretting the absence of that *disciplina ac severitas* which had characterised the regime of mothers such as Cornelia and Aurelia. Mothers might desperately mourn dead children and really think them perfect,[44] but they were not regularly expected to be overly indulgent or patient. These were not their defining characteristics.

The great difficulty is to find maternal features without a paternal equivalent. Fathers were also expected to mourn even young children, and to be blind to their faults (Hor. *Serm.* 1.3. 43-58). In fact, the strongest argument for a peculiarly maternal role in the Roman upper class is the tendency to 'replace' a deceased, absent or divorced mother with a female relation — in modern jargon, to supply a 'mother surrogate'. The rule of thumb in the case of divorce at Rome was for the child to remain with the father. At least one exception is known — that of the young son of Oppianicus who remained with his mother Papia but was taken up by the father on public holidays (Cic. *Clu.* 27). This must have been a special arrangement, for Oppianicus himself retained a younger child from a subsequent marriage. Cicero's daughter Tullia was already divorced when she returned to the home of her former husband's adoptive father to give birth, then to leave for her father's villa without the new-born child.[45] Livia appears to have taken her young son Tiberius, as well as Drusus (whom she was expecting at the time of her divorce from Drusus Nero) with her into her marriage to Octavian (Suet. *Tib.* 4), but perhaps Octavian had already assumed a potentate's dynastic approach to such things. Octavia reared Antonius' children from other unions (Plut. *Ant.* 87). The imperial family seems to have had its own way of doing things — or perhaps it is just that we know more of their arrangements.

Octavian himself had been reared by his grandmother Julia — presumably on his mother's remarriage — until her death, when he joined the household of his mother and stepfather (Nicolaus 3.5; cf. Suet. *Aug.* 8). The young Gaius might have been partially reared in the home of his imperial grandparents, for Suetonius (*Gai.* 8. 4-5) cites a letter written by Augustus to Agrippina (maior) which refers to the tiny Gaius being sent to his mother, to accompany her to Germanicus in Gaul. On Germanicus' death, Gaius lived with his mother until her exile, then with his grandmother Livia. On *her* death, he went to his paternal grandmother Antonia and, at the age of 19, to Tiberius at Capri (Suet. *Gai.* 10). Nero's childhood was similar: his father died when he was three and his mother was subsequently exiled, whereupon he went briefly to the home of his paternal aunt Domitia Lepida (Suet. *Nero* 6; Bradley 1978: 49-50), thus laying the foundation of a family feud between his aunt and his mother which was to be played out over him in years to come. Vespasian was reared by his paternal grandmother, presumably because his father was dead, although his mother survived to his adulthood (Suet. *Vesp.* 2.1-2). Bradley (1985a: 508 n55) has a useful collection of evidence on the childhood of Julio-Claudian emperors.

Many young children must have lost their mothers through death. Pliny's young wife Calpurnia[46] was reared by her paternal aunt, in the household of her grandmother (Plin. *Ep.* 4.19).

Quintilian, whose wife had died, referred to his young son as being reared by a grandmother[47]: it is not clear whether she was Quintilian's mother or his wife's. It is possible that some of the women termed *mammae* were fostering children orphaned at birth — inscriptions set up by *mammae* are usually to young children.[48]

Indeed, the number of inscriptions in which *nutrices, mammae, educatores, nutritores* or *nutricii* figure, either alone or together with parents, suggests that Romans did not take an exclusive view of the functions of the parents as we do. It is not always possible to see why different people seem to be involved in rearing children: possibly parents had sometimes to be relieved for their work or had difficulty in managing to feed another mouth but did not wish to cede parenthood altogether. This reinforces the impression that motherhood was not defined strongly in terms of relations with the young child, even in the lower social groups — a significant difference from our own cultural emphasis.

Literary stereotypes which do resemble our own include that of the anxious mother[49] but this is paralleled by images of anxious fathers.[50] There is also the figure of the mother who aspires to have her children exceed her own learning (Hor. *Epist.* 1.18. 26-7) — the nearest approach to our own idea of maternal self-sacrifice. Yet in general such stock characteristics are shared by fathers and are quoted in relation to adult children as much as young ones.

Human children are, as Lucretius rightly pointed out (5.288 ff), more helpless in their early stages than any other species. Thus, although cultures vary greatly in the extent to which they watch over children or consciously destroy or foster 'childish' characteristics, it must always be necessary to make special arrangements for feeding and cleaning them. It is evident from the disparate references in inscriptions and Latin literature that these tasks, and some general custodial function, could be performed in the wealthier household by a mercenary or slave nurse and sometimes relegated to others, even by parents of the lower classes.

Bowlby's disciple Ainsworth has attempted to test his findings on infant attachment in different settings. Where Bowlby confined his argument to institutions, Ainsworth looked at societies in which fostering and other systems of changing the people caring for small children were normal practice, embedded in kinship and other existing social networks. She found (Ainsworth 1967: Ch. 25) that Bowlby's conclusions held and that children in those settings did show signs of disturbance as a result of being unable to 'attach' to a specific person. Margaret Mead, the great apostle of cultural relativism, argued on the contrary that many cultures in which children routinely grow up with a variety of tenders and helpers produce people quite as socially adjusted as those in which infants 'fix' upon a single figure (Mead 1962). Each situation would necessarily involve a host of variables. Pre-industrial conditions of mortality, coupled with the absence of the father (and, in imperial times, the mother) on official appointments, would necessitate a less rigid arrangement than current demographic and economic circumstances impose on the modern family. There is no real evidence that children actually prefer the limited modern social situation. Gathorne-Hardy, who is generally critical of parental neglect, mentions very favourably the home of an acquaintance, run on traditional English upper-class lines, since it functions as a cheerful, chaotic and constantly active miniature community.[51] Sir Kenneth Clark (1974: 2-4) has highly unpleasant recollections of his early years when he was left to the ministrations of servants, but the reverse could equally have been the case. Those casual, permissive slaves so despised by Vipstanus Messalla[52] might have provided a welcome counter to the distance and discipline of parents in some homes. Or parents might leave the unpleasantness of day-to-day discipline to servants and appear to the children as attractive collaborators.

The only conclusive finding of this chapter is that the Roman mother's relationship to her young child, particularly within the upper class, was not similar to the modern one. She was not the exclusive formative influence which Sociology and Psychology, developed within a few highly urbanised, wealthy modern countries, assume her to be. This is not to say that she was *not* affectionate and anxious about young children, but that she was not thought to be more so than the father or nurse of the children. The authors who consider her importance to the budding orator view her as one of many influences on the young child.

It will emerge from subsequent chapters that the Roman mother was deemed a greater influence on the adult child than is usual or approved in our society. Where we refer to typically maternal characteristics in relation to small children, Roman literary stereotypes tend to focus on mothers and adolescent or adult children, particularly male ones. It will emerge that adult sons were expected to show (and *did* show) considerable affection and respect for their mothers. It would seem that the special character of the relationship developed over the life cycle, rather than being set by a close, exclusive relationship in infancy. It would be wilful to see this pattern as aberrant simply because it differs from our own.

The question of a connection between the 'basic' form of child-rearing and the ideal personality of the top social group is really too difficult to answer. Certainly restraint, distance and a firm adherence to the social *status quo* were expected of wealthy Romans and although, to their credit, some were unable to measure up to these standards[53] they were conscious of their existence. Both Favorinus and Soranus observed a relationship between breast-feeding and maternal affection[54] and, indeed, women engaged in the activities of the social and political élite who did not feed their own children and were not connected with the daily care of them would really have enjoyed a relationship more akin to that which we associate with fatherhood.[55]

There must have been great individual variation. Nero's aunt Domitia Lepida pursued quite a different style of 'mothering' from that of her sister-in-law Agrippina minor.[56] We have already noted the expressions such as *in gremio matris* which imply a notional intimacy between the mother and the small child. On the Ara Pacis frieze we see children of the very highest social group automatically seizing the hands and clothing of their relations. For what it is worth, this suggests an assumption of physical intimacy and spontaneity quite different from that imposed on nineteenth-century children of the English upper class. There is ample evidence, moreover, that, although patronage and marriage choice had a strong formal element, both friendships and conjugal relations were warm and analogous to those we now aspire to.

There is no evidence that the Roman aristocracy produced a great proportion of sociopaths — although one might plausibly argue that their presence was masked by legitimate channels such as punishment of slaves and imperial conquest. In the face, then, of a smattering of information gleaned from inscriptions and the literature of adult men, it is possible to piece together a general impression of relations between the Roman mother and her young child, but it cannot be sufficiently stressed that the information gleaned is highly selective and inconclusive, both about the details of the relation itself and its consequences for the adult.

Notes

1. Stone (1977: 70): 'to preserve their mental stability, parents were obliged to limit the degree of their psychological involvement with their infant children'.

2. E.g. by MacFarlane pp. 106-7 of his review essay (1979) of Stone's book. Hopkins (1983: 222-3) shows mild scepticism, while Pollock (1983: 127-8) firmly rejects the idea of parental indifference to infant death and illness.

3. Gibbs (1960: 73-4) describes the funeral of the infant Prince Octavius. Since court mourning was not observed for small children of the English royal family, only the wet-nurse attended his interment. Compare the account (p. 73) of the burial of Squire Custance's baby daughter. The body was taken to church with only the nurse and house-keeper in attendance. Small children required baptism and a Christian burial, but were not accorded social recognition at death.

Shorter (1975: reprinted 1979 in paperback, from which the pagination is cited) points (p. 174) to an Anjou parish where neither parent would necessarily attend the funeral of a child under five years. All of these examples belong to the eighteenth century.

4. I have been unable to secure Heurgon's *Capoue Préromaine* (1942), which Price (1978) cites as her source for the information about the statues. Price herself acknowledges (p. 168) the influence of the cities of Magna Graecia and Sicily in producing types so similar to those found in mainland Greece. Most of the finds she cites in this section are Hellenistic.

5. A mother is shown suckling her baby in Fig. 4 of Kampen (1981) — a scene from a sarcophagus, while the mother holds a swaddled baby in Figure 5 (Plate 7 of this book). Figure 80 (Kampen) shows a stele to Scaevinia Procilla, who is depicted standing, holding a baby which may be her own. She is not described as a *nutrix* and her dedicators describe themselves (or possibly her) as PAR. PIENT ('most pious parent/relation').

6. Shorter (1979) has some typical pictures (before p. 177) but any women's magazine would yield a number of them and art galleries are rich in the theme.

7. Kleiner (1977) Fig. 52 appears to be such a family; Fig. 54 shows an older couple with a young man; compare Fig. 80, which represents a married couple, flanked by a man and woman. Hanfmann (1967) Plates 284 54-50 BC) and 312 (AD 250) both depict married couples in typical styles — the former, standing sculpture; the latter, heads on an elaborate sarcophagus.

8. Part of the Ara Pacis frieze is depicted in Plate 2. The portraits of the imperial heirs and some of the imperial women have been inferred from inscribed statue-bases by Hanson and Johnson (1946). Cf. the issue of a *denarius* showing Augustus' daughter Julia with her sons Gaius and Lucius *RIC* Augustus: 166 (17-13 BC. See 404/405 of the 1984 *RIC*). See also Pollini (1985) and the references cited by Kleiner (1978: 773-4).

9. Kleiner (1977) Figures 64, 71, 81-5 inclusive.

10. Cicero further cited the two Muciae and the Liciniae, while

Quintilian added Hortensia. See the discussion below.

11. Quint. *Inst. Or.* 6 *pr.*, esp. 10-11; Plin. *Ep.* 5.16 points out that Minicia combined matronly diginity with girlish sweetness: 'matronalis gravitas erat et tamen suavitas puellaris'. The girl was thirteen, according to Pliny; twelve, according to *ILS* 1030.

12. Lattimore (1942) p. 160: 'When the younger generation watches its elders die and buries them, there is generally no occasion for extreme grief (save when parents die very young).'

13. Cic. *Att* 10.18:

Tullia mea peperit XIII Kal. Iun.puerum ἑπταμηνιαῖον. quod εὐτόκησεν gaudeam; quod quidem est natum perimbecillimum est.

Compare his remarks on the 'natural' quality of love of children, *Att.* 7.2.4, and more serious philosophical argument, *Off.* 1.11; *Fin.* 3.62 and consider Étienne's view (1973) of ancient callousness to the small child from the medical and philosophical viewpoint.

14. See the collection of literary references in Lattimore (1942: 187-8); and deMause (1974: esp 17-18), for a sinister interpretation of this kind of 'reversal', where a parent entertains expectations of services a child will render. As to the relationship between commemoration and feelings, Hopkins (1983: 220-4) has an interesting discussion of the problem, but also fails to come to a conclusion.

15. See Freud and Breuer (1909); Freud (1918); Malinowski (1916), (1929); Jones (1924; reprinted 1964); Stephens (1962); Parsons (1964); Mitchell (1974).

16. E.g. Aristophanes *Eq.* 716-8; Soranus *Gyn.* II.xii (32) 19 [263]; Ariès (1962: 374); Badinter (1980: 106-36); Shorter (1979: 176-84).

17. (Favorinus) *NA* 12.1.6; Soranus *Gyn.* II. xi (31) 17 [260].

18. See *CIL* VI 19128, commentary; also for the similar inscription, deemed by Mommsen to be a forgery based on this one.

19. E.g. Badinter (1980: 176 ff); Sussman (1975).

20. With the exception of Sen. *Contr.* 4,6 — which makes no attempt to simulate a realistic setting and *NA* 12.1.22 — which could be taken to imply the child's removal.

21. Rawson (1986c); Bradley (1986). Cf. Plaut. *Mil. Gl.* 696; *Dig.* 32.99.3 (Paul).

22. Perhaps three: cf. Quint. *Inst. Or.* 1.1.16, citing Chrysippus: '*quamvis nutricibus triennium dederit*' — but these ages have a suspect formulaic quality. Probably the choice of age was not rigid, and philosopher-fathers were not necessarily consulted.

23. As in *CIL* VI 21347; *CIL* VI 23078 and Aul. Gell. *NA* 12.1.

24. Cic. *de Or.* 2.39.162: '*omnia minima mansa, ut nutrices infantibus pueris, in os inserant*'.

25. See 'The child's tie to his mother: Review of the psychoanalytic literature', pp. 361-78. Appendix to the 1969 ed. of *Attachment and loss*, vol 1, and *Mental health and maternal deprivation* (1952) *passim*.

26. Stone (1977) stresses architectural changes (such as the corridor), as well as the economic transformations acknowledged by Badinter

(1980: 195-236) and stressed by Shorter (1979: 204-62. Cf. Medick (1976).

27. As demonstrated by the story of the miracle which occurred when Octavian was a baby — Suet. *Aug.* 94.6. Compare the reference in Chapter 1, n. 12. Hanawalt (1977) documents a number of examples of accidents in medieval English villages which reveal the absence of the modern notion of constant vigilance over babies and small children.

28. While Shorter's gruesome picture of the indifference of mercenary French nurses is somewhat excessive, he certainly produces evidence that the nurse's affectionate involvement with the nurseling cannot be taken for granted — see Shorter (1975: 185-6).

29. See e.g. Saller (1982: 7-11) on analytic uses of the term 'patronage'.

30. '*Similiter ceteros aut affinitate aliqua sibi aut propinquitate coniunctos ... Tuscum nutricis filium relegavit, quod in procuratione Aegypti balineis in adventum suum extructis lavisset.*' (Suet. *Nero* 35. 4-5)

31. E.g. Plin. *Ep.* 6.3; *CIL* VI. 10229 (lines 35, 47 ff); *CIL* VI. 4352 and see Chapter 6 for a discussion of the relationship and comparison with relations with foster-parents and others.

32. '*Sed munusculum meum, quod esse quam fructuosissimum non illius magis interest quae accepit quam mea qui dedi.*' (Plin. *EP.* 6.3.2)

33. '*Ut nutrices ut paedagogos, ut praeceptores pro suo quemque officio diligebat!*' (Plin. *Ep.* 5.16.3)

34. E.g. Aul. Gell. *NA* 12.1.5; Soranus *Gyn.* II. xi (31) 18 [260].

35. The proverbially dirty *nutricis pallium* of Plautus' *Bacchides* 434 reappears three centuries later in Fronto's letters at *Ep. ad Marc. Ant. de Orat.* (= Naber p. 155) 12.

36. Roman inscriptions to *nutrices* include *CIL* VI. 21151 by a husband and *CIL* VI. 29550 by a son.

37. Plin. *Ep.* 2.17.22, where he refers to the *voces servolorum*.

38. E.g. Tac. *Agric.* 4: '*mater Iulia Procilla fuit, rarae castitatis; in huius sinu indulgentiaque educatus ...* '; Cic. *Brutus* 211: '*legimus epistulas Corneliae matris Gracchorum: apparet filios non tam in gremio educatos quam in sermone matris*'; Tac. *Dialogus* 28: '*nam pridem suus cuique filius, ex casta parente natus.. in gremio ac sinu matris educabatur ...*'

39. Cf., e.g. *Agric.* 29, where Agricola is praised for solacing himself with warfare for the loss of his infant son, rather than in the usual masculine way (*ambitiose*) or the usual feminine way: '*neque per lamenta rursus ac maerorem muliebriter tulit*'; cf. also Cic. *Fam.* 9.20.3: '*patriam eluxi iam et gravius et diutius quam ulla mater unicum filium*'; and even Seneca, in reproaching Marcia for her grief, cites numerous instances of extravagant mourning by other mothers, *ad Marciam* 16; and elsewhere concedes in passing that women in general and mothers in particular are expected to mourn most bitterly — Sen. *ad Helviam* 16.1-2.

40. Of a sample of 500 inscriptions in the *CIL* VI collection by mothers to children, 106 were dedicated to children up to the age of fifteen. Of these, 88 were to children of ten years and under. Fathers were joint dedicators of 21 of those 88. This is not conclusive — it is just included to give some idea of the social value parents put on young children.

41. Plin. *Ep.* 8.18, looking back on the marriage of Domitius Tullus,

who was incapacitated when his wife married him; and cf. Plin. *Ep.* 3.16. 3-5 on Arria's behaviour when her husband and son were seriously ill. The son is termed *puer*, but no age is indicated. Compare the letter attributed to the Empress Faustina the younger (no. 10 in the collection included in the *Life* of Avidius Cassius (Vulc. Gall.) — vol. 2, p. 316 of the edition of Haines (1963)).

42. Quintilian recounts his ten-year-old son's final delirium, *Inst. Or.* 6 *pr.* 11 ff, and Pliny tells how the dying Fundania had tried to solace her sister and father, Plin. *Ep.* 5.16.4. There is a suspicious similarity in the patient docility of the subjects, but specific detail attests the parent's attendance in both cases.

43. E.g.

All mothers are accustomed to abet their sons' wrongdoing and assist them in doing harm to their fathers.

... matres omnes filiis
in peccato adiutrices, auxilio in paterna iniuria
solent esse ...

(Ter. *Heaut.* 991-2)

or

His mother controls him cleverly on a tight rein, as fathers usually do.

... illum mater arte contenteque habet,
patres ut consueverunt.

(Plaut. *Asin.* 78)

— where the role-reversal implicit in the latter is the joke running through the whole play.

44. Pseudo-Quint. *Decl.* 18.9; 'quid enim non est formosus filius matri?'

45. Plut. *Cic.* 41.7; Cic. *Fam.* 6.18.5; *Att.* 12.40.

46. I believe she was his third. See Sherwin-White (1966: 71, 92) for discussion.

47. *Inst. Or.* 6 *pr.* 8: *aviae educati.*

48. Fifteen of the 18 inscriptions in *CIL* VI specifying age are for children under twelve years — see Chapter 6 and cf. Rawson (1986c) on *alumni.*

49. Ov. *Rem.* 547-8; Hor. *Carm.* 4.5.9 ff; Sen. *ad Marciam* 24.2.

50. E.g. Ov. *Met.* 2. 91-2 where Apollo states that his concern for Phaethon's safety shows true fatherly feeling.

51. Lady Antonia Fraser is the friend — see Gathorne-Hardy (1972) pp. 142-3 and especially p. 143: 'If a child can't find love or sympathy with one of the girls or his mother, there is always someone else to go to.'

52. '*Horum fabulis et erroribus virides statim et rudes animi imbuuntur; nec quisquam in tota domo pensi habet quid coram infante domino aut dicat aut faciat*'. *Dial.* 29.1.

53. Compare Cicero's dejection at the death of an engaging slave boy, *Att.* 1.12.4: '*nam puer festivus, anagnostes noster, Sositheus, decesserat meque plus quam servi mors debere videbatur commoverat*'. Pliny (*Ep.* VIII 16.3) confesses to being distressed at illness and death in his *familia*: '*nec ignoro alios eiusmodi casus nihil amplius vocare quam damnum, eoque sibi magnos homines et sapientes videri*'.

54. *NA* 12.1. 21-2: *Gyn* II. xi (31) 18 [260].

55. Gibbs (1960) recalls her own desperation at having to bring up her small children herself — a feat for which her education had unfitted her. Compare the narrator in Mitford's novel *The pursuit of love* who, like Gibbs, found it easier to get used to the idea of housework than of child care: 'So we worked hard, mending and making and washing, doing any chores for Nanny rather than actually look after the children ourselves. I have seen too many children brought up without Nannies to think this at all desirable.' (p. 204, 1980 Penguin ed., Harmondsworth)

56. Tac. *Ann.* 12.64. Vespasian's grandmother and mother presented a similar contrast — Suet. *Vesp.* 2. 1-2.

6

Mother Substitutes

The Concept of Substitution

We have already seen in Chapter 5 that the mother's presence and intimate physical involvement with the small child was not prized as much by the ancients as by modern experts. This view in part reflects a difference in theories of learning. While the idea of small children learning the fundamentals of a discipline was not unknown in the ancient world — witness especially Quintilian *Inst. Or.* 1.1.19 — serious learning was seen as beginning later. The modern stress on the importance of the early years for emotional and social development was to an extent paralleled by ancient ideas on moral development. Where Bowlby (1952) argued that small children deprived of a mother or mother substitute would develop into delinquents and social misfits, Favorinus claimed that babies would imbibe low servile morals with a nurse's milk, (Aul. Gell. *NA* 12.1.17) and Quintilian feared for the foundations of grammar learned at the knee of a foreign-born nurse or *paedagogus*.[1]

Perhaps the most significant difference in the two attitudes to childhood — and therefore to those who care for the very young — lies in the influence of the people who propagated these ideas in the two cultures. Favorinus obviously impressed Aulus Gellius with his eloquence on the subject of mothers nursing their own children, but it is not certain that either he or the family of the new-born child who had inspired his eloquence acted on Favorinus' views. The usual social practice among the well-to-do — and perhaps also among the lower social orders — was probably to give babies over to a slave or mercenary nurse (Bradley 1986). Bowlby and Spock, on the other hand, had a great impact

141

on child-rearing practices in modern societies where baby health centres and books have been taken seriously as centres of wisdom on the subject (Reiger 1984). To an extent, the proliferation of uniform prescriptions on child health has coincided with the historical emphasis on childhood as a formative stage and on an almost exclusively sentimental view of children's role in the family.

Although it was deplored by moralists, their denunciations reveal the currency of the practice of handing over small children to the least important member of the hierarchy of a *familia*.[2] The smaller the child, the less important it was. As it progressed through the early stages of life, it progressed, too, to teachers and custodians whose status improved correspondingly. A *paedagogus* was probably more important than a nurse, a *grammaticus* than a *paedagogus*, and so on.[3] Philosophers could mingle on equal — or politely acceptable — terms with members of the senatorial aristocracy. *Paedagogi* were not considered suitable dinner guests, although the position could lead to great opportunities within a wealthy household (Bonner 1977: 38-46; Bradley 1985a: 497). The younger Cato allegedly obeyed his *paedagogi* from respect (Plut. *Cat. min.* 1), but the function of the *paedagogus* altered over the life cycle of his charge. The disciplined child inevitably asserted his social superiority as an adult. Martial XI.39 provides a light-hearted version of the process:

You used to rock my cradle, Charidemus, and you were the constant guard and companion of my childhood. But now my neckcloth is darkened by my clipped beard, and my girlfriend complains that my upper lip prickles her. But I have not outgrown you. My bailiff and steward fear you, the very household trembles before you. You forbid me play and dalliance. You permit me nothing, but all licence for yourself. You denounce me, you keep close watch, you complain, you heave sighs. You barely refrain from seizing the cane in your fury. If I have put on purple clothes or gelled my hair into a fashionable style, you cry out, 'Your father would never have done that!' With a frown, you count my drinks as if the jar came from your own store. Cut it out! I cannot bear having a Cato as my servant. My girlfriend can tell you that I am now a man.

Cunarum fueras motor, Charideme, mearum

et pueri custos adsiduusque comes.
iam mihi nigrescunt tonsa sudaria barba
    et queritur labris puncta puella meis;
sed tibi non crevi: te noster vilicus horret,
    te dispensator, te domus ipsa pavet.
ludere nec nobis nec tu permittis amare;
    nil mihi vis et vis cuncta licere tibi.
corripis, observas, quereris, suspiria ducis,
    et vix a ferulis temperat ira tua.
si Tyrios sumpsi cultus unxive capillos,
    exclamas 'Numquam fecerat ista pater';
et numeras nostros adstricta fronte trientes,
    tamquam de cella sit cadus ille tua.
Desine; non possum libertum ferre Catonem.
    esse virum iam me dicet amica tibi.

The characterization of Lydus and Mnesilochus in Plautus' *Bacchides*, suggests that this might have been a stock picture of the relationship between a youth and his ageing *paedagogus*. Ideally, the young man's assertion was benevolent and he showed a proper regard for his dependant. Cicero (De *Amicit.* 74) makes the point that friendship does not automatically develop from longstanding intimacy. If it did, nurses and *paedagogi* would have a strong claim! (See Bradley 1985a: 505)

As an upper-class Roman girl passed out of the very early stage of childhood, her mother probably began to play an increasing role — if only more closely supervisory — in her upbringing. The tasks of tending to her physical needs or listening to her undeveloped speech was not, in spite of the views of a few educational philosophers, expected of the mother. This probably enhanced the mother's status in the child's eyes, for, like the father, she would become associated particularly with the business of becoming more grown-up and interesting. It need not mean that the mother was a more distant and forbidding figure than a nurse[4] but she might gain in authority and perhaps in importance to the child's everyday experience as he or she moved up through the stages of life. Thus maternal and paternal roles were not absolutely distinct, a trend noted earlier.

From this, it follows that nurses and those who tended babies and toddlers were not, in Roman eyes, the 'mother substitutes' of Bowlby's works. In the case of Quintilian's own motherless children, the 'substitute' for the mother was the woman of their own class: their grandmother. In addition they were tended by nurses and 'all those who normally take responsibility for those age groups' (*'omnes qui sollicitare illas aetates solent'* — *Inst. Or.* 6 *pr* 8). Or, to put it more accurately, his five-year-old son was tended by such people. His elder son, who survived to the age of nine, was taught by *praeceptores* and Quintilian's detailed knowledge of his performance (*Inst. Or.* 6 *pr* 10-11) makes it clear that he, as the father, closely monitored these studies. The role of the *avia educans* ('grandmother who was bringing him up') is not clearly defined. Quintilian might mention her in relation to the younger boy simply as a rival for the child's affections or because she would be expected to play a greater role with a child of that age than his father would.

In Chapter 5, we reviewed the example of Pliny's young wife, Calpurnia, apparently reared by her paternal grandfather and aunt because her parents were both dead. To the aunt, Pliny (*Ep.* 4.19.1-2) wrote that the young woman was a credit to her upbringing. Later, he reassured the aunt about Calpurnia's health after a miscarriage:

Since I believe your attachment to your niece to be even more tender than a mother's fondness ...

cum adfectum tuum erga fratris filiam cogito etiam materna indulgentia molliorem ...[5]

while the grandfather's interest appears to be less sentimental.[6] In this case, then, the 'mother substitute' was given reports of her niece's health and her progress in wifely skills. Presumably the young orphan had also had the attentions of nurses and others, but her aunt was the more authoritative, but fond, figure who appears to have taken primary responsibility for her.

Pliny's letter about the death of the girl Minicia Marcella is also interesting. It makes no mention of a mother, and it seems reasonable to assume she was dead. Among the girl's virtues, Pliny (*Ep.* 5.16.3) lists her proper regard for the various attendants involved with her:

How she loved her nurses, *paedagogi* and teachers in precisely the proportion due to each of them!

ut nutrices, ut paedagogos, ut praeceptores pro suo quemque officio diligebat!

It would be helpful to have an elaboration on the proper limits of such attachments, and their relative strength and manifestations.

Nurses[7]

On the proper relations with *nutrices* it is possible to make some pronouncements. The relationship with a *nutrix* seems to have lasted throughout life, though it changed with the age of the nurseling. Nero's burial rites were administered in part by his *nutrices* (Suet. *Nero* 50). In childhood, a nurse would tend to a baby's needs,[8] wean it on to solid food[9] and perhaps become fond of the child.[10] The child, however, became an adult, in a position to bestow favours on the nurse as a social inferior: thus nurses were included in family vaults[11] or given substantial gifts.[12] That is, they were seen as *clientes*, family retainers, often former slaves, with a claim to largess and consideration and an obligation to provide loyalty and service. The title *nutrix* appears on tombstones erected by husbands,[13] as a professional description, just as it does on epitaphs erected by the nurseling's family long after the nurse has provided her services.[14]

Both the combination of tasks and the 'phasing out' of the job as the child progressed through the life cycle are characteristic of motherhood in our own society. Fronto's assertion (see n. 10) that foolish nurses typically love their charges more as children and lament their transition to the outside world resembles the maternal stereotype of our own culture. Yet as we have seen in the preceding chapter, this was not the typical image of the Roman mother, who was characterised by disciplinarian skills rather than indulgence or over-protectiveness, even towards small children. Interestingly, Horace, whose satires tell us of his father's role in his education but not of his mother's, uses the typical good mother as the example of one who wishes her child to exceed her own learning and talents (*Epist.* 1.18.26-7): the reverse of Fronto's image of the nurse. It is difficult to know whether he is appealing here to a universal sterotype of the *pia mater*, adapting it to an upper-class audience or generalising from his own experience. It could easily have been applied to women such as Cornelia, Julia Procilla, or Agrippina (minor), who arranged to have their sons taught rhetoric or philosophy,[15] skills unlikely to have been acquired formally by the mothers themselves — and then taken it upon themselves to set appropriate limits to the sons' involvement in such advanced studies.[16] This authoritative, supervisory role, so often linked with ideal maternal behaviour, is at odds with the fond physical attendance of the socially inferior nurse.

Mammae and *tatae*

What, then, of the lower classes, where one might expect mothers to carry out the physical offices for their own children unless death forced their replacement. There is evidence that lower-class children were also reared sometimes by people other than their mothers. Within the *CIL* VI collection, there are 44 inscriptions to a *mamma*,[17] 27 inscriptions by a *mamma* to a dead child,[18] 11 inscriptions to or by *educatores*[19] and 44 inscriptions involving someone who had 'nurtured' a child[20] — variously described as a *nutricius*, *nutritor* or *qui eam nutrierunt* (as in *CIL* VI 34421).

Not all of these inscriptions involve children whose mothers have died (Cf. Bradley 1986: 208-9). There are, for example, inscriptions erected to a child by parents, *mamma* and *tata*, such as *CIL* VI 35530 to three-year-old Ti. Iulius by the slave Anthus, his *tata*, his *mamma* Rhoxane, his father Terminalis and his mother Iulia Euphrantice. Such examples suggest that the small child was given over to foster-parents in the early years to free the parents for their work. The terms *mammae* and *tatae* appear to be associated with childhood, for most of the inscriptions erected by a *mamma* are to small children[21] and the term is sometimes associated with *alumni* (eg. *CIL* VI 14347, 38769), a word generally applied to children who are very young, but not infants,[22] although inscriptions to *mammae* appear to have been erected by adults.

On the whole, the names of the children and the *mammae* are those of slaves and freed slaves. Where a *mamma* is styled *patrona*,[23] the children could have been bought by the *mamma* to perform a specific function within the family. Alternatively, a maternal type of relationship might have developed within a slave household which eventually moved the *mamma*, on gaining her freedom, to redeem the child. Sometimes the relationship appears to have been assigned, perhaps by an owner: the imperial *verna* Ianuaria erected a marble tablet to her husband

Ulpianus, also an imperial *verna*, and to others, including Aelia Helpis, who had been *mamma* to them both.[24] The two men Tiberius Iulius Eunus and Tiberius Claudius Deuter included the imperial freedwoman Claudia Cedne in *CIL* VI 37752, dedicated to their *parentes*. She is characterised as *mamma* (Claudia Aug l Cedne *mamma*). Others included in the dedication are characterised by a professional description (e.g. *medicus auricularius*) or status indicator (*verna*), so it is possible that *mamma* here, like *nutrix* elsewhere, signifies a function within the *familia*. If her function were to look after the children of a certain age, she might also have fostered the dedicators. One of the men, Tiberius Claudius Eunus, is described as a *cunarius*, which probably signified a nursery position.[25] Alternatively, she might have been their mother.

A *mamma*, then, could be a woman called upon by a master, a child's parent or her own inclination to take responsibility for a child, probably after it had grown beyond infancy, but not reached the stage at which it might be seriously trained for future work. The fact that a few *mammae* are also described as *nutrices*[26] simply confirms that the functions were usually different, because there would be no need otherwise to distinguish between them with additional terms.

Varro claims that children sometimes called their mothers '*mamma*',[27] but this is not really borne out by inscriptional usage. The child and *mamma* sometimes bear a common gentile name, as in the case of Turrania Prepusa and Turrania Polybia in *CIL* VI 27827 cited below. This could reflect their membership of the same *familia* rather than biological kinship. *Mamma*, paired as it is with *tata*, does seem to represent a maternal type of relationship, whether between social equals or kin. Mourning *mammae* tend to use affectionate language for the dead children on epitaphs[28] and to describe themselves as miserable and deprived. Although the epitaph *CIL* VI 11592 is damaged, it appears to have the deceased *verna karissima* Ampliata address her owner with the formula

Do not mourn, Mamma

NOLI DOLERE MAMMA[29]

CIL VI 25808 is quite long for a sepulchral inscription. Addressed to Salvidiena Faustilla by the *libertina* Salvidiena

Hilara, it stresses that the learned girl's death has left her *mamma* in a wretched state.[30] Turrania Polybia, mourning the death of seven-year-old Turrania Prepusa, laments the cruel fate which snatched the child away and thus prevented her from discharging her obligations — presumably funeral rites, or comfort in old age — to her *mamma*:

> To the memory of Turrania Prepusa, who lived seven years, three months. Turrania Polybia created it to her dear and most delightful spirit, suddenly taken by the malevolence of the Fates, so that she was unable to fulfil the offices she was intended to perform for her *mamma*.

:MEMORIAE
TVRRANIAE PREPVSAE
VIX ANN VII MENS III
TVRRANIA POLYBIA
DELICATAE ANIMAE
DVLCISSIMAE INIQVITATE
FATORVM SVBITO
RAPTAE VT NON POTVERT
CONSVMMARE IN SE
DESTINATA BENEFICIA
MAMMAE SVAE:

(*CIL* VI 27 827)

This style of tombstone is very reminiscent of the lament of some bereaved parents, that they are performing the very office for a dead child which the child ought to have performed for them.[31]

In general, then, the *mamma* appears to have had with a young child a kin-like relationship, sometimes shared with a *tata*. 'Foster-parent' is probably the best English term to apply, as long as this is understood to cover both substitute parents for a child whose own parents were dead or had abandoned it and temporary substitute parents in the case of a child whose parents apparently retained responsibility for the child but allowed it to be reared for part at least of its childhood by a *mamma* and, sometimes, a *tata* as well. Again, the inscriptions throw little light on whether the parents and foster-parents would have lived under the same roof in such a case.

As we might expect from the nature of the inscriptions, there is evidence only of affectionate relations. If *mammae* and *tatae* played a disciplinary role, this is not alluded to in the epitaphs. Bonds of sentiment and obligation appear to have been associated with the relationship, but where the mother was alive the *mamma* seems to have supplemented rather than entirely replaced her. In spite of the etymological connection between *mamma* and the breast, *mammae* appear not to have breast-fed children.[32] This could mean that lower-class children were more likely to be breast-fed by their own mothers before being passed on to a foster-mother or minder but even that task might have been assigned to specialist nurses in a large slave household.[33]

Nutritores, nutricii and *educatores*

To the modern mind, the expression 'mother substitute' implies a woman. For this reason, I have so far concentrated on *nutrices*, *mammae* and the female relations of motherless children, but there are also examples of men associated with the rearing of children and perhaps eligible for such a term, as Bradley (1985a) has shown in his valuable study. In his scornful account of contemporary customs, Vipstanus Messalla is made to describe a typical arrangement in a prosperous household as follows:

> These days an infant is handed over at birth to some Greek maidservant with the addition of some fellow from the great body of slaves, usually the most worthless, who is not fit for any responsible charge.

> at nunc natus infans delegatur Graeculae alicui ancillae, cui adiungitur unus aut alter ex omnibus servis, plerumque vilissimus nec cuiquam serio ministerio adcommodatus.
>
> (Tac. *Dial.* 29.1)

CIL VI 21334, to Licinia Lampetia Basilioflora,[34] was erected by C. Mussius Chrysonicus and Aurelia Soteris, styled *nutritores lactanei*. Another sepulchral inscription *CIL* VI 11005 to Aemilianus was erected by his parents Secundus and Successa and by Sutius and Sutia '*isdem nutritores*' — presumably 'nurturers' of Aemilianus, whose age has been lost from the end of the inscription, but who would appear from the description to be a child. In these instances, the *nutritores* seem to be jointly associated with feeding — and probably tending — a young child. Similarly, *CIL* VI 29191, to four-year-old M. Ulpius Felicissimus, was erected primarily by M. Ulpius Merops, an imperial freedman and Flavia Phoebas as well as by M. Ulpius Primigenius and Capriola, his *nutricii*, to their pious *alumnus*. The first two are probably the parents and the second two (one free, one probably a slave) assigned to look after the child.[35]

That the *nutricius* or *nutritor* was not necessarily just the husband of a *nutrix* is suggested by the fact that husbands dedicating inscriptions to *nutrix* wives do not adopt the term, while a woman is included in the term *nutricii* in *CIL* VI 29191, quoted in n. 35 above.[36] Similarly, in *CIL* VI 34421, to the much lamented three-year-old Anteis Chrysostom, the primary dedication is by her parents Faenomenus and Helpis. Their names are followed by:

> Porcius Maximus and Porcia Charita and Porcia Helias and Sardonyx and Menophilus, who nourished her right up to the day of her death.

> PORCIVS MAXIMVS ET PORCIA
> CHARITA ET PORCIA HELIAS
> ET SARDONVX ET MENOPHI
> LVS QVI EAM NVTRIERVNT
> IN DIEM MORTIS EIVS:

This could refer to all four, or to Sardonyx and Menophilus particularly. In either case, it suggests that the little girl was tended by male and female fellow-slaves of her parents.

As we shall see below, *nutritores* and *nutricii* were usually social inferiors of the children they tended. In this case, however, the group of dedicators almost represents a self-constituted extended family, revolving around the charming and loquacious little Anteis Chrysostom (or perhaps '*chrysostom*' is a descriptive nickname, similar to the adjectives *loquax* and *garrula*, which follow). Compare *CIL* VI 10170, by the imperial gladiator and freedman Trophimus to himself, to his free-born wife, to his *nutricius* C. Tadienus Secundus (who is free-born) and to his freed *verna* Pindar (or Pindarus). Other examples are *CIL* VI 9625, by A. Sempronius Laetus, a building surveyor,[37] to himself, his wife, his beloved freedmen Orestes and Orestillus, to Octavia Acme, described only as 'nourished by us', '*nutrita ab nobis*', and to his *liberti* and their descendants according to the usual formula. A smaller group is involved in *CIL* VI 6324, which seems to have been erected by Atticus, son of the nurse Stacte, as *conlacteus* to his mother's nurseling, the four-year-old Sisenna.[38]

These seem to be examples of people towards the lower end of the social spectrum, prepared to adopt familial relations with others. There is a certain logic in some of the combinations: a married couple take up an *alumnus* or *verna* almost as a child of their own, then the *nutricius* or *nutritor* to whom the child is assigned for daily care is himself absorbed into a special relationship, and particularly associated with family dedications to a dead child, rather as a nurse or *mamma* might be. In the case of *CIL* VI 9625, it is not clear whether Octavia Acme, whose name bears no relation to any other on the inscription, was *'nutrita'* by Sempronius Laetus and Sempronia Metrothea, his wife, or by the two *'carissimi'* freedmen as well.[39]

On the whole, there is an identifiable status distinction between parents and nurturers, but owners or patrons readily express appreciation of their services. An attractive example is *CIL* VI 21279a, to Licinius Meropnus, about fifty years old at the time of his death. The marble tablet was erected by his *patrona* Licinia Veneria. Her high opinion of him is attested not only by the length of the inscription, but by the descriptors she applies — *bene merens* and *dulcissimus*. He had been the *nutritor* of her children and of her *alumni*.[40] This suggests that he occupied a specialised function in the household, with responsibility for young children.

Most of the dedications fall into the mould of being addressed to or including a valued family retainer, again analogous to the place occupied by *nutrices* in sepulchral inscriptions. Typical examples are:

To the shades below. P. Aelius Placentius erected this to the worthy *nutritor* of his children, the well deserving Marcus Aurelius Liberalis.

:D M
P AELIVS PLACENTIVS
NVTRITORI FILIORVM SVORVM
DIGNISSIMO M AVRELIO LIBERALI
B M F:

(*CIL* VI 10766)

Here lies Gnaeus Cornelius Atimetus and Gnaeus, the freedman of Lentulus Gaetulicus and his faithful procurator. Gnaeus Cornelius Cossus and Lentulus Gaetulicus dedicated this to their faithful procurator and dutiful *nutricius* on their own account as well as a memorial in the Bruttian villa on their Sabine estate.

> :CN CORNELIVS
> ATIMETVS
> CN LENTVLI GAETVLICI
> L ET PROCVRATOR
> EIVSDEM FIDELISSIMVS
> HIC SEPVLTVS EST
> COSSVS CORNELIVS
> CN E LENTVLVS
> GAETVLICVS
> PROCVRATORI SVO
> FIDELISSIMO ET
> NVTRICIO PIISSIMO
> DE SVO FECIT ET
> MONVMENTVM
> IN SABINIS SVIS
> IN VILLA
> BRVTTIANA:

(*CIL* VI 9834)[41]

It is difficult to tell from the inscriptions whether these *nutritores* and *nutricii* were mother substitutes in the sense that they cared for children whose mothers had died or been separated from them. This would obviously not apply in the case of the inscription by Licinia Veneria to Licinius Meropnus,[42] where the mother actually engaged the *nutritor* for her own children. The dedicators of *CIL* VI 10450, M. Aberrinus Fortunatus and Aemilia Peiagia, appear to be a married couple who had availed themselves of the services of M. Aberrinus Philadespotes/us to care for their daughter:

To the shades below: to Marcus Aberrinus Philadespotes/us, thirty-five years old. Marcus Aberrinus Fortunatus and Aemilia Peiagia, former owners (patrons) dedicated this to their freedman who did his duty well by them and was *nutricius* of their daughter.

DIS MANIBVS
M ABERRINO PHILA
DESPOTO VIX A XXXV
FECIT ET M ABERRI
NVS FORTVNATVS
ET AEMILIA PEIAGIA
PATRONI EIVS LIBER
TO DE SE BENE MERITO
ET NVTRICIO FILIAE SVAE:

CIL VI 28593 was inscribed on a marble altar erected by Memmia Tertulla to her *nutricius* Neonianus (an imperial *verna*) and to her mother Memmia Panther(a).[43]

In such cases, the *nutritor* could no more be styled a mother substitute than could a wet-nurse or *paedagogus* with responsibility for young children. The fact that inscriptions are dedicated only by a father or by the person who had been cared for by a *nutritor* in childhood raises the possibility that they provided maternal care, but it need not follow. Where two members of a *familia* honour the same *nutritor* or *nutricius*,[44] there is a suggestion that slave children were relegated to him at a particular stage, perhaps after they had left the care of a nurse or mother, but in general the *nutritor* or *nutricius*, like the *nutrix*, seems to have extended the relationships open to a young child rather than replaced others. Again, this argues against the more rigid modern notion of certain kinds of care being classed as 'maternal'. The essential distinction for the Roman child seems to have been one of status. Mothers and fathers provided discipline and affection — so, to an extent, did a variety of people with whom the small child mixed. A certain grateful *pietas* and affection might be shown by that child as an adult towards these early figures, but it does seem anachronistic to try and make the label 'mother surrogate' or 'mother substitute' fit the ancient case. That we have inscriptions to *nutricii* and *nutritores* suggests that adults felt an obligation to honour their memory, whether for the care those adults had received as children or in appreciation of services extended to their own children. The high rate of manumission among such servants confirms this (Treggiari 1976: 96; Table 8.1; Bradley 1986: 204-6).

There seem to have been nuances between the terms derived from *educare* on the one hand and *nutrire* on the other. Bradley's discussion (1985a: esp. 498-500) is essential reading on the topic.

153

He presents a thorough social analysis of the categories *paedagogi, nutritores, nutricii* and *educatores*. But '*educator*' and its cognates were not confined to child care professionals. The terms could be applied to distinguished teachers like Seneca (Bradley 1985a: 500) and even to relations — that is, to social equals of the child. Thus Quintilian spoke of his young son being cared for by an *avia educans* ('a grandmother who was bringing him up'; *Inst. Or. 6 pr.* 8) — an expression almost paralleled by *CIL* VI 1478 to Oscia Modesta, described by her distinguished grandson as '*avia carissima*' and '*educatrix dulcissima*'. The object of *CIL* VI 1527,a (= 37053), (the so-called '*laudatio Turiae*') is characterised as a model of family feeling. Not only did she dower her female relations, but she brought some of them up in her own home:

> NAM PROPINQVAS VESTRAS D
> FICIIS DOMIBVS VESTRIS APVD NOS
> EDVCAVISTIS
>
> (lines 44-5)

It would be unwise to generalise too freely from such small samples; for some flexibility is apparent in the usage. Just as a *mamma* could be a patron or a *liberta*, so *nutritores* and *educatores* could vary somewhat in their standing. In a general sense, *educare* seems to have meant 'bring up' or 'train', while 'nutrire' meant not only 'to feed' but to tend in a basic, physical way.[45] The social difference would then emerge from the distinction between those who looked after infants and those who were responsible for their overall upbringing. Thus Quintilian's small son was probably fed and cared for daily by his *nutrices* and the unspecified 'others', but his grandmother would have overseen their activities. It was strict supervision which Vipstanus Messalla had in mind in his statement:

> This was the way in which Cornelia oversaw the upbringing of the Gracchi, Aurelia oversaw that of Caesar and Atia that of Augustus.

> sic Corneliam Gracchorum, sic Aureliam Caesaris, sic Atiam Augusti praefuisse educationibus.
>
> (Tac. *Dial.* 28.6)

where *educationes* virtually has the meaning 'methods of child-rearing', characterised immediately afterward as *quae disciplina ac severitas.* To be *educatus litter[is] Graecis quam et Latinis,* like the six-year-old L. Valerius Turnus of *CIL* VI 28138, was almost to be 'educated' in the English sense of the word. In *CIL* VI 34386, where the deceased child addresses his parents, the term *educastis* appears to mean 'brought up' in every sense, but in *CIL* VI 19128, Graxia Alexandria is praised by her husband, the imperial freedman Pudens, because *etiam filios suos propriis uberibus educavit* — so that the verb there is almost equivalent to *nutrivit.*

Bradley has shown (1985a) that terms could be elastic but that one could generalise that *educare* could cover the various aspects of bringing up a child, while *nutrire* usually had a more basic meaning, and was therefore more suitable for application to small children whose physical requirements were obvious. The ministrations supplied to meet such needs were seen as servile and of a 'lower' order, as one would expect in a society which associated such physical tasks with hard necessity. This does not mean that children did not develop strong affection for those who tended them in the early years, but they must have learned to distinguish the status of those who ministered to them and those who dealt with them without carrying out such tasks. Again, as in the last chapter, the story of the infant Tiberius is instructive, for it displays both the familiarity of the child with mother and nurse alike and the difference of function, for he endangered them during their escape in the civil war by crying:

> When he was removed hurriedly first from his nurse's breast, then from his mother's embrace (or lap) by friends who were trying to relieve the poor women of their burden in this dire emergency.

> semel cum a nutricis ubere, iterum cum a sinu matris raptim auferretur ab iis, qui pro necessitate temporis mulierculas levare onere temptabant.
>
> (Suet. *Tib.* 6.1)

The wicked stepmother

The term 'substitute mother' is then most suitably applied to relations such as aunts or grandmothers who took on the kind of function appropriate to a mother — such as Nero's aunt Domitia Lepida, Quintilian's mother (or mother-in-law) or the aunt of Pliny's wife Calpurnia. As far as can be discerned, such women were readily accepted by children as replacements for their dead or absent mothers. It is, therefore, notable that stepmothers were viewed so differently. Unlike a *nutritor* or *nutrix*, a stepmother necessarily occupied the same social position which the biological mother of a child would have held. She must have performed some of the same roles within the family and household.

Stepfathers also had a dubious reputation. As we saw in Chapter 3, Apuleius (*Apol.* 71) felt bound to answer charges that he might have acted in the *way* that stepfathers often did and the law eventually gave widowed mothers certain rights on condition that they not remarry.[46] Stepfathers who took a paternal interest in their stepchildren were accorded a wondering admiration by the literary sources, as if this were unexpected (e.g. Nicolaus 3.5). There was none the less a great difference in the assumptions about stepfathers and stepmothers, stemming probably from the fact that stepmothers usually lived in the same household as the stepchildren and because of the presumption that a woman would always advance the interest of her own children over the interest of a strange woman's children. Such tension would have been more evident from the necessity for children to live side by side with their stepbrothers and sisters, rivals for the father's attention and property if the stepmother produced children from the marriage with him. If the reputation of stepfathers was ambivalent and shady, that of stepmothers was regularly and explicitly malign.

Cicero's allegation that Sassia required Oppianicus to murder his three sons before she would consent to marry him (*Clu.* 26-7) need be taken no more literally than Juvenal's insistence (6.626-33) that stepmothers always try to poison their stepchildren. It does, however, indicate the kind of thing which could freely be imputed simply on the basis of the relationship and one imagines that impressionable children, filled with such tales would have been terrified in advance of a new stepmother. If she then showed favouritism to her own children, this would reinforce childish expectations and the most routine discipline, if contrasted with an idealised version of a dead mother's behaviour (or the attentions of a divorced mother who did not take responsibility for her children's day-to-day conduct) might have furthered the idea. If psychoanalytic views of infantile resentment of parents have any basis, it could be that the persistent stereotype of the evil stepmother might represent fears of real mothers untempered by guilt. It does not sufficiently explain the difference in the view of stepfathers, since paternal discipline would surely arouse equal resentment in the childish mind and therefore the adult unconscious.

Whatever its explanation, the representation of stepmothers pervades Latin literature. Tacitus refers routinely to *novercalia odia* ('stepmotherly hatred') as a self-explanatory term for Livia's alleged antipathy to Agrippa Postumus,[47] yet she seems to have been the protector of Agrippina (maior) and her children. It was not until after Livia's death that they suffered extreme persecution from Tiberius.[48] Agrippina minor actually offended her own son by befriending her stepdaughter (and daughter-in-law) Octavia.[49] The fact that there *were* benign stepmothers does not seem to have altered the dominant prejudice. Augustus's sister Octavia received some credit for her care of M. Antonius' children from other unions, but that was chiefly because it was so important for Augustus's own propaganda that she should appear as a model of womanly virtues and a wronged wife (Plut. *Ant.* 87.1). Seneca's mother had been reared from early childhood by a stepmother. Unable to think of any criticism to offer of this stepmother, Seneca (*ad Helviam* 2.4) still counts this as a hardship:

> You grew up under a stepmother whom you compelled by your total obedience and dutiful affection (equal to that which a daughter might display) to be a mother to you but even a good stepmother is a hard thing to endure.

> crevisti sub noverca, quam tu quidem omni obsequio et pietate, quanta vel in filia conspici potest, matrem fieri coegisti; nulli tamen non magno constitit etiam bona noverca.

That is, even though he admits that the stepmother behaved like a mother, the credit for this goes to the stepdaughter. Pliny took it for granted in *Ep.* 9.13 that Fannia was a good stepmother to Helvidius Priscus — yet in court he played up to the popular image of stepmothers as scheming seductresses bent on cheating stepchildren of their patrimony.[50]

It is notable that there is only one epitaph in the *CIL* VI collection (no. 30123) explicitly mentioning a *noverca* (or *noberca*, in this case). Stepfathers figure a little as dedicators and as objects of dedication,[51] so the apparent neglect of stepmothers is marked.

There are some indications that dedicators honoured individual stepmothers while avoiding the opprobrious '*noverca*'. It is a small sample on which to base an argument, but there are four inscriptions which seem to involve a stepmother without using this term. Thus Sentia Viva erected *CIL* VI 26211 in her lifetime for herself, her daughter Plaetoria, her sister Plaetoria and her stepdaughter Sentia, but does not characterise herself as a stepmother.[52] *CIL* VI 14367 was erected by Oculatia, '*privigna*'.

MEMORIAE
CANTABR

which could signify a female name, such as Cantabria, *CIL* VI 11816 is quite explicitly erected by C. Turranius Primus '*privignus*' to Annia Restituta, while *CIL* VI 29679 was erected by Zoticus, an imperial *verna*, to Labiena/e, who appears to have been his stepmother:

D M
ZOTICVS AVG
N VER L LABIENE VI
TRICI COGNATAE
BENEMERENTI ET MAIA
MATR   FILIA

The inscription is on a fragment from an eleborately decorated marble sarcophagus. It does look rather as if Zoticus and his stepsister combined to erect the memorial to Labiene/a. He seems to have thought that *vitrix* was the feminine of *vitricus*. It is possible that '*vitrici cognatae*' is quite correct Latin for 'relation of his stepfather' or a *cognomen* (for Victrix, cf. Chantraine 1967: 196-7), but I incline to the view that Zoticus has tried to coin a neutral expression for the relationship of stepmother, avoiding the traditional odium of '*noverca*'. The fact that analogous inscriptions were recorded to stepfathers and mothers and fathers-in-law makes the argument more dubious, but these other relationships are explicitly represented in *CIL* VI commemorations to a greater degree.[53]

Considering the flexibility noted elsewhere in the readiness to add to the family unit, the apparent reluctance to include stepmothers in dedications, or perhaps to avoid naming them as stepmothers, is suggestive. It is difficult to know whether the legendary reputation of stepmothers generated such reserve, or the reputation arose directly from experience. Epitaphs yield little evidence of fond feelings between stepmothers and stepchildren even at death. At best, the relationship appears to have been guarded, and well summarised by the emperor Marcus' analogy with his feelings for palace life and philosophy:

> If you had a stepmother and a mother at the same time you would pay your respects to the stepmother out of good manners, but to your mother your visits would come from your heartfelt wish.

> εἰ μητρυιάν τε ἅμα εἶχες καὶ μητέρα, ἐκείνην τ'ἄν ἐθεράπευες καὶ ὅμως ἡ ἐπάνοδός σοι πρὸς τὴν μητέρα συνεχὴς ἐγίνετο.

(*Med.* 6.12)

Conclusion

Where children in modern urban cultures tend to be reared primarily by their mothers and to be intimately involved with them in their early years, Roman children seem to have had a more varied experience. Not only did maternal mortality and divorce impose actual separation from the mother, but custom and economic circumstances dictated both separation and alternation with other custodians. Poor women like the mother of M. Antonius Gnipho might have abandoned their children from poverty or fear of disgrace (Suet. *Gramm.* 7). Suetonius tells us that C. Melissus was exposed simply *ob discordiam parentum*. This might mean his family disagreed about rearing him, or that his parents separated and neither wanted the burden of a child (Suet. *Gramm.* 21).

We have seen (in Chapter 2) that slave children could be taken very young from their parents for sale, and there are indications that specialist *nutrices* and *nutritores* or *nutricii* were given the care of slave children — sometimes, too, of *alumni* and the free children of a household (Bradley 1986; Rawson 1986c). *Mammae* and *tatae* appear to have been foster-parents, sometimes owners or patrons of slave alumni, sometimes acting in concert with a child's parents, and conceivably their relations or good friends (Bradley 1985a: 520-3).

I have argued that the concept of a 'mother substitute' is

inapposite for many of these relations, partly because they could supplement the usual role of the mother and partly because the mother's role was not itself viewed as the exclusive dispensation of care for the infant or small child. Certainly no conflict is apparent in the numerous examples of joint dedications of inscriptions to dead children.

'Substitution' is more suitably applied to social equals who actually took the place of a dead or absent mother, such as the *mamma* of an orphaned or abandoned child, or the *avia* (or *amita* 'aunt') *educans* of a motherless child. Yet, even in those cases, men sometimes fulfilled a similar role. Social status seems to have been a more important determinant of the relationship than gender — again, perhaps, because the role of the mother was less closely associated with the exclusive care of the small child than in our own society.

The child's attitude to those who offered care and took responsibility seems also to have been determined by relative social station. An *alumnus* could be an object of affection and perform a role similar to that of a son or daughter, but it was for the adult of superior station to determine that the relationship should take this form rather than one of more conventional *clientela*. An upper-class child would show proper benevolence as an adult to the *nutrix*, whether former slave or free, who had provided milk and care in his infancy. The duties owed an aunt who had performed a mother's office of education seem to have been akin to those owed a mother — respect and affection, and the consciousness that one's behaviour reflected on her training. The duty of performing funeral rites is apparent in all the relationships — necessarily, since it is often through the sepulchral inscriptions that we know of relations with *alumni*, *nutrices*, *nutritores*, *educatores*, *mammae* and *tatae*. Dio 48.33 records the award of a state funeral to Augustus' *paedagogus* and both Cicero (*De Amicit* 74) and Pliny (*Ep.* 5.16.3) assume that nurses and others who care for the young have certain claims on their charge in later life.

Those associated with a child's early years tend, on the whole, to have been of lower status, engaged as they were in tasks judged servile and demeaning. Their services were valued by parents and child alike, but parents who could afford to do so seem to have escaped the more routine aspects of bringing up small children and contented themselves with directing others in these offices. As children grew older and were deemed fit for 'proper' training, they passed into the hands of those with higher standing, whether parents, teachers or foremen.

In our society, removal from the mother or even occasional replacement of the mother by a professional is regarded as a hardship for a young child. There must have been circumstances in which it was wretched for small children in ancient Rome, particularly for children born into poor or slave families, but the overall impression gained is that there was a wider network of people involved with the various stages of a child's life. It could be that some children were able to enjoy pleasant, casual relationships with a number of adults at once. Schoolmasters have a severe reputation in Latin texts, and famous mothers were characterised more by firm direction than indulgent affection. Literature seldom takes the child's viewpoint, and there is no chance of reconstructing the emotional setting of childhood in the ancient world. Perhaps the portrait of the 'wicked stepmother', who unaccountably looms large as the great horror of childhood, was a symbol of the uncertainties of life in pre-industrial conditions.

Notes

1. *Inst. Or.* 1.1.4: '*ante omnia ne sit vitiosus sermo nutricibus*'. Quintilian was conscious of being in a minority in urging that learning in the early years counted for something. He cites the example of Chrysippus, who had conceded that the nurses who should tend a child for the first three years could form its character and asks: '*cur autem non pertineat ad litteras aetas quae ad mores iam pertinent?*' *Inst. Or.* 1.1.16-17.

2. Favorinus in *NA* 12.1.17-19; Vipstanus Messalla in Tac. *Dial.* 29.

3. Bonner (1977: 46) points to the low status of the *paedagogus* schoolmaster compared with the *grammaticus*. Cic. *Off.* 1.150-1 rationalises such status distinctions in general as stemming from the benefit to humankind which each job category provides and the suitability of the task to a given rank in life. The production of clothes and food were lesser arts. I have unfortunately been unable to obtain the study of the status of the Roman paedagogue by the Dutch scholar R. Boulogne *De plaats van de paedagogus in de romeinse cultuur* (Groningen 1951).

4. Gathorne-Hardy (1972: 77-8) gives examples of English children such as Winston Churchill and the autobiographical portrait of Compton Mackenzie in *Sinister Street* to show that the process could make the mother more adored, because she was not associated with humdrum activities and discipline.

5. *Ep.* 8.11.1 and cf. *Ep.* 4.19.1.

6. *Ep.* 8.10. The contrast is pointed out by Phillips (1978: 74-5).

7. *Nurses*: although literary references to nurses occur in this

subsection, most of the examples are drawn from the sepulchral inscriptions (or those classified under the monumental tombs) of *CIL* VI.

Inscriptions dedicated *to* a nurse include:

1354;	5063;	5201;	5939;	6072;	6323;
7290*;	7393;	8660;	8941;	8943;	9901b;
10909;	11265;	12023;	12133;	13683;	15655;
16128;	16329;	16440;	16450;	16592;	17564
19155;	20042;	20883;	21151;	21661;	21710;
21988;	23128;	24073;	24297;	24232;	27262;
29497;	29550;	35037;	38999;		⚊ 27557

I have excluded metaphorical uses of *matrix* and inscriptions to a *mater nutrix*, 'nursing mother) (21347; 13321; cf. 29550), who (unlike a mother who is also a nurse, e.g. 8943) is not a 'mother substitute'.

Twenty-two inscriptions were dedicated by a *nutrix*, many of them by nurse and parents jointly. In such cases, the nurse usually appeared at the end of the list of dedicators (e.g. 35123; 12366):

15377;	17490;	22638v;	28120;	7618;	7741;	6686;
20938;	12366;	18032;	34383;	12299;	23589;	4352;
25301;	17157;	1516;	7355;	15952;	25728;	26539;
35123						

8. Producing the proverbially dirty nurse's cloak — Pl. *Bacch.* 434, Fronto *de Orat.* 12 (= Naber p. 155).

9. Quint. *Inst. Or.* 10.1.19; Cic. *de Or.* 2.39.162.

10. Fronto *Ep. ad Ant.* 1,5 (= Naber p. 102), but note Bradley's excellent caution (1986: 220-2) against glossing over the relationship with a veneer of historical romanticism.

11. As in the case of the nurse Prima — *CIL* VI 4352.

12. Like the little farm Pliny gave his nurse — Plin. *Ep.* 6.3.1 or the legacy to the nurse Dasumia Syche — lines 35, 42 ff of *CIL* VI 10229.

13. E.g. *CIL* VI 21151; 16592; 12023 (a *contubernalis*).

14. Cf. *CIL* VI 8660 by Epictetus to his nurse, 82 at the time of her death; 16450 by Cornelius Dolabella Metillianus to Servia Cornelia Sabina, a *libertina*; 16128 to Cornelia Prima, nurse of Scipio. Ages are not usually given, so it is difficult to be certain, but most of these appear to be epitaphs erected to a faithful servant who continued to be styled *nutrix* because that was her job. Cf. Bradley's Table 8.1 (1986: 204-6).

Nutrices could become dry-nurses — *nutrices assae* — and still practise the job when unable to provide milk. (Cf. the scholiast on Juv.14.208, where Juvenal characterised the *assa* as *vetula*.) Nonius *de Prop. Serm.* I. 57 M (Teubner text) defines *assae* in terms of attendance and associates such terminology with positions of a service character. See also Dixon (1984c).

15. Plut. *Tib. Gr.* 1. Cf. Cic. *Brutus* 211 on Cornelia; Tac. *Agric.* 4 on Julia Procilla; Tac. *Ann.* 12.8 on Agrippina.

16. Julia Procilla and Agrippina are both known to have done this —

Tac. *Agric.* 4.4-5; Suet. *Nero* 52.1.

17. *CIL* VI	2210;	4567;	4639;	4850;	5040;	8021;
	10368;	11487;	12321;	12771;	12840;	13831;
	14347;	15326;	15349;	15507;	15585;	16043;
	16450;	17026;	17223;	17439;	18698;	20578;
	20603;	20632;	20823;	23350;	23556;	24329;
	25276;	25324;	26001;	26008;	27208;	27844;
	28047;	28206;	28241A;	28447;	29116;	35270;
	37752;	38891.				
18. *CIL* VI	5425;	7726;	10016;	11592;	14720;	15345;
	15471;	16926;	17800;	18032;	19473;	20318;
	21405;	26594;	29634;	33538;	35530;	36353;
	38598;	38638+A;	38769;	25808;	20909;	11714;
	6973;	12366;	27827.			
19. *CIL* VI	34386;	1478;	4871;	9792;	10714;	13221;
	15983;	16844;	18848;	27198;	30915.	

In addition, 1527.A (= 37053) refers to relations being reared in the home of the subject of the dedication ('Turia'), while 34386 and 19128 refer to parents who have reared their own child in a particular way. 28138 describes the dead child as:

EDVCATVS LITTER
GRAECIS QVAM ET LATINIS:

The other inscriptions listed describe someone as *educator* or *educatrix*. Latinists accustomed to published editions of literary texts will often find the syntax wanting. I have not presumed to correct authenticated inscription readings.

20. *NVTRITOR/NVTRITORES* (25): *CIL* VI 19054; 1332=31632; 19547; 38952; 24089; 13151; 31918=1746; 8425; 19007; 1365; 11005; 8925; 17471; 37078; 37775+9967 = 33818; 10766; 10848; 14083; 16446; 21279, a and b; 25302; 37055.
These include *NVTRITORES LACTANEI*: 31833 = 1623; 1424; 21334.

NVTRICIVS/NVTRICII (16): *CIL* VI 29191; 15104; 16574; 5405; 8486; 9834; 10450; 33249=7271; 38598; 10170; 20433; 21432; 27298; 27365; 28593; 34159, A = 25371.
From parts of the verb *NVTRIRE* (3): *CIL* VI 9625; 21695; (34421).

21. 27 *CIL* VI epitaphs are dedicated by a *mamma*, eight of them jointly with a *tata*. The age of the deceased charge is given in sixteen of those cases, of which only two were over fifteen years, while most of the ages (thirteen) were under eight years. Cf. Bradley (1985a), esp. pp. 496, 501; and see the Table of Inscriptions.

22. On the age of *alumni*, see Rawson 1986c, esp. pp. 179-81 and n. 31. Of the *CIL* VI inscriptions by a *mamma*, 60% range from age one year 16 months to seven years (*CIL* VI 29634; 18032). Compare the use of *verna*, a slave born into the *familia* — but see Chantraine (1967: 125-7; 170-4).

23. As in *CIL* VI 20603 to Iulia Filete; 12840 to Aufidia Veneria or 15349 to Claudia Alexandria.

24. *CIL* VI 29116:

> D   M
> VLPIANO AVG N VERNAE Q
> VIXIT ANIS XXXV IANVARIA
> AVG N VERNA MARITO SVO
> INCONPARABILI CVN QVO
> VIXIT ANNIS XV DE SE BENE MER
> FECIT ET AELIAE HELPIDVTI MAMMAE EO
> RVM ET FAVSTO AVG N LIB ET CL IVLIANO
>
> LIBERTIS LIBERTABVSQVE POSTERISQ —

and cf. *CIL* VI 27208, by the *libertus* M. Terentius Restitutus and his *liberta* Crocale to Carvilia:

> MAMMAE SVAE BE
> NE MERITAE DE SE:

25. Reasoning from *cunae* f.pl. meaning 'cradle'. It could conceivably mean 'someone who makes cradles'. It does not appear in Lewis and Short. The *OLD* gives the meaning 'attendant on infants', citing the feminine *cunaria*, which appears in *CIL* VI 27134. Cf. Treggiari (1976: 89).

26. E.g. Servia Cornelia Sabina, a *libertina*, described in *CIL* VI 16450 as *nutrix et mammul b m* by her high-born charge (possibly her *patronus'* son) Servius Cornelius Dolabella Metillianus.

27. *De Hon. et Nove Vet. dictis* — frag. preserved at Nonius 81,4. 'Grandmother' is given by Forcellini's *Lexicon Totius Latinitatis* (reprinted 1965 from the Padua 1926 edition) as a transferred meaning of *mammula* and by Lewis and Short as a usage of *mamma* in inscriptions, but there is nothing to demonstrate this usage apart from the Greek use of the term μάμμη — cf. Phrynichus 110, Pollux 3.17.

28. As in *CIL* VI 33538 to Claudius Successus, who, at 24 years, is the oldest object of a dedication by a *mamma* in the *CIL* VI collection. He is described as *optimus adulescens pientissimus et infelicissimus*. Compare *CIL* VI 11592 by Pedania Primigenia to the four-year-old Ampliata, '*verna karissima*', and see the discussion in the text below.

29. Editors are agreed that the stone shows:

> NOII DO--E- MAMMA

which is a variant on the more common '*noli dolere mater*' as in *CIL* VI 20182,D;28523. Similar sentiments are put into the mouth of a dead child at *CIL* VI 23551; 27227; 35126.

30.   : V SALVIDIENA Q L HILARA
> SALVIDIENAE FAVSTILLAE
> DELICIAE SVAE

ERVDITAE OMNIBVS ARTIBVS
RELIQVISTI MAMMAM TVAM
GEMENTEM PLANGENTEM PLORANTEM
  VIX AN XV
MENSIB III DIEB XI HOR VII
VIRGINEM ERIPVIT FATVS MALVS
DESTITVISTI VITILLA MEA
MISERAM MAMMAM TVAM:

31. E.g. *CIL* VI 12307 by Aricinia Nais and C. Curtius Antiochus to their son Aricinius Bassus; 26901 — by Successus to his nine-year-old son and his wife Caesia Gemella, buried with him. See Lattimore's (1942) discussion of the theme, pp. 188-91.

32. Caelius Aurelianus used *mamma* to signify 'wet-nurse' in his translation of Soranus 2.11 (31), but that could represent a much later development. As I argued above, inscriptions such as *CIL* VI 18032, where Flavia Euphrosyne describes herself as *mamma idem nutrix*, suggest that the terms described distinct functions.

33. Cf. Plaut. *Mil. Gl.* 697:

nutrici non mussuru's quicquam, quae vernas alit?

Dig. 32.99.3 (Paul) on the definition of a rural or urban slave, raises the case (whether hypothetical or typical is, as always, open to debate) of the child:

qui natus est ex ancilla urbana et missus in villam nutriendus

and *CIL* VI 21695 (first line dubious)

... COMPSENI VICARIAE
NATA PICENO NVTRITA
ROMAE MORTVA PRAENESTE
V AN XX:

— although *nutrire* is not an informative verb, and could well refer to the sustenance of a child after it had passed the breast-fed stage. Compare the discussion in the text below of *nutritores*, *nutricii* and *educatores*. These disparate references all imply that slave children could be sent out to nurse. Bradley (1986: 207-13) has an excellent discussion of the arrangements for care of slave children and the economic motives of the owners.

34. *Cil* VI 31833 and 1623 represent the same inscription, with a slightly different version of the first few lines, but these do not seriously affect the reading of the dedication as a whole. Editors are agreed on the last six lines.

35. : M VLPIO FELICISSIMO VIXIT ANN IIII DIEB V
M VLPIVS AVG LIB MEROPS ET FLAVIA PHOEBAS
INFELICISSIMI ET M VLPIVS PRIMIGENIVS ET
CAPRIOLA NVTRICII ALVMNO PIISSIMO:

36. And cf. *CIL* VI 1365, where Amycus and Chrestina are described as *nutritores*.

37. Or perhaps an inspector or architect (= *mensor aedificorum*). The *OLD* suggests 'a surveyor of building works'.

38. Though the text could be read differently:

: ATTICVS F
STACTES NVTRICIS
SISENNAE F CONLACTEVS
V ANN IV:

and compare *CIL* VI 25377, which does not contain a *nutricius* or *nutritor* but shows a similar flexibility in grouping the dedicator Rasinia, who set it up to herself, her patron P. Rasinius Celadus, her apparently infant son Rasinius Memor, her twenty-three-year-old *verna* Rasinia Aucte and D. Rasinius, described as *libertus idem cognatus*. Perhaps she or Celadus freed this 'blood' relation.

39. : A SEMPRONIVS LAETVS MENSOR
AEDIFICORVM SIBI ET
SEMPRONIAE METROTHEAE VXORI ET
ORESTI ET ORESTILLO LIBERTIS CARISSIMIS ET
OCTAVIAE ACME NVTRITAE AB NOBIS
LIBERTIS LIBERTABVS POSTERISQVE EORVM
...

40. ...
LICINIVS MEROPNVS QVI VICSIT ANNIS PLVS MINVS
L
MENSIBVS III DIEBVS XX LICINIA VENERIA FECIT
LIBER
BENE MERENTI ATQVE ET DVLCISSIMO ET
NVTRITORI FILIORVM
MEORVM QVAM QVOD ET ALVMNORVM MEORVM:

41. And see n. 20 above for a list.

42. *CIL* VI 21279a, discussed above and quoted in part in n. 40.

43. Cf. *CIL* VI 13151, where the *nutritor* is a secondary dedicator, whose name follows those of the parents. In *CIL* VI 11005 Sutius and Sutia are added after the parents and styled *nutritores*.

44. As in *CIL* VI 5405, from a *columbarium*, set up by Euhodus and Evander, members of Domitian's *familia*, to Ti. Claudius Epaphus '*nutricio suo bene merenti*'.

45. Thus Seutonius uses *nutritor* of the man who reared and manumitted the *grammaticus* M. Antonius Gniphus (Suet. *Gramm.* 7), and the participle *nutritus* of the child Nero, reared by his paternal aunt during his mother's exile (Suet. *Nero* 6.3). *CIL* VI 15983, by Memphius Iraenaeus and Renatus, *alumni* and heirs of Coelia Palaestine, apparently distinguished between her and their *educatores*, the imperial freedmen Aelius Provincialis and Aelius Viator. I am not persuaded by Bonner's

suggestion (1977: 42) that *nutricius* and *paedagogus* eventually became synonymous, but Bradley's thorough discussion of the categories (1985a: 499-500) suggests that there is no firm distinction between an *educator* and a *nutritor*.

46. That is, the mother's right to an inheritance from the husband, or to *tutela* of the children, was eventually forfeit if she remarried, because of the presumption that a new husband would attempt to undermine her children's rights. See Chapter 3 and Humbert (1972: 387-446) for later rulings (to the fifth century AD). As I argue in the earlier chapter, these laws were very late and possibly to be associated with the Christian stress on widows' chastity, but the fear of stepfathers is reflected in the literature centuries before.

47. Tac. *Ann.* 1.6. Hallett (1984: 257-8) argues with some justice that there was little tension between stepmothers and stepdaughters, but the *stereotype* was uniformly forbidding.

48. Phillips (1978: 76) makes this point. She notes, too, that it was Livia who had made an allowance to Julia the younger in her exile — Tac. *Ann.* 4.71.

49. Tac. *Ann.* 13.18 — admittedly this was provocative.

50. Esp. *Ep.* 6.33 where Pliny boasts of his advocacy in a 'test case' for the distinguished Attia Viriola, whose octogenarian father, '*amore captus*', had made a new will within days of his remarriage. Presumably the speech he enclosed with this letter dwelt even more shamelessly on stereotypes.

51. I have found eleven sepulchral inscriptions in *CIL* VI *by* stepfathers to *privigni*: *CIL* VI 3541; 7377; 7547; 11374; 14289; 15446; 18912; 15205; 19333; 21554; 28376 and five by stepchildren to stepfathers: *CIL* VI 11739; 13091; 24501; 29433; 39025 (two of these to the mother as well, one set up by the mother/wife *and* stepchild together). *CIL* VI 22356, to a *privignus*, does not specify the dedicator. Harrod (1909) gives additional examples (p. 59) because he takes '*patraster*' to mean 'stepfather', while I take it to mean 'uncle'. (Consider *CIL* VI 14105 by Umidia Onesime to her *patraster et tutor*, in spite of the great unlikelihood of a stepfather occupying the position of *tutor*).

52. :SENTIA A F VIVA FECI
SIBI ET
PLAETORIAE L F FILIAE SVAE
PLAETORIAE L F SORORI SVAE
SENTIAE L F PRIVIGNAE SVAE:

This is a rather confusing inscription in any case. It would make better sense if the second Plaetoria were the *privigna* and Sentia the *soror*.

53. Harrod (1909: 59) gives similar circumlocutions for 'stepfather' in *CIL* VI 12581 and 26279 and compare his entries (59-60) on *socer* and *socra*. Chantraine (1967: 196-7) draws attention to the difficulties of reading *CIL* VI 29679 with great certainty. He finds it improbable that vitrici should bear the meaning 'stepmother' here, but is reluctant to accept the *CIL* VI Index interpretation of the words as part of a name.

7

The Roman Mother and the Adolescent or Adult Son

The mother's role in her son's transition to manhood

He was left a fatherless ward in the care of guardians until his fourteenth year — but he remained perpetually in the guardianship of his mother.

pupillus relictus sub tutorum cura usque ad quartum decumum annum fuit, sub matris tutela semper.

(Sen. *ad. Marciam* 24.1)

In many modern cultures adolescence and the early adult years are seen as causing special difficulties within families. It is a time of mutual testing, of the generation gap. There is some evidence of similar strain in Roman families, but adolescence was not always distinguished from other stages of life and ancient accounts often leave the reader in doubt as to whether the 'children' discussed are infants or young adults.[1] Incidental details sometimes tell us that the subject is a young man in the early stages of a political and military career, while tombstones occasionally specify a youth's age at death. Those incidents which are passed on tend in the main to be anecdotal and, as with other sources on family relations, they fall too often into stock categories: pious acknowledgements of the contribution made by a mother to the moral development of a famous man, or sensational tales of gross breaches of the usual relationship, with scandalous detail supplied, but even these have their uses in reconstructing notions of what constituted the proper relationship between a mother and her adult or nearly adult son. The tombstones and letters provide a welcome supplement to the richer but more suspect yield of imperial biographies. They help us to form a picture of male adolescence at Rome and of the role a mother might play in her son's life as he progressed from childhood, through youth, into the proper pursuits of manhood, from many of which she was excluded.

In *pro Caelio* 18 Cicero answered the charge that Caelius chose to live apart from his father in order to lead a dissolute life. Both the idea that such a charge might be made and Cicero's insistence that many young men now live in their own apartments are suggestive. In planning the allowance due his own son Marcus to further his studies in Athens in April 45 BC, Cicero pointed out that he would have set aside a similar sum if Marcus, not quite twenty at the time, had been occupying a bachelor apartment in Rome (*Att.* 12.32.2). Nicolaus of Damascus 4 tells us that the young Octavian continued to live with his mother and stepfather even after he had assumed his *toga virilis*, as if this, like Atia's close interest in his daily activities, was both particularly commendable and somewhat unusual.[2] This is suggested, too, by Cicero's assertion elsewhere:

> ... that he should live with his own family, especially with his father — for in my judgement family feeling is the basis of all the virtues ...

> ... ut vivat cum suis, primum cum parente — nam meo iudicio pietas fundamentum est omnium virtutum ...
>
> (*pro Plancio* 29)

although his own son and nephew lived apart from their parents. All of this indicates that separate residence was normal, but there was still some idea abroad that keeping sons at home was more desirable.

The adult son, then, might have lived apart from his mother even if she and the father were alive and lived together. In the case of a divorced mother, the son might not have lived with her for many years before he came of age. Yet widowed, remarried or divorced, a mother was apparently entitled to regular visits from her son. The young Quintus Cicero reported to his uncle after such visits (e.g. *Att.* 13.42) and young Marcus Cicero was encouraged to attend the divorced Terentia (*Att.* 12.28.1). As an older man, Tiberius was criticised for *not* visiting his aged mother (Suet. *Tib.* 5.1) and Seneca spoke of the pleasure a mother gained from such visits (*ad Helviam* 15.1). The emperor Marcus used the analogy of visits to a stepmother, which would emanate from obligation, in contrast to the visits to one's mother, which would be provoked by genuine feeling (*Med.* 6.12). Such visits, then, were seen as an earnest of family feeling and respect and their omission a ground of disapproval and offence.

By modern standards, the lives of young adult senatorial males were a curious mixture of freedom and dependence. If, as Nicolaus implies, they could establish their own households at an age between fourteen and seventeen, their actual behaviour might have been consonant with their legal status as 'independent', *sui iuris* and no longer in need of a *tutor* to manage financial affairs, in the case of a fatherless boy, who thus became a *paterfamilias* at law regardless of his marital or parental status.[3] Quintus and Caelius, whose fathers were alive when they left the paternal home, show that separate residence was in any case not uncommon by the age of seventeen or eighteen. The difference would be that a fourteen-year-old *sui iuris* and living 'alone', would conduct his own financial affairs, while the son *in patria potestate* was dependent on the father's allowance.[4] Both would have their physical needs attended to by slaves and their financial arrangements mediated by professionals, whether slave or free.

The senatorial male began his public career early. Even before embarking on the ladder of office, he might serve on the staff of a governor or consul,[5] and prosecutions were launched by youths of nineteen.[6] Even allowing for the fact that some husbands fostered their young wives' learning,[7] the great difference between male and female education within the upper class dated from adolescence. At an age when girls were married and embarked on the social duties and pleasures of a Roman matron's life, boys continued their formal education by attaching themselves to an established orator at Rome (Plut. *Cic.* 3; Tac. *Dial.* 30.3) or seeking the philosophical and rhetorical refinements offered by Rhodes or Athens. They might learn through practical application the skills of the law court, the battlefield or the provincial assizes.

Given the formal exclusion of women from these areas, it is all the more interesting to find a continuing stress in the literary sources on the good mother's attention to her son's development throughout this phase. Not only was she praised for attention to his morals, as in the case of Atia's supervision of Octavian (Nicolaus 4/10) but she might take it upon herself to direct the course of his studies. Neither Julia Procilla, mother of Agricola, nor Agrippina minor, mother of Nero, appears to have had any training in philosophy, yet each checked her son's study of the subject on grounds of propriety (Tac. *Agric.* 4; Suet. *Nero* 52). This was both a social and a political judgement and acquiescence in it shows the authority which the mother, as an experienced member of the older generation, could legitimately wield over a young son. Apparently philosophy exercised the kind of fascination on the younger generation at Rome which has been attributed in this century to Communism, Existentialism and the Counter-Culture. Even Domitia Lucilla, mother of the future emperor Marcus, reputedly had difficulty in persuading him to sleep on a normal couch rather than the floor because of his stoic leanings (SHA, Iul. Cap. *Marcus Ant.*). Not only is the maternal check approved by the sources in these cases, it has the retrospective support of at least one son. Tacitus states that his account is based on Agricola's own reminiscence of his youth.[8] The mother is not depicted as an ignoramus warding off the 'real world'[9] but as the saner voice of the older generation, alert to social realities.

One of the most intimate portraits of a mother and son is passed on by Pliny *Ep.* 6.20, on the occasion of the eruption of Vesuvius in AD 79. Pliny, then seventeen, had pursued his studies under his mother's eye on open ground while they awaited the return of her brother from his rescue operations. The mother eventually agreed that the situation was too dangerous and urged her young son to leave without the encumbrance of an ageing mother, although she had earlier resisted a friend's advice to flee. In the end, both mother and son gained safety in flight. The account, passed on for its relevance to the obvious historical aspects of the natural disaster, establishes the level of a mother's responsibility. Pliny's mother Plinia Secunda was a widow staying with her brother and clearly held responsible for her son's actions and safety. She was able to make the important decisions for him, even in such dire straits, just as she continued her more normal activity of seeing to it that he pursued his studies. An Athenian mother would probably have taken orders from her seventeen-year-old son (cf. Lacey 1968: 117).

Martial's flippant reference to the unprofitable tendency of his own education[10] intimates that it was not only widows who could exercise their judgement. In Martial's mock lament, as so often in the Roman sources, the parents are linked, with no firm division between the maternal and paternal role in making decisions which would affect a young man's career. The emperor Marcus seems to have owed his philhellenic training to his mother Domitia Lucilla and his maternal grandfather.[11] The information is too meagre to draw firm conclusions about the relative contributions of male family members. Certainly widows could call on their male relations for help. Iunius Mauricus asked for Pliny's advice on a suitable teacher for his fatherless nephews (and niece, perhaps)[12] and the Emperor Marcus attested his maternal great-grandfather's involvement in the choice of his teacher (*Med.* 1.4). Pliny the elder appears to have had a say in the studies of his nephew (Plin. *Ep.* 3.5.15). Yet in each case it was the widowed mother who took final responsibility — and therefore the ultimate credit — for her son's education. Thus Cornelia (*mater Gracchorum*) was given some of the honour due for the skilful oratory of her sons, while escaping any stigma for their revolutionary policies (Cic. *Brutus* 211; but cf. Plut. *Tib. Gr.* 8.7). By the same token, Caesar's widowed mother Aurelia was acknowledged for her moral support of his career and her strict methods of education, without being held to account for his active sexual reputation (Tac. *Dial.* 28).

It is interesting to compare this with Cicero's more detailed comments on his nephew Quintus. He suggests that paternal indulgence had 'spoilt' Quintus (e.g. *Att.* 10.6.2) but in the end absolves fathers of blame for their children's flaws:

> But it is definitely not our fault. No, nature is the fatal element. That was what corrupted Curio and Hortensius' son, not any failing of their fathers.

> sed nulla nostra culpa est, natura metuenda est. haec Curionem, haec Hortensi filium, non patrum culpa corrupit.[13]

This differs from the modern tendency to attribute responsibility to parents *only* for the flaws and problems of the adult child and to view the mother as the chief formative influence. We have already seen that even proverbially influential mothers were cited as an afterthought and Licinia and Hortensia were assumed to have acquired their gifted speech from their eloquent fathers.[14]

The information about Atia's involvement in the education of the youthful Octavian is more detailed — presumably because it was based on his own memoirs available to Nicolaus. Each evening she checked which teachers he had frequented and what he had learned (Nicolaus 3/6). Agrippina was later to take the lead in appointing suitable teachers to the young Nero.[15] Both of these women had remarried by the time their sons reached their adolescence and embarked on advanced studies, but their stepfathers appear to have played a secondary role in crucial educational decisions. Perhaps if the fathers had lived *they* would have made the key decisions about the specifically masculine training imposed from the age of about sixteen. A mother's wishes had more force than those of a youth's uncles or stepfather. It is difficult to estimate how they compared with those of a father, beyond the observation that both parents tend to be linked in the presumption of educational responsibility.[16]

The relative independence of the Roman matron in the economic sphere might have enhanced her position in her son's eyes, even when he had attained adulthood. In most cases, she became *sui iuris* on her father's death. If in her husband's control (*in manu mariti*), she gained independence on the husband's death, when her dowry and any property he chose to leave her would revert to her. Even if the father were alive, wealthy young men of the Roman upper class had financial 'expectations' of their mothers as well as their fathers. We have seen in Chapter 3 that sons felt — and were generally thought to be — hard done by if passed over by maternal testaments (Val. Max. 7.7-8), although their claim to an intestate mother's estate was weak. A son might look to his living father for a liberal allowance and to a dead father for his estate, but he would also hope to benefit handsomely on his mother's death. Cicero (*Att.* 12.28) thought it could be in young Marcus' interests to wait on Terentia while she was considering her new will in 45 BC.

Perhaps if a mother had contributed substantially to her daughter's dowry the son's eventual expectations (at the mother's death) would be greater than his sister's. Technically gifts other than dowry between living people were void at Roman law but there is some evidence of mothers contributing sometimes through their own dowries, administered by the husband to a son during the mother's lifetime. On Terentia's divorce from Cicero, part of her dowry was retained to contribute to young Marcus's comfortable life-style (*Att.* 15.20.4). Perhaps it would have been put to the same use if the marriage had continued. Seneca (*ad Helviam* 14.3) speaks of his mother's generosity to her children during their period *in tutela* and to himself when he ran for political office, a very expensive business. Pliny appealed to Trajan (*Ep.* 10.4) on behalf of a friend whose mother had unwittingly neglected the necessary formalities in transferring to her son sufficient wealth to raise his status. Prudence as well as affection would urge a wealthy young man to defer to his mother's judgement. Again, we can descry a connection between the ideal of *pietas in matrem* and economic advantage.

A mother's continuing authority could derive also from her ancestral distinction. This could be as advantageous as wealth for political and social purposes. A mother such as Aemilia the elder, daughter and sister of great generals, or Cornelia, daughter of Scipio Africanus maior, conferred a signal political advantage on her sons when they solicited high office. The son of Sulla was allegedly honoured by playmates as a boy because of the prestige of his mother Caecilia Metella.[17] Julius Caesar's praise of his maternal and paternal ancestry at his aunt's funeral is a well-known example of political exploitation of this factor (Suet. *Iul.* 6.1). A respectable maternal line could help ensure a good marriage (Plin. *Ep.* 1.14.6). In the lower orders a mother's status was conferred on her children if marriage between the parents was not formally recognised.[18] This could sometimes lead to epigraphic emphasis on the mother's position (Rawson 1966: 76-7). The fact that a mother might not be engaged in the same trade as her son or have shared his studies was not, therefore, necessarily a bar to her intervention in his adult activities. A mother could legitimately lend support and advice for activities such as law and politics which were essentially male preserves,[19] or make binding decisions on the direction of an education — such as philosophy — which she had not herself experienced. Her financial position, her descent, her own reputation and the partnership she enjoyed with her husband ensured that her counsel was taken seriously.

The difficulty experienced within imperial families of producing a direct male line of succession led to an emphasis on descent through the female line from early in the Julio–Claudian regime. Some emperors — notably, Tiberius and Nero — owed their position not so much to their birth as to their mothers' marriages. In the second century the adoptive emperors Hadrian and Marcus had been first married to princesses of the former imperial family. Thus the native wit of a chosen heir, already related to the emperor or his wife, was united with the inherited credentials of an imperial bride in an attempt to produce new Caesars still linked by 'blood' with an established regime.

This stress on descent was given a new twist by the two Julias, Soaemias and Mamaea. They insisted on the illegitimate but imperial paternity of their sons — Elagabalus and Alexander Severus respectively — to support a claim to the throne. The influence of mothers whose own descent or marriage had established a son's claim to the throne could be great. So could the influence of an adoptive mother like Trajan's widow Plotina. In either case, gratitude could move a ruler to honour and defer to the woman who had secured his elevation. We saw in Chapter 4 that emperors celebrated such women on coinage from *pietas* and a desire to emphasise their own right to the succession. In this chapter, we shall also see examples of rejection of mothers, such as Livia and Agrippina minor, who traded unduly on their past services to their sons.

There seems to have been a fine distinction between acceptable maternal ambition or advice in the political sphere and female intrusion. Perhaps it is not surprising that mothers and sons sometimes disagreed about where the distinction ought to be drawn. Hallett (1984: esp. 243-5) has pointed out that Roman matrons tended to focus their ambitions on their sons rather than their husbands. To an extent, such ambition was applauded — as in the case of Cornelia, mother of the Gracchi, or Aurelia, mother of Caesar. Sons expected their mothers to support their political aspirations and showed their appreciation of the support. Yet Seneca drew attention to the contrast between the proper aid lent him by his mother[20] and the improper ambition of other mothers:

> who exploit their children's influence with female irresponsibility, who fulfil their ambitions through those sons because women cannot hold office.

> quae potentiam liberorum muliebri impotentia exercent, quae, quia feminis honores non licet gerere, per illos ambitiosae sunt.

> (*ad Helviam* 14.2)

This description of excessive maternal ambition would apply as much to the highly praised Cornelia as to Agrippina minor. In a later subsection we shall examine examples of conflict between mothers and son which seem to have revolved around this distinction between proper maternal ambition and 'interference' in the son's life. The most thoroughly documented examples tend, inevitably, to emanate from the imperial family but there is some evidence to suggest that the problem was more general, to do with the changing role of the mother throughout her son's life cycle.

Indeed, an examination of conflict between mother and son over the proper limits of her authority exposes ways in which it did differ from that of the father. As we shall see, her power has defined socially rather than legally and could be attacked. From her point of view, it was best to avoid a serious challenge. Perhaps the prudent mother, who had overseen her son's education, helped establish his political career and given him advice when consulted, refrained from demanding too much in return.[21]

My argument, then, is that maternal authority altered throughout a son's life cycle, but that it did not follow the pattern familiar in some modern societies. The association of the mother and small child was not as strong as the modern one, but the mother's status did not decline rapidly in ancient Rome as the son approached adulthood, nor was the relationship dependent on co-residence. Sons were expected to visit their mothers regularly after they had left home, or if the mother had moved because of divorce or remarriage. The respect accorded the mother by her adolescent or adult son appears to have been strengthened by the general social esteem in which a Roman matron was held and her association as partner rather than obvious subordinate in parental activities. Her individual standing could be enhanced by her descent or wealth — both of which could be useful to an ambitious son — or her personal qualities. Women such as Cornelia, Atia and Arria won a respect from their peers which had no equivalent in an ancient culture like that of classical Athens, where there was little social intercourse between the sexes outside the family circle and it was impolite to speak of respectable women by name in public.[22]

Such factors combined to produce some formidable women, particularly in the well-attested upper social echelons. While they were required to defer to their fathers and to an extent to their husbands, such women stood in an authoritative relationship to their sons, in whom they invested their ambitions. A mother's authority was enhanced by widowhood but it did not derive wholly from that state. The mother was apparently expected to participate in decisions concerning an adolescent son's training and career even if his father were alive, though her role was probably more decisive if she was a widow. She was generally expected to show a keen and detailed interest in her son's activities, to encourage and identify with his aspirations and to correct any wrong-headed youthful tendencies. These characteristics can be discerned in a number of mothers and sons, but are most spectacularly illustrated by examples from the imperial family. Such examples — and others — also show the other side of the coin, for sometimes adult sons *did* become impatient of a mother's intervention in their lives and challenge her authority. In many cases, such challenges must have been settled without any overt breach between mother and son. If a mother really fought her son's rebellion and he persisted, this exposed the ultimate weakness of her position. Unlike the father, she did not have any form of binding legal *potestas* over her son. Even disinheritance by a mother was not as drastic as the denial of his patrimony. Once a son was established in his career, he could afford to dispense with his mother's advice and could even neglect the usual pious attentions, although that would incur general censure. Let us look now at detailed examples in an attempt to define Roman expectations of the relationship between a mother and her son as he entered adult life.

Marriage, maternal authority and the wider world

The right of parents to impose serious choices on their adult children does not seem to have been questioned as such and mothers had some say in the marriage choices of sons as well as daughters. Yet specific measures might be resisted. The consequences of such family quarrels seem to have varied. Cicero's nephew, young Quintus, did not like the choices his parents presented for his marriage. It is notable that his mother and father, often at odds during their marriage and now divorced, should have been united on this point. His mother Pomponia seems to have none of her acknowledged right to a say in the business (e.g. Cic. *Att.* 13.42.1). Servilia's son Brutus went against her wishes in divorcing his wife and marrying his cousin Porcia. There was a coolness between mother-in-law and daughter-in-law, observed by Cicero, but it did not lead to a serious rift (*Att.* 13.10.3; 22.4. Cf. Africa 1978: 614-15). Although Servilia seems to have favoured close ties with Caesar, she sided unquestioningly with her son and sons-in-law after his assassination. After presiding over a meeting of family and friends — largely tyrannicides — to consider the question of Brutus' grain commission and other tactical points, she undertook to lobby on her son's behalf in his absence.[23]

Sassia's quarrel with her son was not so easily forgotten. The reason for their falling out is not made clear by Cicero, but the two gave no quarter. Having arranged a marriage between her stepson and her daughter, she then had this son-in-law bring a charge of murder against her son by an earlier marriage — Aulus Cluentius Habitus. Nor did family feeling keep him from answering her accusations in kind, through the medium of Cicero (*Clu.* 176, 188-94 *et passim*).

A mother's wishes could be thwarted by events which overtook the son himself. Seneca's mother, who had rallied her following to help him achieve high office, must have suffered at his exile. Her hopes were bound up with her son. The *consolatio* he wrote on that occasion argues away her feelings, demonstrating by cold logic that they are misplaced and unworthy of her, but the need for such a work is testimony in itself to her disappointment. Octavia made no attempt to hide her grief at the death of her son Marcellus. Octavian had marked out his nephew for the succession[24] and Octavia had doubtless looked forward to being mother of the next *princeps* (emperor). Seneca says that she dressed in mourning for the rest of her life and could not hear her son's name spoken. That this was not entirely because she missed him personally is indicated by her aversion to other mothers, and particularly to Livia, whose position was strengthened.[25] This is particularly interesting because Octavia had daughters who could and did continue the imperial line and Livia was already wife of the *princeps*. We have seen in Chapter 4 the special honours heaped on both women, who enjoyed a status comparable with that of the Vestals. Yet it was as mothers of potential *principes* that they vied with each other.

A mother's wishes counted even in that most masculine preserve, the military. Atia saw fit to keep the young Octavian from accompanying his uncle Julius Caesar on military service to Libya in 47 BC because of his poor health (Nicolaus 6/14). He later asked leave to return from a military expedition to visit his mother (Nicolaus 14/31). If Seneca (*ad Marciam* 24.1) is to be believed, Marcia's son Metilius eschewed military service as a youth in order to remain with his mother. Such consideration —

which would be treated with great scorn in many modern societies — is described favourably by Nicolaus and Seneca.

The letters attributed to Cornelia *mat. Gracchorum*, though of dubious authenticity, throw some light on the expectations of a mother's right to appeal to an adult son. The letters were admired in antiquity for their prose style,[26] but, given the approving references to Cornelia as an exemplary mother, there is an implicit endorsement of their sentiments as suitable to the relationship. The mother, elsewhere spoken of as properly ambitious for her sons to distinguish themselves, is here depicted as attempting to sway Gaius from his desperate, radical course. The arguments she employs would today be deemed fit for psychiatric analysis[27] and, more popularly, as improper 'interference' in an adult child's chosen course. Yet it is apparent that no ancient reader saw any impropriety in her insistence that Gaius should fill the place of her many dead children and bring her comfort in her old age, nor in her complaint that he caused her more pain than the family enemies and ought, at least, to have the decency to wait until her miserable remainder of life were finished before embarking on his headlong rush to disaster.[28]

Maternal appeals clearly counted for a great deal among Roman men. Such appeals would have gained somewhat if they came from widowed mothers. As we have observed in Chapter 2, women who survived childbirth were (statistically) likely to become widows eventually. Although remarriage was common and childless widows were obliged by Augustan legislation to remarry, a mother who chose to remain with her young children must have consolidated her influence over them. Even if she did not, she could assert herself over her son while he was a young man, as Atia did after her remarriage. Individual distinction and competition for honours was a feature of Roman aristocratic male life. Yet such individual honours had to be won by a collective effort and mothers were important contributors to that effort. It was perhaps for this reason that sons accepted their advice and strictures even in areas of which the mothers could have no direct, personal experience.

When the mother went too far: conflict

If the adolescent or adult Roman male's life was a combination of dependence and autonomy, his mother's standing, too, veered between authority and powerlessness. We have seen that a mother's force rested not on a legal foundation but on convention and moral force. This was doubtless reinforced in many instances by the fact that the mother had the disposition of a substantial fortune on her death, and in some cases even held a great part of her deceased husband's estate for life, on the understanding that she would eventually pass it on by testament to her children.[29]

Even outside the imperial family, a mother could assist her son's advancement by judicious arrangements for his marriage or her own remarriage: both Octavian and Fulvia's son Clodius benefited from the support of a powerful stepfather.[30] Up to a point, she was expected both to aid her adult son and to dictate to him. Modern Western mothers are obliged by social pressure to observe a sharp distinction between their authoritative relation to young children and a more peripheral role in their adult children's lives. Attempts to bully or even influence older children — especially sons — are regarded as unsuitable and somewhat ridiculous breaches of an unspoken code. The 'rules' governing relations between mothers and adult sons of the Roman propertied class imposed more subtle distinctions, and some mothers appear to have exercised considerable control over their sons' activities.

Yet, in the last analysis, an adult son could successfully defy his mother. Even Octavian, that pious son, eventually disregarded his mother's pleas and departed to gather an army from among Caesar's *coloni* without her permission (Nicolaus 31/132-4). Up to that point, he had depended on her for political news and advice during his time in Apollonia and Brundisium after Caesar's death. It is interesting that Nicolaus, who had represented her earlier cautions as the thoughtful counsel of an elder (6/14-15; 18/52-4), depicts his independent action as a step into manhood, a necessary separation from an over-anxious mother. The attribution of motive — masculine ambition versus womanly timidity — is noteworthy. He concealed his plan from her:

> lest she should hinder his great schemes because of her affection and the weakness typical of a woman — especially of a mother.

μὴ ὑπὸ φιλοστοργίας ἅμα καὶ ἀσθενείας, οἷα γυνή
τε καὶ μῆτερ, μεγάλαις ἐπινοίαις ἐμποδὼν γένοιτο.
(Nicolaus 31/134)

I tend to agree with Hall (1923: 76; cf. Bellemore 1984: 131) that these passages are based on Augustus' own later memoirs, and might represent his view of the situation.

Aulus Gellius (*NA* 1.23) passes on the traditional tale of the youth Papirius Praetextatus, who accompanied his father to the Senate and afterwards refused to tell his mother what had been discussed there. When she continued to press him, he told her that the Senate had been debating whether men should be allowed more than one wife. The next day, the senators were besieged by crowds of women begging them not to pass the law, but to grant women the right to several husbands instead although Praetextatus had sworn his mother to secrecy. On learning the full story, the senators applauded the boy for his public humiliation of his mother, because he had defended the citadel of male political mysteries against female curiosity. Valueless as history, the stock rhetorical anecdote suggests that in spite of the active involvement of women in the real political process there remained a firm notional boundary of what was and was not women's business and that a mother's authority was not unassailable (cf. Hallett 1984: 249-50).

In effect, sons *chose* to defer to a mother. Paternal authority was different. Fathers who disapproved of their son's political actions did not write them emotional letters or stand anxiously at doorways — they could haul them off rostra or execute them (Val. Max. 5.8). The slowly liberalising tendency of the laws and the convention of deference to a formidable mother might obscure the difference, but it was there. Cornelia's appeal to her son, if it was made, went unheeded. Brutus went against his mother's wishes in the direction of his political and marriage alignment.[31] Significantly, such moves tend to be endorsed by the sources as a proper separation of the man from the mother.

Veyne (1978: esp. 36-7) has discussed the possible effect on family relations of the awesome powers of a *paterfamilias*. He argues that the system was tolerable only because most fathers died before their children reached adulthood. Mothers, too, could die but if they survived childbirth might live on to be an aid, then a burden, in the business of adult life. I wish here to examine some of the strains imposed by the continuation through the son's life cycle of that *disciplina ac severitas* which won lip-service from moralists.

Opposition to a mother was a delicate business. A certain respect was due her, regardless of the circumstances. Valerius Maximus 7.8.2. tells of the daughter capriciously passed over in her mother's will who forebore to contest it from reverence for her mother's memory. Cicero is very careful of his wording in attacking Sassia on behalf of her son Cluentius. As counsel he makes the most appalling charges of licentiousness and murder against her, but somehow intimates that these do not emanate from Cluentius, who was reluctant either to make a will which omitted his mother or openly to attack her:

> For I am sensible of the fact that, no matter what a mother is like, still a parent's baseness should scarcely be mentioned in a trial involving her son.

> nam illud me non praeterit, cuiuscumque modi sit mater, tamen in iudicio fili de turpitudine parentis dici vix oportere.
>
> *(Clu.* 17)

Although he tells us (*Clu.* 12) that Sassia was unworthy of that great title of 'mother', still her motherhood conferred certain rights which a pious, though wronged son should observe:

> I readily appreciate that men should not only keep silent about wrongs suffered from their parents, but actually endure them calmly.

> facile intellego, non modo reticere homines parentium iniurias, sed etiam animo aequo ferre oportere.
>
> *(Clu.* 17; cf. *Clu.* 18)

As elsewhere, the duty to mother and father is equated here. The Emperor Claudius had little reason to be fond of his mother Antonia, who is said (Suet. *Claud.* 3.2) to have scorned him as a cripple and fool, but he dutifully authorised a commemorative coin issue after his accession (*RIC* 82; cf. new ed. 66; 65), to emphasise his own claim to the throne and to demonstrate his *pietas.*

The tension is evident in the accounts of the Julio–Claudian reigns. Livia had been a partner in Augustus' rule, but had observed the proprieties in displaying her power. Her husband's death conferred on her not only the usual elevation of widowhood but the title *Augusta* and honours which confirmed her position as comparable with that of the Vestals.[32] She was less inclined to obscure her importance in the reign of the son who owed his position to her. Suetonius claims that Tiberius did consult his mother on matters of state, but disliked having this known, and admonished her that women had traditionally been excluded from the political sphere (Suet. *Tib.* 50).

Grant (1954: 138-9) suggests that Tiberius made an honest attempt to deal with a difficult situation by emphasising the religious element of her distinction, so that she could be sufficiently honoured without any hint that she exercised improper political power. Certainly some allowance must be made for the hostility of the tradition to Tiberius. His resistance to excessive honours for the imperial family was general (Tac. *Ann.* 4.8 and 15). Tiberius' conservatism could explain his annoyance at Livia's name appearing before his on a dedication or his refusal to be honoured as 'son of Livia Augusta'[33] — an interesting contrast to the later acknowledgements, especially on coinage, by Gaius and Nero of their mothers.[34]

Yet there is evidence of serious conflict between mother and son which cannot be explained away by reverence for Republican forms. His denial of a routine request for a favour by Livia, with the remark that he would grant it only on condition that the official document would carry the wording that it had been forced on the Emperor by his mother (Suet. *Tib.* 51) was surely provocative. Livia's angry reaction in displaying old papers of Augustus to show that he had never favoured Tiberius as his successor (a reminder of her own part in achieving his elevation) suggests strong emotional currents in the disagreement (Suet. *Tib.* 51; Dio 57.12). Accusations of his neglect of his mother in the last years of her life, and his failure to attend her in her final illness or celebrate her funeral rites (Suet. *Tib.* 51.2) might be exaggerated, but show that he was thought to have neglected conventional signs of filial respect. Livia appears to have been very popular with the commons and the Senate alike[35] and Tiberius' refusal to grant her the posthumous title of 'mother of her country' in spite of senatorial insistence (Dio 58.2) seems to have been spiteful rather than based on principle. It was left to her grandson Claudius to deify her and elevate her memory to the status of Augustus,[36] although he had more reason than her son to dislike Livia (Suet. *Claud.* 3.2).

Nero's relations with his uniquely distinguished mother,[37] the younger Agrippina, merit special attention. It would be unfortunate to give disproportionate emphasis to palace politics in a discussion of family relations, and inaccurate to suggest that conflict between mothers and sons was common, even within the imperial family. Yet the clash between Nero and his mother is discussed in such detail by the sources, particularly Tacitus, and presents such an interesting contrast to her son's public tributes to her that it cannot be ignored. It encapsulates the problem which must have arisen elsewhere, of the mother who had worked diligently to achieve eminence for her son, only to encounter resentment when she made too many subsequent claims on the basis of her earlier efforts. Agrippina cannot have been the only mother to have had difficulty in adjusting the manner and content of her representations to her son as he grew older and more assured in his manhood and his established position in life. Seneca's praise of his mother and the contrast — both implicit and explicit — with other mothers (*ad Helviam* 14, quoted above) suggests that many women expected to call in the favours they felt were due to them as a result of their earlier contribution.

Agrippina was certainly responsible for Nero's elevation. It resulted from her marriage to the Emperor Claudius in AD 49. This was followed by the adoption in the following year of Nero — who thus gained precedence over Claudius' own son, who was younger — and Nero's marriage to Claudius' daughter Octavia in AD 53.[38] On Nero's accession in AD 54 at the age of seventeen, he duly showed his appreciation of his mother by giving out the password *optima mater* to the guard (Suet. *Nero* 9), and by successive coin issues.[39] This was partly in keeping with other conspicuously pious actions[40] and partly to stress the relationship, through his mother, with Germanicus and Augustus.[41] Perhaps, too, he felt a genuine respect for this impressive woman.

The situation soon degenerated although the external honours continued. Dio tells us (62.17 = Xiph. 156.6 ff) that Nero actually celebrated games for Agrippina as late as AD 59. In describing the developing opposition within the palace to Agrippina and her supporter Pallas, Tacitus comments: 'Yet on the surface a great mass of distinctions was continually heaped on her.' (*Ann.* 13.2). Some authors have thought it significant that Agrippina's portrait confronts Nero's on *RIC* Nero: 9/new ed.1 while his profile is superimposed on his mother's in *RIC* 10/new.ed.6 and her titles are relegated to the reverse (Giacosa 1977: 36-7; Grant 1970: 36).

Clashes centred on issues of policy and Agrippina's public and unconventional displays such as her attempt to receive a foreign embassy in state.[42] The political conflict was exacerbated by personal differences, such as Agrippina's attempt to interfere with her son's affair with the freedwoman Acte (Tac. *Ann.* 13.12). In both cases, Agrippina's customary patrician reserve and masculine political skills (*Ann.* 12.7) deserted her. Her violent and erratic behaviour gave ammunition to her enemies, who launched prosecutions against her favourites,[43] presumably with Nero's blessing. Her reaction, to align herself with various dissident elements much as her mother had done in Tiberius' reign,[44] predictably did her no good and the erstwhile 'excellent' mother was marked as powerless by AD 56 with her expulsion from the palace, the withdrawal of the prestigious German guard and the ban on her reception of petitioners (Tac. *Ann.* 13. 18-19; Suet. *Nero* 34). An obscure interval of three years passed before her inadequately explained murder, on an accusation of plotting against Nero's life, in AD 59. Tacitus (*Ann.* 14.1) attributed the act to the urgings of Nero's mistress Poppaea Sabina. Apart from the intrinsic improbability of Nero's readiness to commit matricide rather than defy his now powerless mother by divorcing Octavia, the story is discredited by the further interval of three years before he did divorce his wife and marry Poppaea (Tac. *Ann.* 14.60). It is less incredible that the redoubtable Agrippina actually *was* plotting against him — or at least that Nero was persuaded by her enemies that this was the case, but there is no firm evidence either way.

In many respects the story reads like a modern Freudian play. This is particularly true of Tacitus' version, which must have coloured the accounts of Suetonius and Dio. It is difficult to separate the melodramatic elements from the rest. Outright accusations of incest, the resemblance of the *libertina* mistress to the young Agrippina,[45] Nero's vacillation before the deed and his fear of material and supernatural reprisal afterwards (Tac. *Ann.* 14.10), the objections of his mistresses to his filial deference[46] — all confuse political, sexual and emotional dependence.

Yet this larger-than-life drama might have been acted out in modified form in other senatorial families. Agrippina was, after all, the very type of the severe and ambitious Roman mother, bearing many similarities to the recurrent ideal represented by

Volumnia, Cornelia, Aurelia and Atia. Her *severitas ac saepius superbia* ('austerity and, more often, arrogance') was akin to that *disciplina ac severitas* ('training and austerity') so praised in the *Dialogus de Oratoribus* 28.3-5. It was not dissimilar to the manner of Livia, Agrippina maior and Antonia (mother of Claudius), who received more favourable treatment from the sources. Tacitus' brief reference to the rivalry between Agrippina and Domitia Lepida is interesting. She was Nero's paternal aunt and had cared for him briefly during his mother's exile (Suet. *Nero* 6.3; Bradley 1978: 49-50). Competition between the sisters-in-law took political forms (Tac. *Ann.* 13.19) but also manifested itself in a difference of style. Where Agrippina was severe with her son, Domitia Lepida was indulgent.[47] Again, this is a type of conflict which might have appeared in a number of families. Agrippina's manner threatened Nero's pride in his maturity and his imperial office.

I have already pointed out in Chapter 1 my dissatisfaction with psychoanalytic explanations which proceed from the premise that Roman sons' deference to mothers was aberrant. Both Hallett (1984: 255-6) and Africa (1978: 599-602) postulate a sexual element in the attachment of sons (particularly to widowed mothers) which I consider misplaced. Yet the ancient sources themselves introduced such elements into the story of Nero and Agrippina. I have also asserted that Romans accepted and admired adult obedience to parents, but it is clear from the accounts of Agrippina's downfall that Nero's rejection of excessive maternal intervention, particularly its display in a public arena, was endorsed. It was his neglect of the politeness due a parent[48] and the matricide which were condemned. Agrippina went too far in the type of intervention she made in her son's sexual life and public offices, but particularly in the arrogant manner in which she asserted herself and in her failure to allow for change over time. Atia had kept a careful eye on Octavian, but even he must have had sexual liaisons if it was possible to mark out a year in his late adolescence when he refrained from sex.[49] Both Agrippina and Nero displayed an impatience with forms which could only result in serious conflict. In the palace, the stakes were higher and the price of failure more drastic, but the situation might not have been so unusual.

Less sensational forms of conflict could reflect a particular stage of the life cycle. A son could assert his manhood by rejecting his parents' demands. Where the conflict was between mother and son, it might have been affected by ideas of proper female behaviour. Seneca's allusion to the excessive ambition and avarice of some mothers is in keeping with disapproving references in literature to women who held court in the provinces and elsewhere.[50] Such references also suggest that petitioners approached wives and mothers as readily as their office-holding male connections, on the assumption that women were in a position to secure concessions and favours. Once again, we are in search of a distinction which was rather fine and not readily agreed on by the ancient Romans themselves.

Fathers must also have made awkward demands of their sons. The status of fathers, however, allowed little room for sustained and serious revolt. The greater fragility of the mother's position, less evident when her son was younger and more tractable, imposed the need for discretion at least in the manner in which demands were made. Some distinguished Roman matrons, accustomed to the obedience of a young son, probably failed to allow for this. They might have overestimated their bargaining position and left an equally proud son without a means of graceful refusal of requests he found excessive. If this approach were not gradually modified as the son grew older, it might have led to serious breaches. Patience and self-restraint were clearly required on both sides. Perhaps there were mothers indefatigably ambitious for their sons and accustomed to being heeded by social inferiors and juniors who found that, like Agrippina, they could endure anything to *get* a son to his goal but could not tolerate his autonomous exercise of that position (Tac. *Ann.* 12.64).

Sons who did not revolt: in search of 'normal' relations

The distinction, though, was a fine one, not to be confused with modern ideas of children 'being left to lead their own lives'. Cornelia's insistence that her sons distinguish themselves was passed on admiringly. Augustus' mother was praised for her aid in his career. Seneca's scorn for over-ambitious mothers must be set against his praise of his own mother's help and encouragement (*ad Helviam* 14.2-3) and his favourable assessment of Marcia's relationship with her son (*ad Marciam* 24.1). Volumnia's insistent exercise of her maternal influence at her son's expense was honoured, according to tradition, by the erection of the temple of Fortuna Virilis (Plut. *Cor.* 37).

Strength and firm moral purpose were the admired character-istics of famous Roman mothers. Some of the examples passed on to posterity actually depicted the frustration of an adult son's hopes, but the male authors and orators who transmitted such stories endorsed the mother's stand, in contrast to modern scholars who clearly identify with the resentment of the thwarted sons.[51] Ancient authors saw it as appropriate for a mother not only to inspire and foster legitimate ambition but to curb mature excesses in her son much as she might check a youthful zeal for philosophy.

Coriolanus' bitterness was evident when he yielded to his mother's plea not to attack Rome (Plut. *Cor.* 36), but she was cele-brated ever after as a national saviour.[52] There was never any hint in the tradition that she had behaved inappropriately or deserved blame for having reared a traitor in the first place. The alleged letters of Cornelia to Gaius Gracchus were thought praiseworthy because she had attempted, albeit unsuccessfully, to correct his political behaviour. M. Antonius' mother Julia interceded insist-ently to save her brother's life. Posterity did not agree with Antonius that this had been the act of an injudicious mother.[53] Even Nero's mother Agrippina received grudging credit from Tacitus who felt that her existence had at least spared Rome the disgrace of a stage-struck emperor performing in public.[54] Frequent, high-handed interference and the public display of political influence by a woman, as mother or wife, were frowned on.[55] Yet this prejudice seems to have co-existed with a firm notion that a mother could continue to act as her son's moral mentor well into his adult life, even on political subjects. This general expectation might not have prevented individual sons from bitterly resenting such intervention, whether they followed the mother's direction or not.

Age and parenthood carried weight at Rome. If a man chose to resist his mother's exhortations, he had to tread carefully. Aeneas, after all, is the prototype of the *pius* son fulfilling his mother's rightful ambitions for him. Vergil's Dido had less success than Tacitus' Poppaea in arguing her lover into a belated revolt against maternal authority. Perhaps most important, the argument of the mistress urging the man to defy his mother is not treated with any sympathy by ancient authors.[56] The example of Agrippina and Nero is extreme. Opposition was not always dramatic and final. Octavian and Brutus disregarded their mother's wishes at significant stages without forcing a breach. Even Aeneas sometimes baulked at his mother's single-minded urging. Most families can accommodate intermittent conflict without disintegration.

A mother's power to pass on wealth could be a source of power over her son — or it could in itself occasion conflict. Valerius Maximus tells the story of Caelius Rufus' exposure of Cornelia, who had refused to pass on to her son Q. Pompeius the properties she had inherited in trust for him:

> Caelius actually read out Q. Pompeius' letter at the arbitration, as evidence of his extreme hardship. It was with this letter that he thwarted Cornelia's unnatural greed.

> recitavit etiam eius epistolam in iudicio ultimae necessitatis indicem, qua impiam Corneliae avaritiam subvertit.
>
> (Val. Max. 4.2.7)

When Pudentilla's sons took Apuleius to court for magical enticement of their mother it was because they feared for their inheritance. P. Aebutius, the youth who sparked off the Bacchanalian witch-hunt of 186 BC, fell out with his mother Duronia, who had allowed his stepfather to appropriate his patrimony. Driven from his home and rejecting their involvement in the Bacchic cult, he sought refuge with his aunt and his freedwoman mistress before denouncing his mother's co-religionists to the authorities (Liv. 39. 9-17). The case of Sassia and her son Aulus Cluentius Habitus seems to have had some strong financial element, in addition to the confused emotional tensions which emerge from Cicero's speech. Even Nero, whose actions can be explained chiefly in terms of political and emotional conflict with his mother, was thought to have coveted her great wealth.

In less drastic circumstances, resentment and esteem might have see-sawed. It is difficult from this distance to distinguish and weigh against each other the constituents of an adult son's regard for his mother. Respect, affection, self-interest and solicitousness are all attested. One of the most valuable insights is provided by the letters Cicero wrote to Atticus about their nephew Quintus and his relations with his mother Pomponia — Atticus' sister. Cicero took an increasingly cynical view of the young man over the years, but at a time when Quintus, then sixteen or seventeen,[57] was staying with him, he stressed to Atticus the importance of taking young Quintus' interests into account in settling his parents' divorce — a prospect which the elders were then discussing seriously amongst themselves. He affirmed the boy's proper affection for his mother:

He seems to me to love his mother fiercely — as he should.

ac mihi videtur valde matrem, ut debet, amare.

(Att. 6.2.2)

Certainly Quintus became violently upset when he inadvertently opened a letter intended for his uncle Marcus and learned that his parents were thinking of a divorce (Cic. *Att.* 6.3.8). He attempted to effect a reconciliation between them (*Att.* 6.7.1). As the divorce became in time a fact of life, Cicero suspected young Quintus of playing off his parents against each other. His father (Quintus senior) was evidently under the impression that the young man was estranged from his mother and was surprised to learn (from Cicero) that he had been corresponding amicably with her (*Att.* 13.41.1; cf. 13.38; 13.39.1). This was in August 45 BC.

By December 45 BC, no more is heard of young Quintus' 'warfare with his mother' (*cum matre bellum* — *Att.* 13.41.1) or 'hatred of his mother' (*odium matris* — *Att.* 13.38.2), for he was at odds with the whole of the older generation, partly because of financial irresponsibility but chiefly, it would appear, because of his failure to agree to his parents' marriage plans for him. His vacillation had exasperated his mother, and therefore his uncle Atticus (*Att.* 13.42.1). He carelessly agreed to fall in with the project in a general way, and the focus of conflict thereafter became political. It might or might not signify anything about her relationship with her son that Pomponia figures henceforth in Cicero's correspondence chiefly as an ally of Atticus. Cicero's preoccupation with the slander spread by the two Quinti about him at a dangerous time would in any case have led him to focus less on everyday family ructions. The conflict between the generations appears to have been general and cyclic in this case. One rather imagines that if the Civil War and death had not intervened, Quintus would have married and produced children, and relations would have entered a calmer phase. There is little evidence of specific mother–son conflict here, or any suggestion that Pomponia's role as such was resented in the arguments about young Quintus' marriage.

Seneca's *consolationes* to his own mother and Marcia respectively, though conventional, give some impression of the usual expectations of an ageing mother's relationship with her mature son. There is — as one would expect from this genre — no reference to conflict, so that we can only speculate about whether it was a continuing aspect of the relationship. The mannered condolences are at least illustrated by examples from the two women's lives which lend the account some degree of verisimilitude. Seneca anticipates Marcia's objection to his arguments — evidently a conventional lament:

> Still, it is a hard thing to lose a young man whom you have brought up, as a protection and adornment to his mother and father alike. Who denies that it is hard?

> grave est tamen, quem educaveris, iuvenem, iam matri iam patri praesidium ac decus, amittere. Quis negat grave esse?
>
> > (*ad Marciam* 17.1)

and, even more interestingly:

> There will be nobody to protect me, to shield me from contempt.

> non erit qui me defendat, qui a contemptu vindicet.
>
> > (*ad Marciam* 19.2)

This is similar to the sentiment attributed to Cornelia (*mater Gracchorum*) in the letter addressed to Gaius Gracchus:

> Of all the children I once had, you are the one who should have put up with their party politics and seen to it that I suffer as little distress as possible in my old age. You should be eager to carry out actions which above all have my approval ...

> quem oportebat omnium eorum, quos antehac habui liberos, partis eorum tolerare atque curare, ut quam minimum sollicitudinis in senecta haberem, utique quaecumque ageres, ea velles maxime mihi placere ...[58]

In differing ways, these express the hope that parents will gain support and solace from adult children, a fitting return for the effort and anxiety of rearing them through youth.

Seneca points out that raising children is not all anxiety. Surely, he says, the affection and caresses of the young are rewards in themselves (*ad Marciam* 12.1)? He goes over the satisfactions Marcia has enjoyed from her son in his lifetime. As an adolescent, he had declined to go abroad on military service because he was unwilling to leave his mother (24.1). His admirable character developed under his mother's watchful eye. Through her agency, he achieved the honour of a priesthood (24.3). Above all, he urges her to remember her son as he was just before he died, when he would delight her with his cheery visits:

> You would do greater justice to the young man himself, who was always so well suited to inspire pleasure in you at the mention of his name or at the mere thought of him, if he should come before his mother in good spirits and cheerfully, as he used to do when he was alive.

> illum ipsum iuvenem, dignissimum qui te laetam semper nominatus cogitatusque faciat, meliore pones loco, si matri suae, qualis vivus solebat, hilarisque et cum gaudio occurrit.
>
> (*ad Marciam* 3.4)

Such visits were part of a mother's usual expectation of an adult son. Livia had similarly been urged by a philosopher to dwell on such recollections after Drusus' death, rather than her sad memories:

> You do not turn your thoughts to the company of your son and his pleasurable visits or his boyish, delightful blandishments and the improvement in his scholarly achievements.

> non convertis te ad convictus filii tui occursusque iucundos, non ad pueriles dulcesque blanditias, non ad incrementa studiorum.
>
> (*ad Marciam* 5.4)

Indeed Seneca detailed, with no pretence of modesty, the delight his own mother derived from *his* visits — her interest in his studies and conversation, and their mutual affection (*ad Helviam* 15.1).

Both Tiberius (Suet. *Tib.* 51) and Nero had marked their estrangement from their mothers by neglect of this crucial mark of respect and affection. Nero, to be sure, had observed the form of visiting his mother after she moved into the palace of Antonia, but his mandatory kiss was formal and the visit always kept short.[59] The examples of Drusus, Metilius (Marcia's son) and Seneca himself suggest that these visits could be very pleasant for the mother, while the Emperor Marcus uses such a visit as an example of a duty which a son enjoyed performing (*Med.* 6.12). Seneca spoke of the spontaneous joy[60] the very sight of his mother inspired in him.

Most references concern the son's obligation and desire to visit his mother, possibly on the assumption that the younger person generally owed this courtesy to an elder. There are examples of mothers visiting married daughters (e.g. Cic. *Att.* 1.5.8; Aul. Gell. *NA* 12.1, of a mother at her daughter's childbed and compare Plin. *Ep.* 3.16) and *ad Helviam* 2.5 might refer to Helvia's trip to Italy to see Seneca. An interesting feature of the descriptions is the boyish good spirits allegedly displayed by sons who did attend their mothers.[61] Even Nero had allayed his mother's suspicions with his *familiaritas iuvenilis* ('youthful intimacy') when he lured her to Baiae with the pretence of a reconciliation (Tac. *Ann.* 14.4). The stereotype of the relationship was a very cheerful, affectionate exchange, marked by embraces and chatter. If the reality did not always live up to it, it is still interesting that this was the characterisation of regular meetings between mother and son. These women, who could be suitably intimidating on occasion, were meant to be charmed by their adult sons.

Sons could also be a worry to mothers — even once they had survived the dangerous years of childhood. The investment of hopes in a son made the impact of his failure or death all the more bitter. Seneca insists on seeing such disappointment as altruistic. He claims to be using the most effective argument against his own mother's grief in assuring her that exile is no real evil for him (*ad Helviam* 4.2). This is of a piece with his reminder to Marcia of the number of mothers who live apart from their children for various reasons, some of them — military service or sea travel — sources of worry in themselves (*ad Marciam* 24.2). This is the image of the *anxia mater* whch recurs in literature.[62] Seneca's mother did live some distance both from him and her other children in Spain. He refers to her past trials, such as the death of her husband, made more difficult to endure 'because all her children were in fact elsewhere' ('*omnibus quidem absent-ibus liberis*' — *ad Helviam* 2.5).[63]

Mothers figure continually as suppliants in accounts of the civil wars. Appian's tales of loyalty and betrayal[64] show (as we might expect) that women *usually* stood by their husbands and *always* went to great lengths for their sons. Yet mothers were not only passive, anxiety-ridden petitioners. When Antonius' mother Julia interceded with him to save her brother L. Caesar from proscription[65] her plea was more like a threat and Antonius granted it grudgingly.

Entreaty and bullying were both maternal techniques and could be employed on behalf of sons or directly on sons. After the fall of Perusia in 40 *BC*, Julia fled to Sextus Pompeius' base in Sicily and helped conduct negotiations between him and her triumvir son. Apparently news of this so disturbed Octavian that he hastily came to terms with Sextus — opening negotiations by sending Sextus' mother Mucia to Sicily as an earnest of good faith.[66] Servilia's behaviour during the ascendancy of her alleged former lover Caesar reveals a combination of maternal concern and a shrewd political sense which was appreciated by her contemporaries. She had had her differences with her son and offended Cicero by her haughty dismissal of his opinions in 44 *BC*, but Cicero wrote respectfully of her to Brutus in the following year, when Brutus was gathering forces outside Italy[67] and his mother was building up support within it. The sarcasm employed by Vespasian's mother to shame him into ambition was contrasted implicitly with the more usual maternal means of achieving that end — *preces* and *auctoritas*, 'pleading' and 'author-ity' (Suet. *Vesp.* 2.2).

We have seen the kind of conflict which could arise between mother and son within the imperial family. Yet even there, con-flict was not typical, and Livia and Agrippina (minor) had begun, like Octavia or Agrippina maior, by exerting themselves to achieve high honours for their sons. Imperial mothers received less attention from the sources between the Julio–Claudians and the Severans, and detail is thin in the absence of a Tacitus or Suetonius. In Chapter 4 we reviewed coins on which emperors celebrated their mothers as a sign of their own piety and dynastic claims. We have seen in Nero's case that public honours did not always reflect private realities, but some coin issues seem to emanate from sincere filial regard. It is interesting, for example, that Titus chose to celebrate his mother Domitilla with the title

DIVA AVGVSTA on his coinage (e.g. *RIC* 70-3) and it is tempting to conclude that this desire to honour her stemmed from
genuine feeling, since she does not appear to have been particularly distinguished and had never been singled out for
honours in her husband's reign.[68] Trajan, like other adoptive
emperors, showed no interest in celebrating his natural mother,
although his father featured on the coinage.[69] Hadrian celebrated
his adoptive parents, particularly Plotina.[70] If their affair was
merely baseless rumour, his relationship with Plotina repeats the
pattern of ambitious imperial mother working to secure her son's
elevation — although in this case he was not her natural son but
adopted favourite. Hadrian seems to have been appropriately
grateful and accepted her authoritative advice, although we do
not have extensive documentation to support this suggestion in
any detail. The main evidence is from the coin issues — and perhaps the gossip based on their collaboration after Trajan's death.

In the great silence of the second century AD, the Emperor
Marcus's jottings to himself give us a glimpse of an apparently
happy relationship with his mother, but his allusions are brief. In
counting his blessings from the gods, he included a good mother
(*Med.* 1.17) and elsewhere expressed his appreciation that she had
lived out the final years of her life with him (*Med.* 1.2.6) He refers
to her importance in his moral training (1.3) and, as we have
seen, spoke of visits to a mother as typically pleasurable (6.12).
None of this, unfortunately, gives us any detailed information of
his relationship with her in his youth and early adult years, but it
does seem to fit the picture painted by Seneca's writings of nearly
a century earlier. The references to her in his letters to Fronto are
brief and conventional, usually concerning her health or her
birthday.[71] The exception is a reference to a long chat he had
with his mother (*matercula mea*) before dinner at their country
house.[72] The tone is twee and Marcus' emphasis is on praising
Fronto and his wife, but the picture of mother and son engaged
in this light gossip as she perches by him on her couch is quite
charming, and again reinforces the impression of cheerful and
affectionate exchanges between mother and son.

In spite of the fact that the younger Faustina was displayed
liberally on coins from an early age and referred to frequently by
her husband in letters, she figures not at all in surviving accounts
of her son Commodus. It was his deeds as emperor after his
mother's death which interested the sources and we lack even the
anecdotal biographic introduction usual in the *Lives* of Plutarch

and Suetonius, which sometimes yields information about mothers and their role in the lives of (in)famous men. Marcus' letters convey an impression of cheerful prosperous family life reminiscent of that of Victoria and Albert, or Nicholas and Alexandra, but no specific detail about the fecund Princess' (then Empress') influence on her sons.

The Severan women achieved a questionable prominence somewhat reminiscent of the Julio–Claudian examples, although this impression could be a result of the chance survival of lurid and largely unreliable source material. Julia Domna enters the imperial scene by means of a romantic story that Septimius Severus chose her as his second wife from her horoscope.[73] Severus associated her with himself on the coinage in a celebration of imperial harmony which presumably linked domestic and imperial peace (e.g. *RIC* IV Severus: 312 and cf. 255) although she was rumoured to have fought hard in palace power struggles, unsuccessfully opposing the praetorian prefect C. Fulvius Plautianus. The marriage of Plautianus' daughter Plautilla to Julia Domna's son Caracalla in AD 202-4 marks Julia Domna's temporary defeat. We are told she withdrew from court intrigue to solace herself with her intellectual interests (Dio 76.15-6) until the downfall of Plautianus in AD 205, although one would expect her to have engineered or at least colluded in the event which restored her to a position of influence at the palace.

She appears to have come into her own on the accession of her sons. It is difficult to determine her place in the fratricide of AD 212, when Caracalla lured his estranged brother to her chamber and had him struck down. Certainly she was afterwards associated with the surviving son, Caracalla, and was honoured with special coin issues and titles.[74] Her role is suspect. It looks very much as if she had been in league with Caracalla. She continued to be closely associated with him, often accompanying him on his travels — as emperor's *wives* had accompanied their husbands previously. Whether the honours granted her in this phase were matched by real power is moot. We have no Tacitus to recount the details of a struggle within the palace. At the time of her son's assassination in AD 217, she was at Antioch, presumably placed to receive news from the Parthian front where he was campaigning. She committed suicide on hearing of his death — in fear of reprisals or obscurity.[75] She had, after all, comfortably survived her other son's murder, so it cannot have been a gesture of maternal sorrow alone.

Her younger sister, Julia Maesa, then in nearby Emesa, was quicker to seize the initiative. She had her daughter Julia Soaemias declare the young Varius Avitus the illegitimate son of his second cousin Caracalla, and therefore a rightful candidate for the purple (Dio 79.30ff). Julia Soaemias and her mother supported the claim with money and energy, rousing the troops camped nearby against Macrinus, the prefect who had plotted Caracalla's overthrow. There could be no doubt that the new Emperor — fourteen years old — owed his position to his mother and, in this case, to his grandmother. The sources claim that the two Julias actually participated in the decisive battle between their forces and those of Macrinus, urging their supporters on (Dio 79.38.4).

The new Emperor, soon known as Elagabalus after the god he served, honoured mother and grandmother alike with the title 'Augusta' and struck issues celebrating them.[76] This is not of itself evidence of his regard for them or their political influence. His three wives were similarly honoured[77] but their term 'in office' was brief and their influence apparently negligible. The theme of the young emperor dominated by an immodest mother has long been a historiographic stock-in-trade, but it seems appropriate in this case. Perhaps the best support for the view is the fact that mother and son were eventually assassinated and their bodies dishonoured together in AD 222. This followed Elagabalus' adoption of his even younger cousin, Gessius Bassianus, who now became the Emperor Alexander Severus at the age of thirteen (Dio 80.20).

This adoption had been engineered by Julia Maesa with a view to supplanting Elagabalus, whose un-Roman preoccupations had caused disquiet. The fact that Julia Maesa recognised Elagabalus' behaviour as politically unsound but that he failed to change his ways suggests that the formidable grandmother had less influence than she would have wished over her daughter Julia Soaemias and her elder grandson. In due course, Julia Maesa died quite naturally in AD 226. Alexander Severus was then seventeen, and continued to be associated in his rule with his mother Julia Mamaea. His mother was with him at the army camp at Mainz in AD 235, where they were both murdered by mutinying soldiers. Again both her presence in the camp and her assassination argue a strong association with her son's rule (Herodian 6.9.5-7).

Certainly the women associated with Severans had a strong

interest in gaining power. The pattern of imperial women enjoying greater success in this as mothers than as wives is interesting. It is surely to be associated with the tendency we have already noted for women to invest their hopes and ambitions in sons rather than husbands. Maternal power over young sons is the marked feature of this dynasty and one is reminded of the struggles between Agrippina and Nero which developed as he grew older and more resentful of her presumption. There is no hint that conflict developed on these lines. We are told that, unlike Nero, who set up a special curtain in the *curia* for Agrippina (Tac. *Ann.* 13.5), Elagabalus encouraged his grandmother openly to sit and even vote in the Senate House.[78] There was no longer much pretence of Republican forms, and honours to the imperial family were great by this time, but this action seems to have given some offence. These Julias were politically astute and capable of imposing their will on their sons, but the sequence of events demonstrates that women, however elevated their rank or formidable their character, still had to exercise power through male media, preferably sons.

In estimating the position of various imperial mothers, residence seems a more reliable gauge of their position than speculation from coins or reliance on gossipy sources. Livia necessarily lived separately from Tiberius during his retirement to Capri, and his failure to visit her regularly was noted as significant (Suet. *Tib.* 51.2). When Nero wished to strip his mother of power and mark his disfavour he not only had her harried with lawsuits — unsuccessfully — but insisted that she move out of his palace (Tac. *Ann.* 13.18-19). Marcus left his mother's home for that of Antoninus on his adoption — though that was not a rejection of her influence, as is shown by his later reference to her spending her last years with him.[79] As wife rather than mother, Julia Domna moved out of Septimius Severus' palace on her political defeat. It is significant that this was marked by the introduction to the palace of a daughter-in-law she had opposed, and that her return to the palace coincided with the daughter-in-law's deportation.

Julia Maesa, Julia Soaemias and Julia Mamaea not only lived with their sons (and grandsons), but travelled with them on military campaigns. Julia Domna, too, had been within reach of messengers even when her son was engaged in frontier warfare. The details of the relationship in each case, the precise limits fought over and any struggles with daughters-in-law are obscured, but the essential association of power between mother and son is evidenced by their constant companionship and their simultaneous deaths. Mother and son could be united, then, in ambition and their unity could survive success even at the imperial level. Ambitious effort by mothers was consistently praised and forceful mothers were tolerated by powerful adult men, even when these men were pressed to make concessions they resented. It is encouraging to learn that relations had a lighter side: mothers took particular pleasure in the visits of their adult sons, and such occasions were ideally gay and agreeable. The historiographic stress on tense and significant encounters between mothers and sons can obscure this aspect, which was probably more typical. Even Cicero's extended discussions of young Quintus' failings and differences with his parents reveal the youth's consistent fondness for his mother. Brutus and M. Antonius had grounds for resentment against their mothers, but continued to act with them in the confident assumption that the mothers would address their sons' interests. More than a general community of interest between the generations,[80] this betokens a particular identification between sons and the mothers who — unable to achieve public honours in their own right — invested their hopes and efforts in them.

'Ordinary' mothers and sons

In attempting to assess expectations of mother–son relationships one might hope for more from the epitaphs, which are less weighted in favour of the sensational and the powerful. Certainly the resultant picture forms a contrast to the lurid relationships of palace politics. The preponderance of *CIL* VI epitaphs by mothers to children and the relative neglect of mothers (and fathers) has been noted in other chapters. To some extent, the discrepancy could be explained away by the fact that many mothers would be celebrated solely as wives, but it was quite possible to remember a woman as *coniunx* and *mater*[81] and we have seen that many husbands must have predeceased wives.

Lattimore has pointed out that in Greek and Roman epitaphs, children did not conventionally express regret at the passing of parents. The parents are the ones who state that they miss their children — it is appropriate for children to outlive parents.[82] Notions of appropriateness must affect the stock terms used on such conventional monuments to piety as tombstones, and need not be taken as a completely accurate reflection of the emotions felt. Even so, the marked lack of lamentation on the loss of a mother and the low incidence of distinctive adjectives is interesting. It was, after all, considered inappropriate for parents to mourn very young children excessively, but we have seen[83] that parents sometimes breached that convention.

Although there are literary examples of mothers — always widows who have not remarried, like Aurelia — living with adult, married sons, these are few. It is tempting to conclude that aged mothers commemorated by sons might have lived with them but the family groupings in epitaphs need not reflect residential patterns. Such inscriptions are testimony to some kind of filial piety, but, as evidence, it is limited and uninformative. This is partly because it is so rare for sons to break the boundaries of the obvious dutiful adjectives, while mothers do sometimes add distinctive adjectives — or even conventional epithets from a wider range — to their sons' epitaphs.

Of fewer than 600 inscriptions erected *to* mothers in the *CIL* VI collection, 476 contain an epithet. Of these, 94 are to MATRI B M (or BENE MERENTI/MERITAE, in full, 'well-deserving') and 180 to MATRI PIAE/PIENTISSIMAE/PIISSIMAE ('pious' or 'dutiful'). Since these all carry the basic idea of doing the right thing, or performing the appropriate role, they shed little light on what children perceived to be the proper role of a mother.

Dedications to MATRI OPTIMAE ('excellent mother') are no more illuminating. Where specific adjectives are present (in 175 cases) they tend to be the same ones which husbands use of wives, such as CARIOR/CARISSIMA ('rather dear'/'most dear') or DVLCISSIMA ('most sweet'). These are the adjectives generally favoured for commemorating women and young children. They also appear as conventional forms of epistolary address, as in Seneca's *ad Helviam*.[84] Mothers, too, tend to describe their children as PIISSIMI or BENE MERENTES, but show greater readiness to dwell on specific virtues and to lament the loss — but then, so do fathers.

This scarcely helps to distinguish any special characteristics of the relationship between mothers and sons from parent–child relations in general. Again, there is a slight difference between the literary stereotypes and the evidence of sepulchral inscriptions. The mother mourning her son is the prototype of bereft misery:

I have mourned for the state now both more grievously and for longer than any mother for her only son.

patriam eluxi iam et gravius et diutius quam ulla mater unicum filium.

(Cic. *Fam.* 9.20.3)[85]

The inscriptions do not support such a strong association between motherhood and mourning, or a significantly greater likelihood that mothers mourn sons rather than daughters. Perhaps the stereotype is based more on the presumption that female, especially maternal, grief is more abandoned in general,[86] and that a son is in all circumstances more precious than a daughter. Polybius 31.28.2 refers to Aemilius Paullus as 'childless' after the death of his two youngest sons, although he had two surviving sons who had been adopted into other houses, and two daughters who might not have been married at the time. If this was a common attitude, the stress on a son being mourned is an emphasis on the more important child, whose death represents the greatest loss. In general, daughters are not as well represented as sons in the *CIL* VI epitaphs,[87] but where daughters are commemorated, it is sometimes by mothers as sole dedicators.[88] The phenomenon seems to be connected to the general under-representation of women in tombstones and the fact that women could be commemorated as spouses from an earlier age than men (Hopkins 1966: 261). It tells us nothing specific about the bond between mothers and sons.

We need not, however, dismiss out of hand the possibility of a special relationship between mothers and sons. We have seen that Octavia spent the remainder of her life passionately mourning the death of Marcellus (Sen. *ad Marciam* 2.3-5). Many another ambitious woman, having invested all her hopes and affection in the child able to distinguish himself in spheres formally closed to herself, would have found his death a bitter blow. Freudians argue that sexual rivalry, however unconscious, makes parents more indulgent to the child of the opposite sex, and if Roman fathers appear to have had a particular fondness for their daughters,[89] the corollary, that mothers doted on their sons, might have held.[90]

The risks attendant on some forms of masculine achievement might have heightened maternal preference. Again, the image of the anxious mother awaiting the son who is off on a voyage is a recurrent one. Horace *Carm.* 4.5.9-13 depicts the mother offering up prayers for the return of the son from a sea voyage and Ovid *Rem.Am.* 547-8 speaks of the mother who fears for her son on military service. Yet, by the same logic, mothers should worry over daughters in childbirth. One is left with the suspicion that authors, as sons, were more aware of maternal behaviour to sons as a group. The *topos* of the mother mourning the only son is a concentrated version of womanly behaviour just as the mother is commemorated by her children for stock womanly characteristics ('sweetness' and so on) rather than specifically maternal ones.

Conclusion

Certain recurrent elements emerge from the study of the Roman mother and the older son. As an upper-class Roman son grew into adolescence, then adulthood, he passed in effect from the world of common childish experience into a more emphatically masculine domain. His mother's advice and help was still relevant in this world, but the possibility of conflict was heightened at a stage in life when a son would be more inclined to assert himself within the family sphere. In most cases, this would amount to little more than intermittent conflict over specific issues such as financial allocations within the family or choice of marriage partner.

A Roman mother might have wielded more authority with a son and perhaps exerted more direct influence on his formal education if his father had died. Yet sons who had come of age virtually attained adult privileges — including the option of a separate residence — if freed from *patria potestas*. The authority of a mother, whether widow, divorcee or *univira* still living with her son's father, was based on an amalgam of custom and individual strength of character as well as family habits of affection and material considerations such as her disposition of part of the family fortune. The delicate balance could at times be upset — sensationally so, in some cases related at length by the literary sources. This should not obscure the fact that the relationship was conventionally depicted as a happy one founded on mutual esteem.

The Roman mother, aristocratic or otherwise, was expected to worry over her son and to urge him on to proper achievements. He was expected to defer to her wishes within recognised limits. Even if both sides breached this understanding, accommodation could be made. Allowing for individual variation, the two hoped for affectionate mutual support, with the mother somewhat in the ascendant. Aristocratic career patterns made it probable that mothers would invest their own ambitions for political power in their sons, which could in itself have proved a source of friction or frustration, but if both learned to moderate their expectations and curb their impatience, the son's ambitions could become a source of continuing mutual satisfaction, since his achievements reflected favourably on his mother.

Notes

1. Children can be designated by general terms such as *liberi, pueri* and *filii*. The stages of childhood and youth are distinguished only in cultures which pay attention to children. Slusanski (1974) attempted an historical analysis of such a development at Rome (esp. 569-78). Cf. Neraudau (1979); Eyben (1977); Gray-Fow (1985). In general, the literary sources distinguish only the broad categories of *adulescens, iuvenis, iunior.* Compare the remarks of Lyman (1974: 77) on the difficulty of determining the age and stage of 'children' in later texts.

2. He later moved into his own residence nearby, but continued to frequent the house of his mother and stepfather — Nicolaus 15.

3. *Dig.* 50.16.195.2 (Ulpian) — although it became customary for a *curator* to check the transactions of people *sui iuris* up to the age of twenty-five. See Crook (1967a: 116-18). In his commentary on the praetorian edict, Ulpian wrote of it as an obligation (*adhibere debet curatores: Dig.* 4.4.7.2) for disinterested adults to attend certain transactions undertaken by minors but as Thomas (1976: 466-8) points out, this was not a formal requirement at law. It had, however, been possible from the second century BC for a young person to plead inexperience as a ground for failing to honour a contract, so it was in the interest of anybody dealing with a youth to have an adult witness to the proceedings. The practice became more binding from the second century AD on. (See *Inst.* 1.23.1-2 and Thomas' commentary on it (1975: 56-7) and Jolowicz (1954: 238-40)).

4. Cf. Cic. *Cael.* 17, *Att.* 12.32.2.

5. Aemilius Paullus' sons and sons-in-law served under him in Macedon (Plut. *Aem.P.* 27). The two young Cicerones, Quintus and Marcus, accompanied Cicero to Cilicia in 50 BC where they pursued their formal studies and presumably learned from observation the duties of a governor. In accordance with the custom of the time, Cicero left behind him in Italy his wife Terentia and daughter Tullia (who was between marriages). The boys were both young — Quintus took the *toga virilis* at Laodicea (*Att.* 6.1.12 — where their studies are also mentioned) and young Marcus took his at Arpinum in the following year, at the age of fifteen (*Att.* 9.19.1).

6. Taylor (1949: 2, n12) lists accusations brought by young men, and

speaks generally of the type of training undertaken by young noblemen (pp. 29-30). Compare Cato censor's praise of a young man for prosecuting his dead father's enemy, Plut. *Cat. mai.* 15.3, and Seneca *de Brev. Vit.* 6.1 on Livius Drusus, whose involvement in the courts preceded his assumption of the *toga virilis.*

7. Cf. Plin. *Ep.* 4.19. 2-4 of Pliny's own wife or *Ep.* 1.16 of the wife of a friend.

8. I recall how he used to tell the story of his inordinate youthful enthusiasm for philosophy — which he would have pursued more avidly than appropriate for a Roman and a senator if his mother's good sense had not checked his burning zeal.

> memoria teneo solitum ipsum narrare se prima in iuventa studium philosophiae acrius, ultra quam concessum Romano ac senatori, hausisse, ni prudentia matris incensum ac flagrantem animum cercuisset.
>
> (Tac. *Agric.* 4)

9. Like the typical mother of Sen. *Dial.* 1.2.5 or the nurse of Fronto *Ep. ad Ant. imp.* 1.5 (= Naber p. 102).

10. Martial 9.73 line 7:

> at me litterulas stulti docuere parentes.

11. Marcus' father died when he was ten. He was then adopted by his paternal grandfather, and returned to his mother's care before his adoption at seventeen by Antoninus Pius, when he continued his studies in Greek literature and philosophy. See Farquharson (1944: 257-8, vol. II (commentary)) and the text of *Med.* 1.3.

12. Plin. *Ep.* 2.18 and see Sherwin-White's note *ad loc.* (1966:199).

13. *Att.* 10.4.6. Compare *Att.* 10.7.3:

> I think you judge that this flaw proceeds from nature, not our lax upbringing.
>
> hoc autem vitium puto te existimare non (a) nostra indulgentia sed a natura profectum.

14. E.g. Cic. *Brutus* 210-12; Quintilian *Inst. Or.* 1.1.4-6 and see the discussion in Chapter 5.

15. Suet. *Nero* 52; Dio *epitome* 61.32.3 (*Exc. Val.* 229, Xiph. 144.7-16 R.St.(Zon)); Tac. *Ann.* 12.8.

16. E.g. Martial 9.73 cited above and cf. Tac. *Dial.* 29, where Vipstanus Messalla condemns the laxity of modern *parents.*

17. Plut. *Cat. min.* 3.1; cf. Juv. *Sat.* 6.161-71.

18. Cf. Rawson (1966); Crook (1967a: 40); Weaver (1986).

19. Consider the role of Caecilia Metella (as patron, not mother) in protecting Roscius of America: Cic. *Rosc. Am.* 27. Examples of political advice from mothers are furnished by the cases of Servilia (e.g. *Att.* 15.11) — in spite of the recent attempt by Hillard (1983) to argue away the evidence — and of Octavian's mother Atia, e.g. Nicolaus 18.52,54.

20. And aunt — cf. *ad Helviam* 19.2.
21. Again, compare Sen. *ad Helviam*, esp. 14.3:

> tu gratiae nostrae, tamquam alienis rebus utereris, pepercisti
> et ex honoribus nostris nihil ad te nisi voluptas et impensa per-
> tinuit.

22. Thuc. 2.46. See e.g. Schaps (1977) and compare Cornelius Nepos
pr. 6-7 for a contrast between contemporary Greek and Roman social
practice.
23. *Att.* 15.11 — though the incident is played down by Hillard
(1983). The sequence of events is examined in detail by Africa (1978).
24. By his marriage to Julia. See *RG* 21.1, Sen. *ad Marciam* 2.3.
25. Sen. *ad Marciam* 2.3-5, esp. 2.5:

> She hated all mothers and fumed particularly at Livia, because
> the promised good fortune seemed to have passed to Livia's
> son.

> Oderat omnes matres et in Liviam maxime furebat, quia
> videbatur ad illius filium transisse sibi promissa felicitas.

26. E.g. Cic. *Brutus* 211; Quintilian *Inst. Or.* 1.1.6.
27. See e.g. Weakland and Fry (1962).

28. ... so that you should consider it wicked to undertake any major
course against my judgement — especially when I have so
little of my life left to live.

> ... uti nefas haberes rerum maiorum adversum meam
> sententiam quicquam facere, praesertim mihi, cui parva res
> vitae restat.

For the full letter see Fragments 59 P.K. Marshall (ed.) *Cornelii Nepotis
vitae cum Fragmentis* (Leipzig 1977) or No. 58, H. Färber *Cornelius Nepos:
Kurzbiographie und Fragmente* (Munich 1925).
29. The clearest example is that of Murdia *CIL* VI 10230, but see
also Aemilia (Polyb. 31.26 ff) who passed on massive dowry payments at
her death, Pudentilla (Apul. *Apologia* 93) and the lawsuit brought by a
son for the *praedia* his mother failed to pass on to him (Val. Max. 4.2.7).
30. Nicolaus 3.5 where Nicolaus comments that the boy was brought
up 'as if at a father's home' (ὡς παρὰ πατρί) — clearly not the usual
expectation. Antonius threatens Cicero with his stepson Clodius in *Att.*
14.13A, suggesting that he has been unable to receive Cicero in his home
because young Clodius also resided there.
31. *Att.* 13.9; 10; 22 and see Africa (1978: 614-15).
32. Suet. *Aug.* 101; Tac. *Ann.* 1.8.2.
33. Dio 57.12. He is also said to have become angered that a statue
commemorating Augustus listed Livia's name before his own on the
inscription Tac. *Ann.* 3.64.

34. The elder Agrippina was commemorated by Gaius as mother of Caesar Augustus in *RIC* 16-19 and the superb commemorative *sestertius* 42 (new ed. I, 13,21,30 and 55). Nero's mother, the younger Agrippina, figured as Augusta, mother of the Emperor, in *RIC* 9-16 (cf. new ed. 1-3 and 6). See Chapter 4 for further detail.

35. Great crowds thronged her residence during her illness of AD 22 — Tac. *Ann.* 3.64 and consider the *dupondius* issued at Rome AD 22-3 with the legend SALVS AVGVSTA. Dio says that the senators sincerely desired to honour her on her death because she had endeared herself to the senatorial order by her gifts to impoverished nobles and her contributions to the dowries of senatorial girls over the years — Dio 58.2 (Xiph. 142.21 — 143.25).

36. Suet. *Claud*. 11.2 and see *RIC* I. 86a/new ed. 101.

37. Tac. *Ann.* 12.42.3. She had been honoured in her brother's rule — e.g. Suet. *Gai.* 15.3; Dio 59.3.4. As wife of Claudius, she became the first woman to be granted the title of 'Augusta' during her husband's lifetime (*RIC* Claudius: 100/new ed. 75).

38. Tac. *Ann.* 12.58. The *denarius RIC* I Claudius: 100, one of the coin issues celebrating Nero's status as *princeps iuventutis*, AD 51 showed his mother's bust on the reverse (or obverse, according to the 1984 rev. *RIC* I. Claudius: 75 and n125), clearly identifying her with his new status.

39. See n. 34 above for coin issues, and Tac. *Ann* 13.2 for other honours granted early in Nero's reign. *RIC* Nero: 9/new ed. *RIC* I Nero: 1 is the first example of the appearance of a living woman's portrait on the coinage with that of the reigning emperor (Mattingly and Sydenham 1923: I. 145).

40. Termed *pietatis ostentatio* by Suet. *Nero* 9.

41. In the coin issues cited noted above, Nero stressed his dynastic claims rather than his offices, as in the legend on the obverse of the *aureus RIC* 9 (new ed. 1):

AGRIPP AVG DIVI CLAVD NERONIS CAES MATER

with reverse

NERONI CLAVD DIVI F CAES AVG GERM IMP TR P

RIC 10/new ed. 6 celebrates Nero on the obverse. The reverse legend is the same as the obverse of *RIC* 9/new ed. I but shows the divine Augustus and Claudius on a *quadriga* drawn by four elephants.

42. Tac. *Ann.* 13.5 (compare *Ann.* 12.37, under Claudius, and Tacitus' disapproving remarks). Furneaux (1907 II: 53 n15) is probably right in assuming that Dio 61.3.2 is a muddled version of the Tacitean account. Compare Nero's self-justification after Agrippina's murder — Tac. *Ann.* 14.11.

43. Furneaux (1907: II. 44 n16) points to the attempt to topple Vitellius, Tac. *Ann.* 12.42, and the condemnation of Tarquitius Priscus, Tac. *Ann.* 12.59, but that was late in Claudius' reign. The anti-Agrippina party seems to have gained ground after Nero's accession, with the support of Burrus and Seneca. Surely the expulsion of Pallas from office

(Tac. *Ann.* 13.14) marks an important stage in this process, while Nero's murder of Britannicus made his own stance clear.

44. Tac. *Ann.* 13.14, 18 and 19 for the behaviour of Nero's mother. For *her* mother's behaviour, see *Ann.* 4.17 ff.

45. Suet. *Nero* 28; Tac. *Ann.* 14.2; Dio 61.11.2.

46. Esp. Tac. *Ann.* 14.1.ff (Poppaea); 14.2 (Aete); Dio 61-12.

47. *Ann.* 12.64 (in AD 54):

> For there was indeed a bitter contest to see whether Nero's aunt or his mother would prevail over him: for Lepida kept trying to win over his immature mind with flattery and generosity in contrast to the stern and menacing style of Agrippina, who was able to secure her son's rule but could not bear him in the role of ruler.

> enimvero certamen acerrimum, amita potius an mater apud Neronem praevaleret: nam Lepida blandimentis ac largitionibus iuvenilem animum devinciebat, truci contra ac minaci Agrippina, quae filio dare imperium, tolerare imperitantem nequibat.

See also Bradley (1978: 48-50). Compare Suet. *Vesp.* 2.1-2 for the contrast between Vespasian's paternal grandmother and his mother.

48. Tac. *Ann.* 13.18 (after Agrippina's removal from the palace AD 55):

> Whenever he did actually come to visit her there, more often than not he would be accompanied by a mass of centurions and he would rush off after giving her a perfunctory kiss.

> quoties ipse illuc ventitaret, saepius turba centurionum et post breve osculum digrediens.

49. Nicolaus 15.34-6. He was then living in his own residence, but in frequent contact with his mother and stepfather.

50. E.g. Tac. *Ann.* 3.33; 4.19; 6.29; Dio 58.24.3; 59.18.4; Plin. *Ep.* 3.9.19. Compare Juv. *Sat.* 8.128.

51. E.g. Africa (1978: esp. 602-3); Hillard (1983: 10).

52. Esp. Plut. *Cor.* 37, on the dedication of the temple of Fortuna in her memory and Val. Max. 5.4.1 (where she is incorrectly called Veturia).

53. Appian *BC* 4.37. Dio records it as Antonius' only laudable act 47.8.5.

54. Tac. *Ann.* 14.13 (he elaborates on the horrors this unleashed in Chapters 14-16).

55. E.g. Suet. *Tib.* 50; Sen. *ad Helviam* 14; Tac. *Ann.* 12.37; 13.5. Compare the references in n. 50 above.

56. E.g. Tac. *Ann.* 14.1; Verg. *Aen.* 4.304 ff.

57. This can be dated from a reference to Pomponia's pregnancy in May 67 *BC* in *Att.* 1.10.5.

58. No. 58 (p. 174), Färber (1925).

59. Tac. *Ann.* 13.18, quoted in n. 48 above.

60. *Puerilis hilaritas!* — a characteristic not suggested by his own surviving writings or Tacitus' portrait of him. See *ad Helviam* 15.1 for the description.

61. *Hilarisque et cum gaudio* ... (Sen. *ad Marciam* 3.4, of Metilius); *pueriles dulcesque blanditiae* (5.4, of Drusus); and Seneca's *puerilis hilaritas*, cited in the previous note.

62. E.g. Hor. *Carm.* 4.5.9, 13-14; Ov. *Rem. Am.* 547-8, quoted below.

63. Though the reference to her grandchildren having played in her lap, *ad Helviam* 2.5, suggests, like 15.3, that she had enjoyed at least one recent visit to Rome.

64. Appian *BC* 4.12 ff, esp. 21 and 23.

65. Appian *BC* 4.12; 37; Dio 47.8.5; Plut. *Ant.* 19.3.

66. Dio 48.15.2; 48.16.3.

67. Plut. *Brutus* 5; Cic. *Att.* 13.9; 10; 40; *Brut.* 1.18.1 and see Africa (1978: 605-6).

68. Cf. the suggestion (Mattingly and Sydenham 1926: II. 318-19) that coins celebrating SABINA AVGVSTA and her deification were authorised by her adoptive son Pius, not her husband Hadrian.

69. E.g. *RIC* II Trajan: 251-2, 727, 762-4. He is always styled DIVVS PATER. Cf. 726-7, where he is linked with Nerva.

70. E.g. *RIC* II Hadrian: 23-33 and the temple dedicated to Plotina.

71. E.g. *ad M. Caes* 5.45 (60) = Naber p. 90; *ad M. Caes* 2.8 = Naber p. 32 (from Fronto).

72. *Ad. M. Caes* 4.6.2 = Naber p. 69. He usually refers to his mother as *domina* in these letters.

73. *SHA* (Ael. Spart.) *Sev.* 3.9.

74. Giacosa (1977: 59), in discussing the coin issues to her as PIA and FELIX, argues that her titles of MATER AVGVSTI/CASTRORVM/PATRIAE belong to the period of Caracalla's sole reign, but several inscriptions were originally to her as MATER AVGVSTORVM/AVGG., with the plural later ineptly obliterated — e.g. *CIL* VI 220; 36932S; 461. This must mean that the titles, at least on inscriptions, preceded the fratricide. On MATER CASTRORVM/SENATVS/PATRIAE see Instinsky (1942: 203-11, esp. 206), and Oliver (1973) on other honours.

75. Herodian 4.13.8. In Dio's version, she attempts to fight against Macrinus (her son's assassin) before killing herself — Dio 79.23.1 ff.

76. E.g. *RIC* IV 2 Elagabalus: 234-43; 249-79.

77. E.g. *RIC* IV 2 Elagabalus: 209-24 (Julia Paula); 225-31 (Aquilia Severa); 399 (Annia Faustina).

78. *SHA* (Ael. Lampr.) *Ant. Hel.* 4.1; 12.3 and Dio 79.17.2.

79. *SHA* (Iul. Cap.) *Marcus Ant.* 5.3; *Med.* 1.17.7.

80. A concept argued persuasively by Baldwin (1976: 221-33). I am not disputing this concept, merely observing an additional dimension to the identification of mothers with their sons' public achievements.

81. E.g. *CIL* VI 36404; 26909; 12776 etc.

82. Lattimore (1942: 190) 'When the younger generation watches its elders die and buries them, there is generally no occasion for extreme grief (save when parents die very young).'

83. E.g. *CIL* VI 14389; 13027; 13284.

84. E.g. *optima mater* — 1; *mater carissima* — 14.1.

85. And compare Cat. *Carm.* 39.5; 64.349.

86. Cf. Tac. *Agric.* 29; Sen. *ad Helviam* 3.2. Women were ordered to observe one year's mourning on the death of Livia, as if mourning was 'women's business' — Dio 58.2 (Xiph. 143.25 — 144.19).

87. Cf. T. Frank (1916: esp. 703); Hopkins (1965a: 323-4 and n. 54). The figures are discussed in some detail in the following chapter.

88. E.g. *CIL* VI 7510; 14 207; 33 170.

89. E.g. Cic. *Mur.* 23; *Verr.* II.i.112.

90. Plutarch's generalisation, at *Con Praec.* 36, that fathers are fonder of daughters because daughters need them, while maternal favour of sons stems from the mother's need for *their* help, has always struck me as very Greek, but Hallett (1984: 246) refers to it as if it was written with Rome in mind. Note that the reference from Sen. *ad Marciam* 17.1, cited above, is to the stock lament of parents at the loss of a son in his prime: such a son would be *iam matri iam patri praesidium ac decus*, not just protector of his mother.

8

Mothers and Daughters

Mothers commonly perform a vital role in training daughters, by precept and example, to fill their place in society. This training ranges from specific craft and domestic management skills to moral education. There is reason to believe that Roman girls did indeed learn from their mothers what was expected of women in their particular social position, but it is important to recognise the limitations of the sources. Balsdon's assertion in his pioneering *Roman women: their history and habits* (1962: 203) that, 'In general a mother's relationship was more intimate with her daughter than with her son,' is intrinsically plausible, but difficult to authenticate with hard evidence.

The surviving literary texts were written overwhelmingly by men, that is, by fathers and sons. Even when they do discuss women in families, they concentrate on fathers and daughters or mothers and sons rather than on the wholly female world of mothers and daughters. It would be difficult to write a book as substantial as Hallett's (1984) on mothers and daughters in Roman society, although Phillips' (1978) paper is a useful study of relations between mothers and adult daughters in the Roman élite (and see Hallett 1984: 261-2). Cicero, who provides an interesting glimpse into his relationship with his son Marcus and a more detailed picture of relations between Quintus junior and senior (his nephew and brother), writes only incidentally of relations between Atticus' wife Pilia and her daughter Attica or even Terentia and Tullia (his own wife and daughter). His feelings for Tullia are plain enough but it is necessary to read between the lines of reported movements and second-hand messages to appreciate the close association of mother and daughter. Tacitus (*Ann.* 11. 37-8) tells us that Domitia Lepida had

210

fallen out with her daughter Messalina but hurried to her side on her downfall in AD 48 and saw to her burial. This bald statement bears no comparison with his detailed treatment of the breach between Nero and Agrippina or of Tiberius and Livia. Biographers noted the influence of an exemplary mother on a great man. They did not record the lives of great women, save as such mothers.

The literary evidence is therefore even less satisfactory than in other areas of family relations and needs to be supplemented with epigraphic and even legal source material. Balancing the different elements can be difficult. We have already seen in Chapter 3 that the Roman mother's capacity to make or break a daughter's marriage was quite strong in fact, although her authority had no legal basis. Phillips (1978) concentrates on literary examples of such maternal power over marriage choices, while Hallett (1984: 259-62) focuses on the affection and support mothers and daughters provided for each other. I agree with these authors that the relationship is characterised by maternal authority and mutual affection. I maintain furthermore that the mother's power of economic disposition was an element of her authoritative standing in the family and that this authority was reinforced in the case of daughters by common social activity. The interests and reputation of mother and daughter were closely identified, even more than those of mother and son or father and daughter — perhaps because of the assumption that the young woman's education, both moral and practical, had been conducted or supervised by her mother and that this process was continued after marriage by visits and consultations. Certainly the identification remained even when the two had little contact — the disgraced Julia was accompanied to Pandateria in 2 BC by her mother Scribonia, although Julia had not lived with her since Augustus divorced Scribonia in Julia's infancy some thirty-six years earlier.[1]

Divorce, or remarriage on the mother's widowhood, must have separated many Roman children from their mothers but we have already seen that childhood was not the crucial time for setting the pattern of the relationship between the upper-class mother and her children. Modern studies of British working-class kinship have documented the continued closeness between women and their married daughters.[2] In the very different context of Roman aristocratic social life, there was a women's world of visiting and talk which was probably more central to the development of a bond between mother and daughter, for it was as a young matron

211

that the Roman girl gained wider social experience and, one imagines, consulted her mother on a range of questions as well as producing that perennial inter-generational bond, a grandchild.

Mothers mourning daughters

You, my daughter, would [more justly?] have dedicated for your mother this epitaph which your mother now sets up for you, poor girl, twelve years old and snatched by the evil day of wretched death, a daughter taken from her mother

... IVS HVNC TITVLVM MATRI TV NATA DICASSES
QVAM MATER MISERAE NVNC TIBI NATA FACIT
BIS SENOS COMPLETAM ANNOS TE FILIA MATRI
ERIPVIT MISERAE MORTIS INQVA DIES ...

(CIL VI 30110)

Funereal ritual and expressions of grief are overlapping but not coextensive categories — a distinction which the word 'mourn' can obscure. Upper-class women such as Seneca's friend Marcia received *consolationes* attempting to reason them out of their grief on philosophical grounds. Their class espoused the ideal of restraint and concealment of emotion in the face of social duty. Those inscriptions erected by parents to children suggest no such restraint. Where the parent is able to afford elaboration, it seldom takes the form of resignation later evident in Christian epitaphs (Lattimore 1942: 327-32). Even the formula *desine mater dolere* ('Cease your grieving, Mother') put in the mouth of the dead child, assumes that the parents, particularly the mother, lament the hard necessity of fate.

In the preceding chapter (on 'The Roman mother and the adolescent or adult son'), I speculated that a mother's regret for her son was stressed by literary sources because of the general emphasis on the importance of males and because upper-class sons were necessarily the focus of a mother's social and political ambition. The loss of a daughter throughout Roman society might rather have signified a loss of companionship. As we shall see, a Roman mother expected to have considerable contact with her married daughter. A daughter's death could also have lessened her interaction with her grandchildren. We know little of the widower son-in-law's obligations, but it seems plausible that

his remarriage would impose a more formal and less partici-
patory role on the maternal grandmother. On the whole, motherless children seem to have been relegated to paternal aunts or
grandmothers.[3] It should also be noted that dedication of an
epitaph by the mother alone strongly suggests that the mother
was widowed (or possibly divorced) and that any such loss would
be exacerbated by loneliness and the fear that the child's death
put her own funeral rites at risk of omission. We have seen that
women were in general expected to mourn more than men, as
being less able to control their emotions[4] and that the mother
who was predeceased by her children was a stock object of pity
and a symbol of desolation.[5]

In his pioneering article 'Race mixture in the Roman Empire'
(1916: esp. 703), Tenney Frank found that 62% of a sample of
sepulchral dedications by parents to children were to sons.
Kajanto's more recent study of Greek epitaphs at Rome
confirmed this tendency: 65.8% of the 2,000 sepulchral
dedications he examined were to sons (1963: 26). Hopkins'
(1965a) study showed a similar trend.[6] Huttunen (1974: 59-68)
tested this finding systematically. His study still showed a preference for sons, but it was not as marked as in the other studies,
possibly because of the differing sampling techniques and foci of
the various scholars.[7] Allowing for these variations, it can be
taken that there was a bias in favour of sons in sepulchral
inscriptions from parents to children, but it is difficult to know
what to infer from this. There seem to have been few hard and
fast rules about epitaphs: parents erected them for adult,
married children but such people could be commemorated by
spouses and sometimes both groups combined.[8] In low-status
inscriptions, fellow slaves and *colliberti* sometimes joined relations,
while other inscriptions could include nurses and family retainers
as dedicators.[9] These considerations make it difficult to draw firm
conclusions from the groupings in the epitaphs. The groupings
would also have been affected by accidents of mortality. Parents
might have buried an adult child because the child's spouse had
also died, because the wedding had been so recent or because
they had more money or greater inclination to commemorate the
death.

Some hypotheses seem plausible at least: that young married
women, especially if childless, were more likely to be included in
their natal tomb (or commemorated by their parents) than
women who died in a long-established marriage — but such

women would in any case be less likely to predecease parents. Certainly it is too flimsy a basis for any strong assumptions about postmarital residence or family identification. Even more difficult is the relationship between convention and grief. While it is evident that parents who use extravagant language are very distressed at the death of a child, it need not follow that terser inscriptions — even the omission of a child's name — indicate a lesser grief so much as economic strictures or a more conventional approach to the forms.

Huttunen's point that people could be commemorated in various social roles — e.g. as sister, wife or daughter — is well taken.[10] He points out also (1974: 59-60) that children, especially daughters, are sometimes subsumed in the term *suis*, possibly because they were generally deemed less important to the family cult than sons.[11] This suggestion is slightly strengthened by the fact that mothers sometimes appear only as *mater* without a name together with a named *pater* as joint dedicator,[12] but *suis* might equally have indicated that other children were still alive at the time a parent erected the family memorial.

Huttunen's contention (1974: 63) that 42% of *CIL* VI sepulchral dedications to daughters were made by the mother alone is intriguing, but difficult to build on. It could mean that mothers were more likely than fathers to commemorate a daughter by name — which might imply a particular attachment between mother and daughter, but the evidence is tenuous, to say the least. We simply know too little about the details of each case to say why all members of one family should figure in some dedications, while others are from one member to another. The under-representation of women, especially daughters, is a fact for which plausible but unprovable explanations can be advanced and the mother–daughter identification can be adduced for Huttunen's 42%, but it is far from conclusive. The low proportion of dedications by children to mothers[13] has been noted already. It reflects a generally low commemoration of parents[14] and gives a curious twist to the literary insistence on *pietas*. In some cases, parents would already have set up monuments for themselves during their lifetimes. Huttunen explains the discrepancy by the fact that parents would have been celebrated as spouses rather than as parents. Yet, even allowing for such factors, the disproportion still seems considerable, given that parents would usually have died before their children. There is no discernible tendency for daughters rather than sons to celebrate mothers.[15]

The mother's duty to her daughter

The primary obligation of a Roman mother to her daughter seems to have been provision of a proper education and of a husband. Although the *paterfamilias* had the right at law to determine his daughter's match and was the only party other than his daughter who could sue for the return of dowry on the dissolution of the match (Ulpian *Tit.* 6.4-5), the sources make it clear from early anecdotes about Cornelia and Sempronius Gracchus[16] that women had long been expected to play a role in the business. The examples of Caecilia Metella, who had her pregnant daughter Aemilia divorce her husband to marry Pompey (Plut. *Pomp.* 9) and of Sassia, who broke up her daughter's marriage so that *she* could marry her erstwhile son-in-law and match her daughter with her stepson from a second marriage (Cic. *Clu.* 12-14), are not presented as examples of admirable maternal behaviour but, as Phillips (1978: 79) has noted, they show that the literary sources took it for granted that mothers had such powers.

Tullia's engagement to Dolabella, arranged primarily by Tullia and her mother while Cicero was abroad,[17] has generally been taken as an instance of his paternal indulgence.[18] Yet the process of betrothal appears regularly to have involved not only the women of a particular family but their female friends. A story circulated that Pompey had approached Cato and been rebuffed by him in spite of the favourable reception of his suit by 'the women' of the family (Plut. *Pomp.* 44). The story is not necessarily true in detail but the process of the women vetting an approach to the family is borne out by other anecdotes and incidental references. Cicero's report of the failure of the suit of one Talna as 'unacceptable to the women' (*'non esse probatum mulieribus'* — *Att.* 13.28) suggests that marriages were, if anything, particularly 'women's business' — primarily, one supposes, the business of mother and daughter.[19] A first marriage could well have been a parental decision, but the examples suggest that — apart from unusually ambitious or formidable women like Caecilia Metella or Sassia — mothers tended to act in concert with adult daughters contemplating a second or third match.

The mother was in many respects the natural ally and protector of her daughter. Even after imperial bans on female representations in court and pledges of surety for third parties, exceptions were made for women helping close relatives (*Dig.*

215

16.1.21; 16.1.8.1). Cicero furnishes an example in *Verr.* II.i.104-6 of a mother protecting the daughter's financial interests (Cf. *CJ* 4.29.6 — AD 229). We have seen that a form of 'maternal *tutela*' evolved and was eventually acknowledged at law. This protective maternal element extended to sons as well as daughters, and in both cases probably applied more to young, fatherless children. By the same token, the mother was expected to include sons and daughters alike in her will, much as fathers did.

Contributing to the daughter's dowry and arranging a match were also important duties for both parents. There was a story that Scipio Africanus the elder unsuccessfully sought leave to return from the war in Spain to arrange his daughter's marriage at Rome.[20] The marriage was somehow settled in the end notwithstanding[21] and, whatever the dotal agreement, part of the large sum pledged for both of his daughters was paid many years after his own death from the estate of his widow Aemilia.[22] Cicero's worry about Terentia's financial machinations in 48 BC involved the payment of Tullia's agreed dowry to her husband Dolabella.[23] It has been suggested[24] that this concerned a pledge from Terentia to pay part of the dowry, which she was slow to do. Dowry seems commonly to have been constituted from contributions from both parents, and sometimes by other kin and even family friends.[25] Livia's practice of contributing to the dowries of senatorial girls, which so endeared her to that order, was really an extension of the maternal role to a wide group within the élite and acknowledged as such in their informal use of the title 'mother of her country'.[26]

Unfortunately, dowry was one of those aspects of life so taken for granted by the sources that it is referred to only allusively. Details like the amount of dowry, its composition and the amount and style of payment are seldom given.[27] The law, compiled over the centuries from real or imagined cases, is more forthcoming on the subject but is not as reliably tied to everyday custom, since odd contingencies and almost insoluble problems dominate the chapters of the *Digest*, edited furthermore to suit sixth-century AD conditions. What does emerge constantly from the rulings of earlier jurists, however emended, is the presumption that dowry was a vital obligation. A mother's gift to a daughter was excepted from the *lex Cincia* restrictions if it was dowry[28] and maternal contributions to dowry figured in legal examples as a matter of course.[29]

Dowry is inextricably tied to the whole business of arranging a marriage: fielding candidates, assessing their claims, enquiring into their means and determining the appropriate dowry payment. Statius' wife Claudia had offered this urgent process as the excuse for failing to join him, as he wished, in his native Naples. She felt she had to remain in Rome to negotiate a marriage for her daughter.[30] Once the marriage had been arranged and taken place, the mother's responsibility continued, though probably at a less energetic pace. Pliny's *Ep.* 4.19 to his young bride's aunt virtually reports on her progress. He praises the girl to the woman who apparently reared her from early childhood in such a way as to allay her fears and assure her that the young wife does her credit. This assumption that a bride's behaviour reflected on the training given her by her mother (or, in this case, mother substitute) suggests another aspect of the relationship between mother and daughter.

There are indications that, if they were not separated by travel, they had considerable contact after the daughter's marriage. The way in which Cicero's sister-in-law Pomponia and her mother are linked suggests Pomponia might even have returned to her mother's home in Quintus' absence on a provincial command. After his return, the mother apparently stayed for a time with her married daughter and son-in-law in Rome in 67 BC.[31] This was the era before wives began to accompany husbands on such tours of duty. Tullia, too, appears to have stayed with her mother not only between marriages but after her union with Dolabella, on his frequent trips abroad during a turbulent period. This cannot have been based on fears for the daughter's chastity or safety — Tullia, for example, travelled across southern Italy to visit her father, then back to her mother before returning to Rome in a time of famine and some disorder (Cic. *Att.* 11.17; 17a). The inference is that these young matrons sought companionship from their mothers rather than from their peers in the capital.

Presumably the visiting would become more intense once the married daughter had children. Aulus Gellius' account of his visit to a friend's home after the birth of the friend's first child reveals the presence of the mother-in-law, who had clearly overseen her daughter's confinement. Although the philosopher Favorinus challenged her course of action, she appeared to be authoritatively concerned with her daughter's well-being.[32] Whatever the outcome of this encounter, the portrait glimpsed so incidentally appears to be conventional. It does not seem too fanciful to conjecture that the (grand)mother would continue from her own home to provide the young mother with advice and support. If the Empress Faustina the younger hurried to attend her young daughter in an apparently minor illness,[33] it is plausible that childbirth and grandchildren's illnesses occasioned the same attention. Seneca's *Consolatio ad Marciam* 16.6-8 also makes it clear that married daughters were expected to visit their mothers regularly. This could be classed as a duty owed by the daughter to her mother, but might reasonably be assumed to entail counsel from the mother, whether on domestic questions, wifely duty or political expediency. Doubtless many mothers supplied such advice unasked.

Similarly mothers could be counted on to act in the daughter's interest in an emergency, even if the daughter had other ideas. Valerius Maximus 6.7.3 tells the tale of Sulpicia, who was locked up by her mother during the Civil War, but managed to escape and flee into exile with her proscribed husband. The mother of Cicero's repudiated bride Publilia urged her daughter's case.[34] We have already seen that Scribonia, mother of Julia, and Domitia Lepida, mother of the Empress Messalina, came to their daughters' aid at a time of crisis and disgrace, to help them endure their extreme trial, although in both cases the mothers had had limited relations with their daughters.[35] Again the emphasis seems to have been on the duties imposed by the fact of maternal relationship, even when it was not reinforced by early upbringing, co-residence or even visits.

Yet, all things being equal, support in adversity would be accompanied by intimacy and affection. It is fortunate for historians that Pliny was on such good terms with the remnants of the Stoic opposition who survived Flavian rule. His friendship with Arria and Fannia has left us with a portrait of two ageing women — Arria minor and her daughter Fannia — who had supported each other through more than a generation of persecution. More, they had preserved the tradition of the prior generation in the story of the famous Arria (maior), staying with her married daughter after the condemnation of her husband Caecina Paetus and determined to kill herself. In response to her son-in-law's ultimate appeal — surely she would not expect her own daughter to commit suicide if he, Thrasea Paetus, perished? — she affirmed that she would, if her daughter (the younger Arria) had enjoyed such happiness in marriage as her mother (Plin. *Ep.*

3.16.10). This could scarcely be viewed as typical motherly advice, but the style of the son-in-law's argument shows that a mother would be expected to have her daughter's interests at heart. In that sense it recalls Seneca's assumption (*ad Helviam* 4.2) that his own mother's chief cause of distress at his exile lay in the idea of her son's suffering. In AD 66 Thrasea Paetus dissuaded Arria minor from imitating her mother by reminding her that *their* daughter Fannia would need her after his suicide.[36] Pliny wrote admiringly (*Ep.* 7.19.4) of the relationship between that mother and daughter which endured so many years of hardship, including a common exile.

In the case of mother and daughter, this presumption of altruistic motherly concern was accompanied by the force of example. A mother might worry about son and daughter alike but her behaviour was more likely to inspire emulation in the child of her own sex. Thrasea Paetus' appeal to his mother-in-law demonstrates this as well, for it took the form: 'Is this the sort of behaviour you would impose by your example on your daughter?' The idea is explicit in Propertius' artificial epitaph, placed in the mouth of the noble Cornelia and containing death-bed advice to her daughter:

And do you, daughter — whose birth marked the year of her father's censorship — see to it that you follow my example in having only one husband.

filia, tu specimen censurae nata paternae,
fac teneas unum nos imitata virum.

(Prop. 4.11.67-8)

Compare Seneca's exhortation to his mother to forget her misery by concentrating on the education of her motherless grand-daughter Novatilla:

Now is the time to form her moral habits and shape her. The principles which are impressed in the tender years go to the inner core. Let it be *your* speech to which she becomes accustomed; let her be moulded to *your* standard. You will bestow a great gift on her, even if you give nothing more than your own example.

219

nunc mores eius compone, nunc forma; altius praecepta
descendunt, quae teneris imprimuntur aetatibus. tuis
adsuescat sermonibus, ad tuum fingatur arbitrium;
multum illi dabis, etiam si nihil dederis praeter exemplum.

(ad Helviam 18.8)

Ironically, Juvenal confirms this view of the relationship with his
denunciation of mothers who help their daughters to commit
adultery: what more can you expect of this generation of women,
he asks, when their mothers set them such an appalling
example?[37]

The inscriptions already analysed in this chapter reveal
another duty a mother owed her daughter — indeed, any of her
children, if the unfortunate necessity arose of performing their
funeral rites. This could not be classed as a specifically maternal
task. The variation in dedications indicates some priorities in
what Huttunen neatly calls 'Roman burial etiquette' (e.g.
1974: 65). The father seems to have been the usual person to
commemorate a child, with the mother often the secondary dedicator, but it was really the duty of any close family member to see
to the rites of any other member.[38] In sum, then, a mother's duty
to her daughter was to train her for married life, to take a leading
role in arranging her marriage, to provide her with companionship and further counsel or training in early married life, to
attend her in childbed and come to her aid in time of emergency.
There was a certain obligation on the mother to set a good
example to the daughter — as part of the training process — and
perhaps to share the shame of any conspicuous failure by the
daughter. This, and the presumption of a selfless concern for the
daughter's welfare, underlay the expectation that the mother
would come to her in time of need. Although the obligation held
regardless of the quality of the personal relationship between the
two, there seems usually to have been a strong bond of companionship and mutual concern between mother and daughter.
The young upper-class matron, married in her teens to a man
already embarked on a political career, must have derived some
comfort from the support of her mother as she became
accustomed to the task of supervising an existing household of
some complexity, learning the niceties of the more extended
social life of a married woman and dealing with motherhood
herself.

The daughter's duty to her mother

Family relationships, though often unequal, are none the less reciprocal. The catalogue of a daughter's duty to her mother is necessarily a complement to that of the mother's duty to her: each is obliged to provide funeral rites; the daughter is obliged to pay visits and the mother to receive them and so on. The exception to this pattern is obedience. The daughter was socially — if not legally — obliged to follow her mother's decision on the choice of husband and even — in the case of Aemilia (Caecilia Metella's daughter) — the decision to leave the husband. Such matters would not generally be decided capriciously and once a girl passed beyond the age of first marriage she is more likely to have been an equal partner in discussions with her mother, like Tullia or those unnamed *mulieres* of Cicero's letter *Att.* 13.28.

Even the father's legal right to end a happy marriage was eroded over time[39] and a determined woman could doubtless defy her mother's insistence that she leave her husband. But the relationship of mother and daughter seems to have been a fairly tight one — even where affection was low, the authority relationship was clear. The daughter, unlike her brother, could not argue that the mother was overstepping her proper bounds. She had acquired her standards from her mother and serious disobedience or an open breach must have been a grave step, virtually a rejection of her upbringing.

In his letters to Atticus, Cicero implies that Terentia sometimes behaved badly to her daughter[40] but that Tullia bore this well. Cicero considered her a dutiful and cheering companion in his times of trial during the Civil War and he gave her credit for her *pietas* toward her mother.[41] Such *pietas* was expected of children of all ages and both sexes. In the case of daughters, the expectation was probably reinforced by frequent contact with the mother and greater dependence on her, reinforced by gratitude for dowry contributions.

Submission to the mother's will won praise. We have seen in Chapter 3, 'The maternal relationship and Roman law', that daughters and sons alike expected to be beneficiaries of the mother's testament. In the case of Aebutia such expectations were disappointed, for the mother named only one of two daughters heir. Valerius Maximus, who recounted the incident (7.8.2), had no hesitation in labelling such favouritism insanity and asserted that the excluded daughter could have gained her 'rights' by appeal to the praetor. Her refusal to do so and her determination to abide by the testament is presented as an instance of her admirable *pietas* and a proof of the injustice she suffered, since it showed how little she deserved the disgrace of exclusion. It is notable that a previous chapter of Valerius Maximus' work (7.7.4) includes sons who *did* challenge a maternal will successfully. It would be ill-judged to make too much of a couple of incidents but this does support the general impression of the sources, that the daughter, as being particularly under the mother's tutelage, was expected to be submissive to her. The son was expected to be dutiful and obedient, too, but the daughter's obligation to the mother was more far-reaching because they experienced the same kind of life and because obedience was a particularly feminine virtue. We have seen that the daughter's performance as a young wife was a reflection on her natal family and particularly on the upbringing and example of her mother. She therefore had a duty to show herself a worthy product of this upbringing.

Terentia and Marcia enjoyed regular visits from their married daughters, as we have seen. These were an obligation on the daughter but one hopes that they were enjoyable to all parties. In consoling Marcia for the loss of her son, Seneca (*ad Marciam* 16.6) elaborates on the comfort she can derive from still having two daughters and granddaughters to solace her. Indeed, if women were the prime mourners, they were also the comforters of Roman society. The formidable Arria (maior) was taken into the home of her daughter in time of crisis (Plin. *Ep.* 3.16) and was protected against her own suicidal designs rather as Sulpicia had been protected, against her will, by her mother during the Civil War'(Val. Max. 6.7.3).

Sometimes a mother's death would be commemorated by her daughter but the convention of not expressing regret at the death of a parent (Lattimore 1942:190) robs these memorials of any personal value. Even the stock expressions of our own society's epitaphs — 'fondly remembered by', 'still sorely missed' and so on — are more revealing of varied relationships. On the whole dead mothers receive the same tributes as dead wives — they are *optima, bene merens, pia/piissima* and, very occasionally, *dulcissima*.[42]

The daughter's duties to the mother can be summarised, then, as obedience, support and company. It is tempting to elaborate on these, but the concrete examples are essentially those of the previous subsection, on the mother's duty to her daughter. One imagines that ageing mothers, especially if widowed, relied increasingly on their daughters' attentions but this is an extension of the evidence, not a straight reading of it.

Conflict and community of interest

In the preceding chapter we examined instances of conflict between mother and son. There is no parallel in the literature of extreme conflict between mother and daughter. It is always possible that Tacitus' casual reference to the breach between Domitia Lepida and her daughter Messalina might represent the tip of an iceberg, but such conflict would not usually have interested the historians. Tension between mothers-in-law and daughters-in-law occupied more of their attention if it revolved around a man at the centre of political activity (in Republican sources) or an emperor.[43]

Even if some daughters were less dutiful than the ideal, the strong impression remains that there was a general community of interest between mother and daughter. Apart from general references to women's visits and consultations about marriages, this is evidenced by shows of solidarity in political situations. At Milo's trial for murder, the victim's widow Fulvia and her mother Sempronia moved the onlookers with their affecting testimony and conspicuous grief.[44] Sassia's daughter apparently aligned with her mother against her brother Cluentius in the family feud which Cicero's speech has preserved for posterity. Cicero (*Clu.* 190) claimed that the daughter's husband had been induced by Sassia to bring the charge against Cluentius in the first place. In the political uncertainty after Caesar's assassination, Servilia presided over a meeting of her son and sons-in-law as well as two of her daughters (Cic. *Att.* 15.11). Caesar's mother Aurelia and sister Julia both testified against Clodius Pulcher at his trial after the Bona Dea affair (Suet. *Iul.* 74.2).

To men, this association could appear sinister. Rumour accused Scipio Aemilianus' wife Sempronia of conspiring with her mother Cornelia to poison him because of his opposition to C. Gracchus, her brother.[45] Juvenal (6.231-41) elaborates on the lengths to which a mother will go to abet her daughter's adultery. Both of these instances are gossipy exaggerations, but display the presumption of common interest. It is difficult to believe that a great number of mothers encouraged adulterous or homicidal daughters, but a general readiness to provide sympathy and practical assistance to the daughter is apparent. It could have been demonstrated in the face of maltreatment by a husband or even, as in Juvenal's example, by the mother playing the part of pander generally assigned in literature and law to a maidservant.

The rumour about Cornelia and Sempronia is interesting for its assumption that a married woman would align politically with her natal family rather than with her husband (cf. Hallett 1984: 45, 259). To be sure, Appian (*BC* 1.20) makes a point of stating that there was no love between the childless Sempronia and her husband. In the better-documented politics after Sulla, alignment of brothers and sisters (including half-relationships, as that between Brutus and the two Iuniae) is evident. The curious thing is that politically motivated divorces — such as that of Mucia by Pompey or of Octavia by Antonius — must have separated children from their mothers so that the mother in years to come could well be on the other side of the political fence from the sons and daughters-in-law chosen in part for their usefulness to the current politics of a father such as Pompey. The part played by a *divorced* mother in arranging matches for her children is not clear. We know that the widowed Servilia expected to play a continuing role in Brutus' alignments — although she was thwarted in this.[46] It seems reasonable to assume that she tried quite as hard to involve herself in the marriages of the daughters by her second marriage. The example of Quintus and Pomponia, discussed in the preceding chapter, shows that divorce did not in itself keep a mother from the process of arranging a child's marriage.

It would be particularly interesting to know whether mothers attempted to rescue daughters from bad marriages in this era of painless divorce. Cicero's anxieties over Tullia's plight are well documented, but it is not always clear how far his worries are about Tullia's happiness and how far they are political. In June 48 *BC* (*Att.* 11.3.1) he feared the return of the full dowry might be difficult if he simply put an end to the marriage, although when divorce did come an amicable agreement was reached.[47] The return of the dowry affected a mother rather differently. If the daughter's father were not alive, the daughter herself received the dowry from the divorced husband. The mother was like any other contributor to it and had no claim to the return of her share.[48]

Presumably mothers also worried over their daughters' plight.

Not Caecilia Metella (Plut. *Pomp.* 9.2) or Sassia (Cic. *Clu.* 12-14) perhaps, but less hard-bitten women concerned at a spendthrift or violent son-in-law's behaviour. The examples of the monster mothers show the moral force which could be applied. A widowed mother could surely have brought pressure to bear either on the son-in-law to improve or on the daughter to end the marriage. A mother might have been less effective if her husband (or former husband) insisted that his own interests were served by the continuation of the marriage. An account of such a case would have increased our knowledge of the relative powers of mother and father and ideas about their proper areas of concern.

Mothers could also be very political and calculating. It would seem natural for a daughter to confide in her mother during their visits. Again, support for this notion comes from an accusation of conspiracy. Tacitus represents the young Livia Julia as reporting to her mother Livilla on her husband's treasonable designs or any hint of them:

Not even his nocturnal behaviour was immune, for his wife used to reveal to her mother Livilla his wakefulness, his sleep, his very sighs.

ne nox quidem secura, cum uxor vigilias somnos suspiria matri Liviae patefaceret.
(Tac. *Ann.* 4.60)

This suggests that daughters did tell their mothers intimate secrets and that mothers were not above using daughters for their own political ends. Antonia's subsequent denunciation of Livilla (who was *her* daughter) in the course of Sejanus' trial is never detailed in the sources (e.g. Dio 58.11.7). It is an exception to the usual solidarity between mother and daughter. These references suggest that women were embroiled in palace politics but that their activities only occasionally interested the chroniclers.

The imperial family furnishes relatively few instances of mother and daughter relations, partly because of the stress already noted on mothers of emperors — that is, sons — and partly because so many imperial women died (naturally or otherwise) by the time their daughters achieved prominence in the sources. This is not true of the two Faustinae, but even in their case we know more of their relations with their husbands — and that of the younger Faustina with her father.[49] On the death of the elder Faustina in AD 141, a foundation established for poor girls virtually gave her a posthumous role of maternal benevolence in the community. It is ironic that we know so little of her relationship with her own daughter, for both women were celebrated officially *as* mothers.[50]

The relationship which is most fully (if not most reliably) documented is that of Julia Maesa with her daughters Julia Mamaea (mother of Elagabalus) and Julia Soaemias (mother of Alexander Severus).[51] In the preceding chapter we looked in some detail at the events following the death of Caracalla, when Julia Maesa and Soaemias secured the succession of the fourteen-year-old Elagabalus in AD 218.[52] This represents a classic instance of community of purpose between mother and daughter and of maternal ambition. But it changed. Julia Maesa seems to have transferred her support to the son of her younger daughter, Mamaea, and to have engineered the plot which resulted in the assassination of Elagabalus and Soaemias and the elevation of Mamaea's son Alexander Severus, then thirteen years old, in AD 222.[53]

The reasons for Julia Maesa's shift are not clear. We noted in the preceding chapter the sources' suggestion (e.g. Herodian 5.5.5) that she appreciated better than Soaemias the ways in which Elagabalus' behaviour offended Roman sensibilities and endangered the regime and the implication that Julia Maesa was unable to impress her understanding on Soaemias and Elagabalus — that is, that her influence with her elder daughter and grandson declined after AD 218. Perhaps Soaemias, who apparently retained great authority over her emperor son, was excluding her mother from policy decisions, but we are left to speculate about the details of possible conflict or coolness between mother and daughter which led to such drastic results. It is doubtful that her younger daughter Mamaea could have managed the successful coup of AD 222 without her mother's support.[54] As in the case of Elagabalus, the new emperor Alexander Severus was very young at the time of his elevation and was probably a passive object of maternal (and grandmaternal) scheming. The details of the sequence may be obscure but Julia Maesa emerges as a spectacular instance of a mother's ability to manipulate her daughters to her own political ends, apparently with their co-operation. Both were women of some force themselves, able to control their young sons, yet as daughters they were generally submissive. In spite of the special character of the power struggle the relations demonstrate in distorted form the usual association between mother and daughter and the presumption of common interest and mutual support.

Conclusion

We are therefore able to reconstruct a picture of sorts of the relationship between mother and daughter in Roman society, particularly at its upper stratum. The mother was above all a figure of authority, to be deferred to even more by her daughter than by her son. In both cases the authority was enhanced by her power of (economic) disposition, particularly at death. The fact that the daughter received dowry at an earlier stage in life (in most cases) and in part, at least, from the mother made for some difference. So did the arrangement of the marriage, an important step in any family and one in which the mother played a leading role. She seems to have been more prominent in the marriage of daughters than sons since first marriage was at a significantly earlier age for daughters, who probably led a fairly restricted social life until that time while sons would be in a slightly better position to discuss choices even for a first marriage.

The pattern of the relationship between mother and daughter was probably established early, with the mother overseeing the girl's training in specifically female areas, both practical and moral. But even if the mother lived apart from the daughter during that phase, by reason of divorce or remarriage after widowhood, her maternal authority still held good, for it was based not on that early association but on the fact of motherhood. The girl's dependence on her mother would have been reinforced rather than severed by marriage. The daughter owed her mother the courtesy of visits and such evidence as we have suggests that the association between mother and daughter was a pleasure, as well as a duty, for both. Once admitted to the relatively free social life of the Roman upper-class matron, the daughter would have had more interests in common with the mother, as well as more questions on which to seek her guidance. We can safely assume that each would have helped the other in time of stress, but there is more evidence of mothers helping daughters than the reverse. Each could commemorate the other's death, although it was more conventional for mothers to express regret and loss at the passing of daughters.

The presumption of the sources is that there was a strong

bond of mutual interest between mother and daughter, even if the details of this are not always clear. In any case, the association of honour and shame existed even where contact between mother and daughter was less frequent or intimate. Similarly, a mother's obligation to come to a daughter's aid in time of trial — whether the major trial of exile or the more everyday but dangerous trial of childbirth — was fixed and not contingent on specific details of a given relationship.

The protective character of the maternal relation to the daughter appears to have been stronger than that with the son, where the mother's power of protection lay chiefly in intercession. It is difficult to refine this element: as with many aspects of Roman motherhood, the main examples are of widowed mothers, who might be presumed to have greater authority and the need and means to give help in the absence of a father. Similarly, the mother's power to make and break a daughter's marriage was considerable but might have been waived in the face of paternal determination.

The temptation to squeeze the meagre evidence is great but to press it any further would be an exercise of creative sentimentality rather than legitimate scholarship. Precise parameters are elusive but we can discern a general framework of reciprocal duty. At best, the relationship between mother and daughter must have been a close companionship maturing over the years. At its most basic level, the mother owed the daughter her help and part of her fortune, and the daughter owed her mother respectful visits and obedience.

Notes

1. Suet. *Aug.* 62-4; Dio 55.10.14; Vell. Pat. 2.100.5 — and see Phillips (1978: 75). There was probably a variety of *ad hoc* arrangements — Cic. *Clu.* 27 shows one small child with a previously divorced mother — but children usually remained with the father after divorce. Consider Cicero's grandson Lentulus (Cic. *Fam.* 6.18.5; Plut. *Cic.* 41.7), or the surprise of Plutarch in recounting that Octavia took Antonius' children with her when she formally left his household. His wonder is general, not merely occasioned by the inclusion of stepchildren (Plut. *Ant.* 57).

2. The classic work is Young and Willmott (1957: esp. 28-43). Compare the findings of Walker and Thompson (1983) on American relationships.

3. E.g. Sen. *ad Helviam* 18.7 and possibly Quint. *Inst. Or.* 6 *pr.* 8 for paternal grandmothers. Consider also the paternal aunt of Pliny's young

wife — *Ep.* 4.19, and Nero's paternal aunt Domitia Lepida — Tac. *Ann.* 12.64; Suet. *Nero* 6.

4. Consider especially Sen. *ad. Marciam* 7.3:

> The same loss injures women more than men, savages more than those of a calm and civilised race, the uneducated more than the educated.

> magis feminas quam viros, magis barbaros quam placidae eruditaeque gentis homines, magis indoctos quam doctos eadem orbitas vulnerat.

and compare *ad Helviam* 16.1.

5. E.g. Cic. *Fam.* 9.20.3 and see the examples of the preceding chapter.

6. Of 5,000 inscriptions from *CIL* VI set up by parents only and giving the age of their child(ren) at death, 156 were dedicated to sons and 95 to daughters — Hopkins (1965a: 324 n54).

7. Only *Sepulcrales* from 24321-26321 were tested by Kajanto, while Huttunen notes (p. 18 n62) that only three parts of *CIL* VI had been published at the time of Frank's study (and he did not use all of the published inscriptions). Huttunen's own study was based on a systematic sampling of one-fifth of the epitaphs from *CIL* VI (1974: 16ff). He eliminated fragmentary and verse inscriptions because of the difficulties in codifying them for computer analysis. Huttunen's sample is skewed by his emphasis on occupational titles, which occur less frequently in inscriptions to or by women (as he points out p. 63).

8. E.g. *CIL* VI 22404 to a woman as mother and wife. *CIL* VI 20957 seems to have been erected by the husband and mother-in-law, although *mater* could just refer to the dead woman's own mother.

9. Consider *CIL* VI 12366 to Cn. Arrius Agapetus by his parents, *mamma* and *nutrix* or 18073 to the thirteen-year-old Flavius Gamos by his father, *nutrix* and one Ti. Flavius Abascantus (possibly his grandfather, if AVS after his name stands for AVVS). See also Flory (1978: 83-4) and, for nurses of the aristocracy and imperial family (among others), Treggiari (1976: 88-9).

10. See esp. pp. 43 and 63. Compare Hopkins (1966: 262).

11. Compare the custom of naming exheredated sons in a Roman father's will but referring to daughters and grandchildren *in potestate* by the blanket term *liberi* — Gai. 2.128; *Inst.* 2.13 *pr.*

12. As in *CIL* VI 3570; 18174; 20079. Eighteen inscriptions in *CIL* VI were dedicated to children by an unnamed mother and unnamed father jointly.

13. Fewer than 600 to mothers, compared with more than a thousand by mothers to children.

14. From his sample, Huttunen (1974: 60-1) cites 239 dedications to either or both parents and 1,050 to sons or daughters, not counting another 657 to *posteris* etc. and 544 to *suis*. Shaw (1987) also notes that young children are more prominent in inscriptions around Rome than from other parts of the empire.

15. E.g. 77 *CIL* sepulchral inscriptions to named mothers celebrated as MATRI BM by children identified either by name or *filius/filia* involve 48 sons and 34 daughters. The categories are not exclusive, e.g. *CIL* VI 7304; 15875; 20671 involve both a son and a daughter, while many include both children and spouses or other connections, e.g. 19749; 21618a; 14898.

16. E.g. Plut. *Tib. Gr.* 4; Liv. 38.57 and see Phillips (1978: 70-1).

17. *Att.* 5.4.1; 5.13.3; 5.14.3; 5.17.4; 6.1.10; 6.6.1; *Fam.* 3.12.2; 8.6.2.

18. See esp. Collins (1952).

19. Tullia's engagement involved suggestions from family friends like Servilia and Pontidia (see references n. 17 above), so discussion might have ranged widely before the more compact unit of mother, daughter and father made the final decision.

20. Va. Max. 4.4.10. Compare Tac. *Ann.* 3.35, where a candidate for the governorship of Africa pleads the necessity to arrange his daughter's marriage as an excuse to escape embarrassing competition with the imperial candidate.

21. According to Valerius Maximus, by Aemilia in consultation with male relations. See Moir (1983) and her bibliography (pp. 139-42); Dixon (1985a: 152-4).

22. Polybius 31.27 ff.

23. E.g. *Att.* 11.2.2; *Fam.* 14.6.

24. In a private communication from Professor J.A. Crook of St. John's College, Cambridge.

25. E.g. 'Turia' to female relations *CIL* VI 1527 lines 42ff; cf. Plin. *Ep.* 2.4; 6.32.

26. Dio 58.2.3; cf. Tac. *Ann.* 1.14.

27. For attempts to piece together such detail, see Watson (1967: 58 ff), based on Plautus; Dixon (1985a), on Polybius; (1984b) on Cicero. See also Saller (1984a), Treggiari (1984), Gardner (1985).

28. *FV* 269; Paul. *Sent.* 5.11.1. The pledge of dowry was also excepted as such from the Claudian ban on female pledges for a third party — *CJ* 4.29.

29. E.g. *Dig.* 23.3.72 (Paul); *Dig.* 23.3.34 (Ulpian); *Dig.* 23.3.62 (Modestinus).

30. Statius 3.5, esp. 54 ff. Compare n. 20 above.

31. *Att.* 1.5.8 — but see Shackleton Bailey 1965: I. 283 *ad loc.*

32. *NA* 12.1, extensively discussed in Chapter 5.

33. Although the evidence comes from the dubious collection of letters in the *Life* of Avidius Cassius (Vulc. Gall. 9-10, to be found in Haines 1963: II.316), it shows none the less that a mother might be expected to tend her daughter if she fell sick, even at this exalted level of society. Certainly the mistrust of the attending doctor has a convincing maternal ring.

34. With a persistence Cicero found exasperating — Cic. *Att.* 12.32.1.

35. For Scribonia and Julia, see the references at n. 1 above. Scribonia's divorce from Augustus had taken place soon after Julia's birth; Tacitus tells us in his account of Messalina's downfall (*Ann.* 11.37-8) that she and Domitia Lepida had been estranged for some time.

36. [Thrasea] admonished Arria, who was trying to share her husband's fate and follow the example of *her* mother Arria the elder, to keep a hold on ife and not to deprive their daughter of her sole support.

Arriamque temptantem mariti suprema et exemplum Arriae matris sequi monet retinere vitam filiaeque communi subsidium unicum non adimere.

(Tac. *Ann.* 16.34.)

37. scilicet expectas ut tradat mater honestos atque alios mores quam quos habet?

(Juv. 6.239-40)

38. See again the variety in the inscriptions cited at n. 8 above. See Kajanto (1963: 26) for the common-sense conjecture that the dedication should be made by 'the nearest surviving member of a family, even if other relatives were alive'.

39. E.g. Pauli *Sent.* 5.6.15; *FV* 116; *CJ* 5.17.5.

40. See e.g. *Att.* 11.2.2 on Tullia's dowry and *Att.* 11.16.5 on Terentia's will. Plutarch's claim that Terentia had not provided her daughter with a proper escort for her travels in Italy, apparently based on a misunderstanding of Tullia's age at the time, could be an echo of criticisms made by Cicero and passed on to posterity by his secretary, Tiro — Plut. *Cic.* 41.3.

41. E.g. *Att.* 11.17 and compare *Fam.* 14.11.

42. E.g. *CIL* VI 11373 (*optima*); 10839, 12776 (*bene merens*); 7968, 22800 (*pia, piissima*); 12238, 10881 (*dulcissima*).

43. E.g. Cicero on Servilia and Porcia — *Att.* 13.22.4; Tacitus on the tensions between Agrippina and Acte — *Ann.* 13.13 or Poppaea — *Ann.* 14.1 — and compare his references to the bad relations between Livia and Agrippina maior — *Ann.* 4.12.

That this continues to be a masculine bias is shown by Giacosa's insistence that Julia Mamaea would not tolerate any daughter-in-law for long. He says (1977: 63) of Alexander Severus:

In 225 he had married Orbiana, but Julia Mamaea, as in the past Julia Domna, was not a woman to tolerate a female presence that was not her own beside her son. It required a couple of years to undermine the marriage.

No evidence is adduced for this reading which is given more space than the account of the overthrow of Julia Soaemias and Elagabalus, which Herodian 5.8.3-10 shows to have been engineered by Julia Soaemias' mother.

44. Asconius *Mil.*, *arg.* 35 (A.C. Clark (ed.), OCT) and compare Cic. *Phil.* 3.16.

45. Appian *BC* 1.20; Liv. *EP.* 59.

46. Cic. *Att.* 13.11.2; 16.2; 22.4. See the discussion in the preceding chapter.

47. Dolabella reneged on the final payment and Cicero was contemplating a legal action for its recovery in 44 *BC* — *Att.* 16.15.2.

48. Ulpian *Tit.* 6.4-5; and see Watson (1967: 66).

49. E.g. Fronto *Ep. ad Ant. Pium* 2.2A.341 pp. 156-7 Van den Hout. Although it is not clear from the text, this has usually been taken to refer to Faustina the younger. See Haines' note to his edition (1962: I.128).

50. Consider the association of Faustina the elder with Vesta on the posthumous issue *RIC*: Pius 1151 and with Ceres *RIC*: Pius 356 in her lifetime. Compare the *aureus RIC*: Pius 511 depicting Faustina the younger on the obverse and Venus Genetrix on the reverse, apparently to commemorate the birth of Commodus.

51. Julia Maesa was the sister of Caracalla's mother Julia Domna. The relationships of the Severans were:

```
Septimius·Severus    Julia Domna     Julia Maesa    Julius Avitus
         └──────┬──────┘                └──────┬──────┘
       Geta   Caracalla    Julia Soaemias   Julia Mamaea
                             └────┬                    │
                            Elagabalus          Alexander Severus
```

52. Herodian 5.3.9 ff; *SHA* (Iul. Cap.) *Macr.* 9; *SHA* (Ael. Lampr.) *Ant. Heliog.* 1-3.

53. Herodian 5.8.3; *SHA* (Ael. Lampr.) *Ant. Heliog* 16-18; *Alex. Sev.* 1.

54. *SHA* (Ael. Lampr.) *Ant. Heliog.* 13-15; Herodian 5.8.3.

9

Conclusion

The central argument of this work has been that the Roman mother was not associated as closely with the young child or with undiscriminating tenderness as the mother of our own cultural tradition but was viewed primarily as the transmitter of traditional morality — ideally, a firm disciplinarian. This forms a contrast with the recurrent stereotype of more recent history which characterises the mother as typically affectionate and the father as typically disciplinarian. Although differences between the parental roles have emerged in this study they have seldom been absolutely clear-cut.

My suggestion that the authoritative role rested in part on the mother's power of economic disposition — that is, her ability to bestow political support, dowry and inheritances — has primary significance for the élite family, for which the sources provide more detailed testimony. It is difficult to balance this against the inscriptional material which provides our major evidence for the lower orders, but it is not impossible that shopkeepers and peasants observed similar inheritance patterns.

The epitaphs tell us that surrogate relations existed in the lower orders, where fostering probably released a young mother for the paid or servile work-force. Within the slave and freed-slave families of Rome, the mother must sometimes have been an anchor in a very uncertain world. She probably occupied an important place within the family structure but it is difficult to determine whether it was one of great authority and, if so, what the authority might have rested on. *Patria potestas* left Roman citizens in a state of dependence on the older generation which must have had some effect on all social levels: even a propertyless day labourer, if he was a *paterfamilias*, was able to indenture his children. The tombstones, like the literary sources, show little difference in the attitudes to mothers and fathers, so women might have benefited from the general stress on deference to the older generation.

Pietas in parentes was a virtue intended to apply until the death of the parents. There was inevitably a difference in the requirements of the relationship according to the age and stage of the child but, by our standards, Roman adults were expected to display great respect and even submissiveness to their parents. The mother's position was not as firm at law as it was within the received morality so, as we have seen, it was possible to defy a mother in extreme cases. For her part, a mother's interests were largely identified with her children's but her loyalties could also be claimed by people from outside her conjugal family — her own blood relations. In the political elite, shifts of alliance could cause a woman to divorce and remarry for the sake of her father's or brother's ambitions (which she would place ahead of her husband's). This would mean that her children did not grow up in the same house with their mother, even though they would normally maintain close contact.

I have attempted in this work to strike a balance between scholarly caution and legitimate extension of the evidence. The prescriptive and anecdotal character of most epitaphs leaves the student of the family frustrated at the glimpses of family life which never form a complete and reliable picture.

Surrogate relationships, especially those involving young, lower-class children, exemplify the problem. The scanty evidence lends itself to over-generalisation from our own cultural attitudes to fill the gaps. I have tried to avoid this but it is very artificial to maintain a pose of complete objectivity and I have inevitably incorporated judgements in my discussion. Because this work concentrates on motherhood and related topics, the chapter on mother substitutes focused on the more benign relationships, but I have presented the material in such a way as to allow readers to form their own conclusions. The evidence strongly suggests that Roman children of all classes were likely to experience a number of relationships outside the nuclear circle. Maternal mortality, custom and the demands of owners or jobs were all contributory factors. It is difficult to know how children felt about this. In a sense, the fact that a condition is common should make it less traumatic but we know that it was considered a hardship to grow up with a stepmother — a situation which many children must have experienced in the ancient world. The separation of slave mother and infant, however common, was probably dreadful for all concerned. We know from nineteenth-century accounts that plantation slaves were not reconciled to family separation. It is possible that surrogate or extended relations which did not involve permanent separation from parents in the ancient world were pleasant. I have cited inscriptions which show that parents and others such as nurses and foster-parents often combined to express their affection for a dead child and it ought to follow that these children enjoyed the attention and love of a number of people while they lived. In the end, we are unable to do more than speculate. Feelings are one of the most interesting and important aspects of family relations in any period but we must accept that these feelings are beyond our reach.

There is more chance of reconstructing the attitudes of adults to their parents. Duty, affection, companionship and loyalty were all hoped for and frequently displayed. It is a pity that the most detailed accounts are not only concentrated in the inner élite but highlight the most spectacular (and probably least typical) kinds of behaviour. Royal and imperial families have seldom displayed the best standards of fraternal and filial feeling, if only because the stakes are so much higher. Conflict which in other families might involve bickering over wills or sulky refusals to visit for a few months, inevitably becomes more violent when whole empires are at stake. It is all the more interesting, therefore, that the imperial family saw itself from the first as a model of 'normal' family feeling and so many rulers identified the stability of their regime with the harmony (*concordia*) of imperial brothers, husbands and wives, parents and children. The coins discussed and illustrated particularly in Chapters 4 and 7 demonstrate this tendency. It was often little more than dynastic propaganda, but the examples of low-born emperors celebrating their natural parents — like the letters of the Emperor Marcus — suggest that this imperial stress was a reflection of the ideals of Roman society.

We have seen that the great mothers of the Roman past often served as symbols of the superior virtue of an earlier age and the imperial women were publicly identified with virtue, just as contemporary women were pilloried by such as Juvenal for embodying the vices of his day. It is therefore interesting that the sporadic attempts from Augustus on to encourage citizen reproduction were not greatly directed at women as potential mothers. But then the legislative programmes designed to reward procreation and punish celibacy, childlessness and adultery were not great models of efficiency. The alimentary schemes examined in Chapter 4 had a relatively short life. In this, as in other legislation, women and children tended to be treated as instruments rather than active agents of social change and moral rejuvenation.

This seems inconsistent with the literary image of mothers as moral guardians. Perhaps if Roman emperors had thought of mobilising female opinion, the dowagers of Rome could have been as effective as women abolitionists and temperance campaigners in eradicating adultery and childlessness! But while Augustus clearly had great respect for his grandmother and mother and for his wife Livia he did not harness the moral force for which such women were known and admired.

This work finishes as it began, with a reminder of the inadequacy of the sources for assembling a complete picture of the maternal relationship and the assertion that it was not characterised by tenderness and affection so much as moral strength. Mothers were entitled to the regard of their children by virtue of the relationship rather than because of any particular services the mother provided in the early years. They retained their position of respect throughout the life cycle, although there was a suggestion that graceful concessions to adult sons eased the strains which might emerge as the mother became older. There is no indication that fostering and separation from remarrying or working mothers caused great instability in the Roman psyche. The diverse sources assure us that Romans attached high ideals to motherhood, but these were not the same as the modern maternal ideal. The reality surely differed from the ideal in any case but we know that many Romans were satisfied with their mothers whom they regularly characterised after death as 'pious' or 'well-deserving', sometimes 'sweet' and occasionally 'beloved'.

Appendix 1

Tollere liberos: the birth of a Roman child*

Something of the ritual surrounding childbirth at Rome has been discussed in Chapter 5, on 'The Roman mother and the young child', while the question of abortion and infanticide was addressed briefly in Chapters 3 ('The maternal relationship and Roman law') and 4 ('Official attitudes to maternity'). For the convenience of the reader, I have drawn together in this short appendix information about procedure on the birth of a child. Those who wish to pursue the subject of infanticide/exposure should consult the bibliography at note 36, Chapter 4, but as I point out there, the subject is usually related to Greek conditions.

The birth of a legitimate child to propertied parents was probably an occasion for rejoicing, but Pliny tells us (*Pan.* 26.5) that poor parents could not afford to rear their children unless they had financial assistance of some kind. Plutarch, writing from a Greek perspective within the Roman Empire, makes a similar assumption (*De Am.Prolis* = 497E *Moralia*) and the philosopher Musonius Rufus (Lutz: 15) refers to infant exposure even within the ranks of the prosperous. Other incidental references in literature fail to specify a social context for child exposure but assume it as part of life (e.g. Tac. *Germania* 19; Aul. Gell. *NA* 12.1.23; Suet. *de Grammaticis* 7.21). Legal writings about the status confusion of free-born children exposed by parents and reared as

---

* This book was already in production when two works on this topic became available to me. They could not therefore be treated in the text, but readers interested in medical aspects of Roman childbirth and the status of midwives are referred to French (1987). Eyben (1986: esp. 323-7) has a useful account of ritual.

slaves or *alumni* by owners (Rawson 1986c) confirm the impression that it was not unusual for children to be exposed at birth for economic or other reasons.

One of the other reasons was doubt about paternity. The sarcophagus reliefs displaying the stages of life sometimes show a mother in a chair immediately after childbirth, with the new-born baby being washed or raised up from the ground by the midwife (see P1.7). Literary sources refer to the *father* as raising (*tollere* or *suscipere*) the child in this way as a formal acknow-ledgement of his paternity and, by implication, of his decision to rear the child. Consider Cicero: 'As soon as we have been brought into the world and raised up . . .' (*Tusc. Disp.* 3.1.2).

Suet. *Aug.* 94.5 refers to the late arrival of Octavius to the senatorial debate about Catiline in 63 BC: he had been delayed by the birth of his son, the future Augustus. Octavius might not have been in the same room during labour, but he could well have been called in immediately afterwards to raise the child. Other references suggest that the child was laid out on the ground, perhaps in a beam of sunlight, ready for the father to perform this ritual. Nero was born at day-break with the result that

> he was almost lit up by the sun's rays before he could be placed on the ground.
>
> (Suet. *Nero* 6.1)

Suetonius mentions elsewhere that Nero's father Domitius Ahenobarbus acknowledged the boy's birth with the usual rais-ing (Suet. *Nero* 5.2.).

The father's rights extended beyond marriage. The traditional ban on the hasty remarriage of widows stemmed from the fear of confusion about the provenance of issue (Plut. *Num.* 12; *FV* 320; Paul *Sent.* 1.21.13. Cf. *Dig.* 3.2.11.1-2 — Ulpian). Cicero's daughter Tullia had been divorced from Dolabella by the time she gave birth in January 45 BC but she went to the home of his adoptive father for the event (Cic. *Fam.* 6.18.5; Plut. *Cic.* 41.7). In the absence of her former husband, his adoptive father presum-ably performed the office of raising up the child. The future emperor Claudius divorced his second wife Plautia Urgulanilla for adultery and suspected murder (Suet. *Claud.* 26.2) and exposed at birth the child she bore several months later:

> The child Claudia was conceived from his freedman Boter.

238

Although she had been begun by another and born within five months of the divorce, he gave orders that the child was to be exposed at her mother's doorstep and cast out naked.

(Suet. *Claud.* 27.1)

Augustus similarly prevailed upon the former husband of his granddaughter Julia to expose the child she bore soon after her exile for adultery (Suet. *Aug.* 65.4). In all these cases, refusal to rear the child was an explicit acknowledgement of its illegitimacy.

A woman who became pregnant from an adulterous affair might have resorted to a secret abortion to avoid such a disgrace. As I noted in Chapter 3, ancient authors tended to associate abortion with adultery (e.g. Tac. *Ann.* 14.63). Cicero alleged in a lawcourt speech (*Clu.* 34) that a widow was bribed by her husband's secondary heir to have an abortion so that her child would not succeed to the estate. Seneca (*ad Helviam* 16.3), Favorinus (*NA* 12.1.8) and Juvenal (6. 595-7) all suggested that society women avoided pregnancy for frivolous reasons such as the preservation of their figures. These references show that abortion was known in ancient times and that men were suspicious of the fact that women could procure abortions without male knowledge but it is difficult to draw any conclusions from such vague gossip. Later legislation censured abortion because it deprived the father of his right to the child (e.g. *Dig.* 47.11.4 — Marcianus), but it is possible that some husbands insisted on abortion as a means of birth control.

Abortion was not clearly distinguished by the ancients from contraception (Hopkins 1965b: 136-7) and there is no way of determining whether procured abortions were more dangerous to women than spontaneous miscarriages and full-term births. My own view is that we know too little about actual cases to draw firm conclusions about the frequency of abortion in ancient Rome. Certainly it was condemned by moralists — but then, so were luxury and celibacy, which those same moralists sometimes practised. Nardi's (1970) comprehensive treatment of the subject reviews all the ancient evidence, including that of the medical writers.

Mental and physical handicaps were another reason for the exposure of new-borns. Cicero (*Leg.* 3.8.19) cites a Twelve Tables clause on the quick dispatch of a deformed infant. Seneca writes (*De Ira* 1.15) that monstrosities were drowned at birth. The medical writer Soranus lists criteria for deciding whether to rear a child (*Gyn.* II.vi.[xxvi]). His text assumes that the midwife or doctor would be consulted about this decision but it probably concerned family members, particularly the older generation. Bad omens might have caused exposure by the superstitious. Dio (62.16.2) reports that a baby was exposed in the forum at Rome bearing a sign 'I will not raise you, for fear you might kill your mother' after Nero's execution of Agrippina. The economic motive would probably have been the strongest for disposing of children.

Aulus Gellius' account of a spontaneous visit to the home of a friend whose wife had just given birth (*NA* 12.1) shows the happier side of birth ritual. Most of it would be familiar to us, for it involved congratulations to the parents and probably questions about naming the child. Reproaching a friend who had not instantly informed him of the birth of a child, Statius (*Silvae* 4.8. 31-41) gives an extravagant version of how he would have reacted to the news. He imagines lighting his own altar, decorating his doorway and celebrating with wine and song. This would presumably precede the party given by the parents! Eight days after the birth of a girl and nine days in the case of a boy, the parents combined a ceremony of purification (*dies lustricus*) with a party for family and friends. This was when the child was named (Suet. *Nero* 6.2; Festus *Epit.* p. 120, under '*lustricus*'). It was also the occasion when the new baby assumed the *bulla*, an amulet worn about the neck to avert unfavourable spirits (Daremberg and Saglio IIA: 1420), the hallmark of childhood among free-born Romans.

Appendix 2: Family Trees*

THE CICERO FAMILY

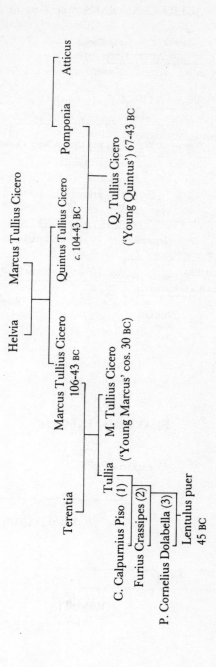

*Note that the trees have been greatly simplified. I have omitted relationships which do not figure in this book. The trees are designed to help readers to follow the relationships mentioned and illustrated in Chapter 4, 'The official encouragement of maternity'.

JULIO–CLAUDIANS 27 BC — AD 68

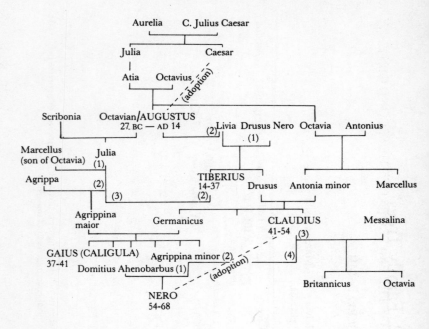

FLAVIANS, AD 69-116

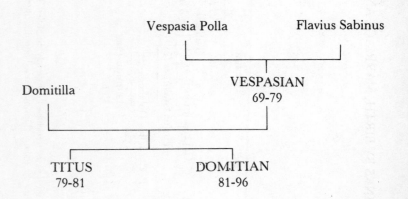

LINKS BY BIRTH, MARRIAGE AND ADOPTION OF THE EMPERORS OF THE SECOND CENTURY AD

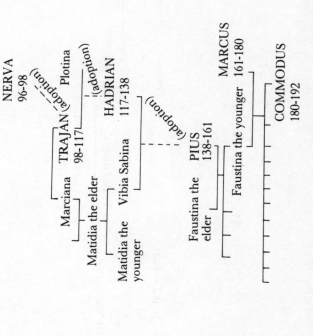

THE SEVERANS, AD 193–235

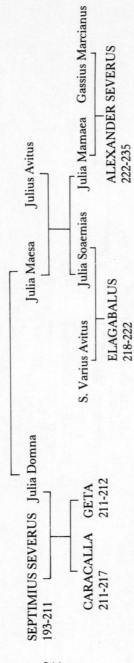

SEPTIMIUS SEVERUS Julia Domna
193–211

CARACALLA   GETA
211–217   211–212

Julia Maesa   Julius Avitus

S. Varius Avitus   Julia Soaemias   Julia Mamaea Gassius Marcianus

ELAGABALUS   ALEXANDER SEVERUS
218–222   222–235

Inscriptions Dedicated by a *Mamma* in *CIL* VI

CIL VI Inscription no.	Age of Child A	M	D	H	Child M	F	*TATA*	Parents M	F	Others
5425	—	—	—		X		—	—	—	—
6973	25	—	22			X	—	—	—	X
7726			—		X		—			—
10016			24		X		X			—
11592	4	6				X	—	—	—	—
11714	9	5	45		X		—	—	—	—
12366	3	—	20		X		—	X	X	—
14720	5	5				X	X	X	X	X
15345	6					X	—	X	X	—
15471		5				X	X	—	—	—
16926 = 26924							—	—	—	—
17800	6	5	26		X		X	X	X	X
18032	7		1	10	X		—			—
19473	2	10	16		X		—	—	—	—
20318		—			X		—	—	—	—

Inscriptions (continued)

CIL VI	Age	Sex	Tata	Father	Mother	Other
20909	10	X	—	—	—	—
21405	15, 4, 13, 7	X	—	X	X	X
25808	—, 3, 11	X	—	X	X	X
26594	7, —, —	—	—	X	—	X
27827	1, 3	X	X	—	—	—
29634	3, 16	X	X	X	X	X
35530	24, 30	X	X	X	X	—
33538		X	—	—	—	—
36353	3, 2, 9	X	X	X	X	X
38598	5(?4)	X	—	X	X	X
38638,A	6, 6, 22	X	—	X	X	—
38769		X	—	—	—	—

Column 1 gives the *CIL* VI number of the epitaph

Column 2 gives the age of the person to whom it is dedicated, where that is indicated: A = years, M = months, D = days, H = Hours

Column 3 gives the sex of the child or object of the dedication: M = Male; F = Female

Column 4 indicates whether a *tata* is listed among the dedicators

Column 5 indicates the inclusion of the parents. These tend to be the primary dedicators, but in 35530 the *tata* and *mamma* precede the father and mother

Column 6 indicates any other dedicators.

The distribution of ages strongly suggests that *mammae* and *tatae* were associated with the early years. *CIL* VI 6571 and 22227 each commemorate a child buried or cremated with the *mamma*.

Some Useful Roman Dates

The Late Republic is usually dated from the tribunate of Tiberius Gracchus (son of Cornelia) in 133 BC.

The imperial period is usually dated from the so-called First Settlement of 27 BC, in which Octavian, who now adopted the title Augustus, took on certain powers on a different basis. The following is a list of emperors divided into dynasties. It will be more useful for this work if combined with the family trees provided:

JULIO-CLAUDIANS

27 BC–AD 14	Augustus (great-nephew, through his mother Atia, of Julius Caesar, who adopted him in his will)
14–27	Tiberius (stepson, son-in-law and adopted son of Augustus, who married Tiberius' mother Livia)
27–41	Gaius (also known as Caligula, great-nephew of Tiberius and son of Agrippina the elder)
41–54	Claudius (uncle of Gaius)
54–68	Nero (great-nephew, son-in-law, stepson and adopted son of Claudius)
69	the year of the four emperors: Galba, Otho, Vitellius, Vespasian

FLAVIANS

69–79	Vespasian
79–81	Titus (elder son of Vespasian)
81–96	Domitian (younger son of Vespasian)

ADOPTIVE EMPERORS

96–98	Nerva
98–117	Trajan (adopted son of Nerva)
117–138	Hadrian (adopted son of Trajan)

ANTONINES

138–161	Pius (adopted by Hadrian)

161–180	Marcus (also called Aurelius; son-in-law and adopted son of Pius)
180–192	Commodus (son of Marcus and Faustina the younger)

SEVERANS

193–211	Septimius Severus
211–212	Caracalla and Geta, sons of Septimius Severus (a brief joint rule until Caracalla killed his brother)
212–217	Caracalla
218–222	Elagabalus (related to Caracalla through his maternal grandmother, who was the sister of Caracalla's mother Julia Domna)
222–235	Alexander Severus (cousin of Elagabalus, who adopted him)

Abbreviations

Abbreviations of journal titles are those of *l'Année philologique*. Abbreviations for ancient authors are those of Lewis and Short *A Latin Dictionary* (Oxford, 1962) and Liddell and Scott *A Greek–English Lexicon* (Oxford, 1961 rep. 1948 ed.). The index of ancient authors includes abbreviations in the alphabetical listing. The list which follows combines works of reference and ancient works which are cited frequently in this book.

ADA	*Acta Divi Augusti*, vol.I, (ed.) S. Riccobono (Rome, 1945).
ANRW	*Aufstieg und Niedergang der römischen Welt*, (ed.) H. Temporini (Berlin, 1972–).
BMC	*Coins of the Roman Empire in the British Museum*, (eds.) H. Mattingly and R.A.G. Carson *et al.* (London 1923-67).
CE	*Carmina Latina Epigraphica*, (eds) F. Buecheler and F. Lommatzsch (3 vols, Leipzig, 1895-1926).
CIL	*Corpus Inscriptionum Latinarum* (Berlin 1862-).
CJ	*Codex Iustinianus*
Coll.	*Mosaicarum et Romanarum Legum Collatio* (vol. II, *FIRA*).
C. Th.	*Codex Theodosianus.*
Dig.	The *Digest* or *Pandects* of Justinian.
FIRA	*Fontes Iuris Romani Anteiustiniani* vols I and II, (eds) S. Riccobono, J. Baviera and V. Arangio-Ruiz (Florence, 1940-43).
FV	(*Fragmenta Vaticana*) Vatican Fragments (vol. II, *FIRA*).
Gai.	The *Institutes* of Gaius.
ILS	*Inscriptiones Latinae Selectae*, (ed.) H. Dessau (Berlin, 1892-1916).
Inst.	The *Institutes* of Justinian.
Med.	The *Meditations* of Marcus Aurelius ('to Himself').
OLD	The *Oxford Latin Dictionary*.
POxy	*The Oxyrhynchus Papyri*, (eds) B.P. Grenfell and A.S. Hunt (London, 1898-).
RE	*Real-Encyclopädie der Klassischen Altertumswissenschaft*,

	(eds) A. Pauly, G. Wissowa and W. Kroll (Stuttgart, 1893-).
RIC	*The Roman Imperial Coinage*, (eds) H. Mattingly *et al.* (London 1923-84), 9 vols, now in thirteen parts.
Sent.	The *Opinions* (*Sententiae*) of the jurist Paul.
SHA	*Scriptores Historiae Augusti*
Tab.	Twelve Tables (vol. I, *FIRA*).

Bibliography

Adelman, I. (1963) An econometric analysis of population growth. *American Economic Review, 53*: 314-39

Africa, T. (1978) The mask of an assassin: a psycho-historical study of M. Junius Brutus. *Journal of Interdisciplinary History, 8*: 599-626

—— (1979) Psychohistory, ancient history and Freud. *Arethusa, 12*: 5-33

Ainsworth, M.D.S. (1967) *Infancy in Uganda,* Johns Hopkins Press, Baltimore

—— (1969) Object relations, dependency, attachment, a theoretical review of the infant–mother relationship. *Child Development, 40*: 969-1025

Ariès, P. (1962) *Centuries of Childhood,* Vintage Books, New York, translated and abridged from the French original, *L'Enfant et la vie familiale sous l'ancien régime* (Librairie Plon, Paris, 1960)

Astin, A.E. (1967) *Scipio Aemilianus,* Clarendon Press, Oxford

Astolfi, R. (1970) *La Lex Iulia et Papia,* Fac. di Giur. dell'Univ. di Padova, Padua

Badian, E. (1985) A Phantom Marriage Law. *Philologus 29*: 82-98

Badinter, E. (1980) *L'Amour en plus: histoire de l'amour maternel, XVIIe-XXe siècle,* Flammarion, Paris

Baldwin, B. (1976) Young and old in Imperial Rome. In S. Bertram (ed.), *The conflict of generations in Ancient Greece and Rome,* North-Holland Publishing Company, Amsterdam: Ch. 13

Balsdon, J.P.V.D. (1962) *Roman women: their history and habits,* Bodley Head, London

Barrett, D.S. (1982) *Greek and Roman coins in the University of Queensland,* Dept. of Classics and Ancient History, University of Queensland, rev. edn, Brisbane

Bateson, G. (1949) Bali: the value system of a steady state. In M. Fortes (ed.) *Social structure: studies presented to A.R. Radcliffe-Brown,* Clarendon Press, Oxford: 35-53

Bauman, R.A. (1968) Some remarks on the structure and survival of the *Quaestio de Adulteriis. Antichthon, 2*: 68-93

Beaucamp, J. (1976) Le vocabulaire de la faiblesse féminine dans les textes juridiques romains du IIIe au VIe siècle. *Revue Historique de Droit Français et Étranger, 54*: 485-508

Bellemore, J. (1984) *Nicolaus of Damascus' life of Augustus,* Classical Press, Bristol

Beloch, J. (1886) *Die Bevölkerung der griechisch-römischen Welt,* Duncker und Humbolt, Leipzig

Benedict, R. (1946) *The chrysanthemum and the sword,* Houghton Mifflin, Boston

Besnier, R. (1979) Properce (élegies II, VII et VIIA) et le premier échec de la législation démographique d'Auguste. *Revue Historique de Droit Français et Étranger, 57*: 191-203

Bogue, D.J. (1969) *Principles of demography,* Wiley, New York

Bonner, S.F. (1977) *Education in Ancient Rome*, Methuen and Company, London

Bowlby, J. (1952) *Maternal care and mental health*, World Health Organisation Monograph Series no. 2, Geneva

—— (1958) The nature of a child's tie to his mother. *International Journal of Psychoanalysis*, *39*: 350-73

—— (1969-80) *Attachment and loss*, Hogarth Press, London, 3 vols (vol. 1: *Attachment*, 1969; vol. 2: *Separation*, 1973; vol. 3: *Loss*, 1980)

Bradley, K.R. (1978) *Suetonius' Life of Nero: an historical commentary*, Collection Latomus 157, Brussels

—— (1984) *Slaves and masters in the Roman Empire: a study in social control*, Collection Latomus 185, Brussels

—— (1985a) Child care at Rome: the role of men. *Historical Reflections/ Réflexions Historiques*, *12*: 485-23

—— (1985b) Child labour in the Roman world. *Historical Reflections/ Réflexions Historiques*, *12*: 311-30

—— (1986) Wet-nursing at Rome: a study in social relations. In B. Rawson (ed.), *The family in Ancient Rome: new perspectives*, Croom Helm, London and Sydney

Brunt, P.A. (1971) *Italian manpower 225 BC–AD 14*, Clarendon Press, Oxford

Buck, C.D. (1949) *A dictionary of selected synonyms in the principal Indo-European languages*, University of Chicago Press, Chicago

Buecheler, F. and Lommatzsch, L. (eds) (1895-1926) *Carmina Latina Epigraphica* = *CE* (3 vols), Teubner, Leipzig

Burn, A.E. (1953) *Hic breve vivitur*: a study of the expectation of life in the Roman Empire. *Past and Present*, *4*: 1-31

Cairns, F. (1979) Propertius on Augustus' marriage law (II.7). *Grazer Beiträge*, *8*: 185-205

Camps, W.A. (1965) *Propertius: Elegies, Book IV*, Cambridge University Press, Cambridge

Carcopino, J. (1928) *Autour des Gracques*, Budé, Paris

Chantraine, H. (1967) *Freigelassene und Sklaven im Dienst der römischen Kaiser*, Steiner, Wiesbaden

Clark, K.M. (1974) *Another part of the wood: a self-portrait*, Murray, London

Cohen, H. (1880-92) *Description historique des monnaies frappées sous l'empire romain*, Paris

Collins, J.H. (1952) Tullia's engagement and marriage to Dolabella. *Classical Journal*, *47*: 162-8, 186

Corbett, P.E. (1930) *The Roman law of marriage*, Clarendon Press, Oxford

Corbier, M. (1985) Idéologie et pratique de l'héritage (Ier siècle avant J.-C. — Ile siècle après J-C.). *Index*, *13*: 501-28

Courtney, E.A. (1980) *A commentary on the Satires of Juvenal*, Athlone Press, London

Crook, J.A. (1967a) *Law and life of Rome*, Thames and Hudson, London, 1967

—— (1967b) *Patria potestas. Classical Quarterly*, *17*: 113-22

—— (1973) Intestacy in Roman society. *Proceedings of the Cambridge Philological Society*, *199* (n.s. *19*): 38-44

—— (1986a) Women in Roman succession. In B. Rawson (ed.), *The family in Ancient Rome: new perspectives*, Croom Helm, London and Sydney: 58-82

—— (1986b) Feminine inadequacy and the *senatusconsultum Velleianum*. In B. Rawson (ed.) *The family in Ancient Rome: new perspectives*, Croom Helm, London and Sydney: 83-92.

Csillag, P. (1976) *The Augustan laws on family relations*, Akademiai Kiado, Budapest

Daremberg, C. and Saglio, E. (1877-1900) *Dictionnaire des antiquités grecques et romaines d'après les textes et les monuments*, 5 vols, Hachette, Paris

Daube, D. (1964) Dodges and rackets in Roman law. *Proceedings of the Classical Association*, 51: 28-30

—— (1969) The *filiusfamilias*. In his *Roman law: linguistic, social and philosophical aspects*, Edinburgh University Press, Edinburgh: 75-91

—— (1976) Martial, father of three. *American Journal of Ancient History*, 1: 145-7

Davis, J.C. (1962) *Decline of the Venetian nobility as a ruling class*, Johns Hopkins Press, Baltimore

deMause, L. (1974) The evolution of childhood. In L. deMause (ed.) *The history of childhood*, Harper and Row, New York: 1-73

den Boer, W. (1973) Demography in Roman history: facts and impressions. *Mnemosyne* (*ser. 4*), *26*: 29-46

—— (1974) Republican Rome and the demography of Hopkins, *Mnemosyne* (*ser. 4*), 27:79-82

des Bouvrie, S. (1984) Augustus' legislation on morals — Which morals and what aims? *Symbolae Osloenses*, *59*: 93-113

de Zulueta, F. (1946-53) *The Institution of Gaius*, Clarendon Press, Oxford, 2 vols (vol. 1, 1946: text; vol. 2, 1953: commentary)

Dickemann, M. (1979) Female infanticide, reproduction strategies and social stratification: a preliminary model. In N.A. Chagnon and W. Irons (eds), *Evolutionary biology and human social behaviour*, Duxbury Press, North Scituate, Mass.: 321-67

Dixon, S. (1984a) *Infirmitas sexus*: womanly weakness in Roman law. *Tijdschrift v. Rechtsgeschiedenis*, *52*: 343-71

—— (1984b) Family finances: Tullia & Terentia. *Antichthon*, *18*: 78-101

—— (1984c) Roman nurses and foster-mothers: some problems of terminology. *AULLA, Papers and Synopses from the 22nd Congress of the Australasian Universities Language and Literature Association*, *22*: 9-24

—— (1985a) Polybius on Roman women and property. *American Journal of Philology*, *106*: 147-70

—— (1985b) The marriage alliance in the Roman élite. *Journal of Family History*, *10*: 353-78

—— (1985c) Breaking the law to do the right thing: the gradual erosion of the Voconian Law in Ancient Rome. *Adelaide Law Review*, *9*: 519-34

Dudley, D.R. (1967) *Urbs Roma*, Phaedon, London

Duncan-Jones, R. (1964) The purpose and organisation of the *alimenta*. *Papers of the British School at Rome*, *32*: 123-46

—— (1974) *The economy of the Roman Empire: quantitative studies*, Cambridge University Press, Cambridge

Durand, J.D. (1960) Mortality estimates from Roman tombstone inscriptions. *American Journal of Sociology*, *65*: 365-73

Earl, D.C. (1963) *Tiberius Gracchus: a study in politics*, Collection Latomus 66, Brussels

Edwards, Mrs A. (1877) *A blue stocking*, Bentley, London

Eliot, George (1980) *Scenes of clerical life*, ed. D. Lodge, Penguin Books, Harmondsworth

Engels, D. (1980) The problem of female infanticide in the Greco–Roman world. *Classical Philology*, *75*: 112-20

Engels, F. (1884) *The origins of the family, private property and the state*, C.H. Kerr, Chicago

Erdmann, W. (1939) Die Rolle der Mutter bei der Verheiratung der Tochter. *Zeitschrift der Savigny Stiftung für Rechtsgeschichte: Romanistische Abteilung*, *60*: 155-84

Étienne, R. (1973) La Conscience médicale antique et la vie des enfants. *Annales de Démographie Historique*, Enfant et Sociétés: 15-61

Eyben, E. (1977) *De jonge Romein volgens de literaire bronnen der periode ca. 200 v. Chr. tot ca. 500 n. Chr.* (with English summary), Verhandl. Acad. voor Wet. Lett. und Schone Kunsten van België, Kl. Lett. 39, Brussels

—— (1986) Sozialgeschichte des Kindes im römischen Altertum. In J. Martin and A. Nitschke, (eds) *Zur Sozialgeschichte der Kindheit*, Verlag Karl Alber, Munich

Färber, H. (1925) *Cornelius Nepos: Kurzbiographie und Fragmente*, Beck, Munich

Farquharson, A.S.L. (1944) *The Meditations of the Emperor Marcus Antoninus* (ed. with translation and commentary), Clarendon Press, Oxford, 2 vols

Field, J.A. (1945) The purpose of the *Lex Julia et Papia-Poppaea*. *Classical Journal*, *40*: 398-416

Flandrin, J.L. (1979) *Families in Former Times*, Cambridge University Press, Cambridge, translation of the French original, *Familles: parenté, maison, sexualité dans l'ancienne société*, Hachette, Paris, 1976

Flory, M.B. (1975) Family and *familia*: a study of social relations in slavery. Yale Ph.D. Diss.

—— (1978) Family in *Familia*. Kinship and community in slavery. *American Journal of Ancient History*, *3*: 78-95

—— (1984) *Sic exempla parantur*: Livia's shrine to Concordia and the Porticus Liviae. *Historia*, *33*: 309-30

Fowler, W.W. (1899) *The Roman festivals of the period of the Republic*, Macmillan, London

—— (1908) *Social life at Rome in the age of Cicero*, London

Frank, R.I. (1976) Augustus' legislation on marriage and children. *California Studies in Classical Antiquity*, *8*: 41-52

Frank, T. (1916) Race mixture in the Roman Empire, *American Historical Review*, *21*: 689-708

French, V. (1987) Midwives and maternity care in the Greco–Roman world. In M. Skinner (ed.) *Rescuing Creusa: new methodological approaches to women in antiquity*. A special issue of *Helios* (n.s. 13.2), Texas Tech. University Press, Lubbock, Texas: 69-84

Freud, S. (1910) Five lectures on psycho-analysis, vol. 11 in J. Strachey (ed.) *The standard edition of the complete psychological works of Sigmund*

Freud, Hogarth Press, London, 1957

―――― (1918) Totem and Taboo, vol. 13. In J. Strachey (ed.) *The standard edition,* Hogarth Press, London, 1955 (and see the new Penguin set of readings)

Freud, S. and Breuer, J. (1909) Studies in hysteria (Journal articles first published in German as *Studien über Hysterie,* Leipzig/Vienna, 1895), vol. 2. In J. Strachey (ed.) *The standard edition,* Hogarth Press, London, 1955

Frey, J.B. (1930) la signification des termes μόνανδρος et *univira. Recherches de Science Réligieuse, 20*: 48-60

Frezza, P. (1930-1) La capacità delle donne all'esercizio della tutela nel diritto romano classico e nei papiri greco–egizi. *Aegyptus II*: 363-85

Frier, B.W. (1985) *The rise of the Roman jurists. Studies in Cicero's 'Pro Caecina',* Princeton University Press, New Jersey

Fromm, E. (1941) *Escape from freedom,* Rinehart and Winston, New York

Furneaux, H.H. (1896,1907) *The Annals of Tacitus,* Clarendon Press, Oxford, 4 vols

Galinsky, G.K. (1981) Augustus' legislation on morals and marriage. *Philologus, 125*: 126-44

Gardner, J. (1985) The recovery of dowry in Roman law. *Classical Quarterly, 35*: 449-53

Garnsey, P. (1967) Adultery trials and the survival of the *Quaestiones* in the Severan age. *Journal of Roman Studies, 57*: 57-60

Gathorne-Hardy, J. (1972) *The rise and fall of the British nanny,* Hodder and Stoughton, London

Geiger, J. (1970) M. Hortensius M.f.Q.n. Hortalus. *Classical Quarterly, 20*: 132-4

George, D. (1925) *London life in the eighteenth century,* Kegan Paul, Trench, Trubner and Company Limited, London

Giacosa, G. (1977) *Women of the Caesars: their lives and portraits on coins,* Milan, translated from the Italian original, *Ritratti di Auguste,* Editzioni Arte e Moneta, Milan, 1974

Gibbs, M.A. (1960) *The years of the nannies,* Hutchinson, London

Golden, M. (1981) Demography and the exposure of girls at Athens. *Phoenix, 35*: 316-51

Goody, J. (1958) *The developmental cycle in domestic groups,* Cambridge University Press, Cambridge

―――― (1969) Indo-European kinship. In his *Comparative Studies in Kinship,* London: 235-9

―――― (1972) The evolution of the family. In P. Laslett (ed.), *Household and family in past time,* Cambridge University Press, Cambridge: 103-24

―――― (1973) Strategies of heirship. *Comparative Studies in Society and History, 15*: 3-20

―――― (1983) *The development of the family and marriage in Europe,* Cambridge University Press, Cambridge

Gorer, G. (1948) *The American people,* Norton, New York

Grant, M. (1954) *Roman imperial money,* Nelson, Edinburgh

―――― (1970) *Nero,* Weidenfeld and Nicholson, London

Gray-Fow, M.J.G. (1985) 'The nomenclature and stages of Roman childhood', Ph.D. Dissertation (Univ. of Wisconsin)

Green, J.R. (1981) *Antiquities: a description of the Classics Department Museum in the Australian National University*, Faculty of Arts, Australian National University, Canberra

Gruber, H.A. (1910) *Coins of the Roman Republic in the British Museum*, Trustees of the British Museum, London, 4 vols (reprinted 1970)

Haase, F. (ed.) (1872-4) *Luci Annaei Senecae opera quae supersunt*, Teubner, Leipzig, 3 vols

Haines, C.R. (1962-3) *The correspondence of Marcus Cornelius Fronto*, Harvard University Press, Cambridge, Mass., 2 vols

Hainsworth, D.R. (1986) *Surrogate kin? Masters and servants in English noble households in the later seventeenth century*, University of Adelaide, Adelaide

Hall, C.M. (1923) *Nicolaus of Damascus' life of Augustus*, Smith College Classical Studies 4, Northampton, Mass.

Hallett, J. (1973) The role of women in Roman elegy: counter-cultural feminism. *Arethusa, 6*: 103-24

―――― (1984) *Fathers and daughters in Roman society: women and the élite family*, Princeton University Press, Princeton

Hanawalt, B.A. (1977) Childrearing among the lower classes of Late Medieval England. *Journal of Interdisciplinary History, 8*: 1-13

Hanfmann, G. (1967) *Classical sculpture*, Joseph, London

Hanson, C. and Johnson, F.P. (1946) On certain portrait inscriptions. *American Journal of Archaeology, 50*: 389-400

Hareven, T. (1977) The family cycle in historical perspective: a proposal for a developmental approach. In J. Cuisenier and M. Segalen (eds), *The family life cycle in European societies*, Mouton, The Hague: Ch. 18

Harkness, A.C. (1896) Age at marriage and at death in the Roman Empire. *Transactions of the American Philological Association, 27*: 35-72

Harris, W.V. (1982) The theoretical possibility of extensive infanticide in the Greco–Roman world. *Classical Quarterly, 32*: 114-16

Harrod, S.G. (1909) 'Latin terms of endearment and of family relationship', Dissertation, Princeton

Henrion, R. (1940) Des origines du mot *Familia. L'Antiquité Classique, 9*: 37-69; *11*: 253-87

Henry, L. (1957) La mortalité d'après les inscriptions funéraires. *Population, 12*: 149-52

Hillard, T. (1983) *Materna auctoritas*: the political influence of Roman *matronae. Classicum, 22*: 10-13.

Hollingsworth, T.H. (1964) Demography of the British peerage. *Population Studies 18, 2 supp. iv*

Hombert, M and Préaux, C. (1945) Note sur la durée de la vie dans l'Égypte gréco–romaine. *Chronique d'Égypte, 20*: 143-5

Hopkins, K. (1965a) The age of Roman girls at marriage. *Population Studies, 18*: 309-27

―――― (1965b) Contraception in the Roman Empire. *Comparative Studies in Society and History, 8*: 124-51

―――― (1966) On the probable age structure of the Roman population. *Population Studies, 20*: 245-64

―――― (1974) Demography in Roman history. *Mnemosyne, 27*: 77-8

―――― (1978) *Conquerors and slaves*, Sociological Studies in Roman History

I, Cambridge University Press, Cambridge

―― (1983) *Death and renewal,* Sociological Studies in Roman History II, Cambridge University Press, Cambridge

Howell, C. (1976) Peasant inheritance customs in the Midlands, 1280-1700. In J. Goody, J. Thirsk and E. Thompson (eds), *Family and inheritance: rural society in Western Europe 1200-1800,* Cambridge University Press, Cambridge: Ch. 5

Humbert, M. (1972) *Le remariage à Rome: étude d'histoire juridique et sociale,* Giuffrè (Universita di Roma, Pubblicazioni dell'Istituto di Diritto Romano) 44, Milan

Huttunen, P. (1974) *The social strata in the Imperial City of Rome: a quantitative study of the social representation in the epitaphs published in the C.I.L. VI,* University of Oulu, Oulu

Instinsky, H.U. (1942) Studien zur Geschichte des Septimius Severus. *Klio, 35 (= n.s. 17)*: 200-19

Jolowicz, H.F. (1954) *Historical introduction to the study of Roman law* (corrected version of the 2nd ed of 1952, based on the 1932 original), Cambridge University Press, Cambridge

Jones, E. (1924; reprinted 1964) Mother-right and sexual ignorance of savages. In *Essays in applied psychoanalysis, 2,* New York: 145-73

Jörs, P. (1882) Ueber das Verhaltnis der *Lex Iulia de Maritandis Ordinibus* zur *Lex Papia Poppaea,* Dissertation, Bonn

Kajanto, I. (1963) *A study [of] the Greek epitaphs of Rome,* Acta Instituti Romani Finlandiae, 2, 3, Helsinki

―― (1970) On divorce among the common people of Rome. *Révue des Études Latines: Mélanges Marcel Durry, 47 bis*: 99-113

Kampen, N. (1981) *Image and status: Roman working women in Ostia,* Mann, Berlin

―― (1982) Social status and gender in Roman art: the case of the saleswoman. In M.D. Garrard and N. Broude (eds) *Feminism and Art History,* Harper and Row, London: Ch. 4

Kanowski, M. (1978) *The Antiquities Collection. Department of Classics and Ancient History, University of Queensland,* Dept. of Classics and Ancient History, University of Queensland, Brisbane

Kaser, M. (1955-9) *Das römische Privatrecht,* Beck, Munich, 2 vols

Kleiner, D.E. (1977) *Roman group portraiture: the funerary reliefs of the late Republic and early Empire,* Garland, New York

―― (1978) The great friezes of the Ara Pacis Augustae: Greek sources, Roman derivatives and Augustan social policy. *Mélanges de l'École Française de Rome: Antiquité, 90*: 753-85

Koschaker (1937) Eheformen bei den Indogermanern. *Zeitschrift für Ausländisches und Internationales Privatrecht, 11*: 77-140b

Kübler, B. (1909-10) Uber das *ius liberorum* der Frauen und die Vormundschaft der Mutter, ein Beitrag zur Geschichte der Rezeption des römischen Rechts in Agypten. *Zeitschrift der Savigny Stiftung für Rechtsgeschichte: Romanistische Abteilung, 30*: 154-83; *31*: 176-95

Kuhn, A.L. (1947) *The mother's role in childhood education: New England concepts 1830-1860,* Yale University Press, New Haven

Lacey, W.K. (1968) *The family in classical Greece,* Thames and Hudson, London

Bibliography

Lambert, G.R. (1982) *Rhetoric rampant: the family under siege in the early Western tradition*, University of Western Ontario, London, Ontario

Langer, W.L. (1974) Infanticide: a historical survey. *History of Childhood Quarterly, 1*: 353-65

Lasch, C. (1977) *Haven in a heartless world: the family besieged*, Basic Books, New York

Laslett, P. and Wall, R. (eds) (1972) *Household and family in past time*, Cambridge University Press, Cambridge

Laslett, P., Wachter, K.H. and Laslett, R. (1978) The English evidence on household structure compared with the outcomes of micro-simulation. In K.H. Wachter *et al.*, *Statistical studies of historical social structure*, Academic Press, London: Ch. 5

Last, H. (1923) Family and social life. In C. Bailey (ed.) *The Legacy of Rome*, Clarendon Press, Oxford: 209-36

Latte, K. (1960) *Römische Religionsgeschichte*, Beck, Munich

Lattimore, R. (1942) *Themes in Greek and Latin epitaphs*, Illinois University Press, Urbana, Illinois

Lawler, L.B. (1929) Married life in *CIL* IX. *Classical Journal, 24*: 346-53

Lévi-Strauss, C. (1963) *Structural anthropology*, Doubleday, Garden City, New York

Lévy-Bruhl, H. (1959) *Nouvelles Études sur le très ancien droit romain*, Publication de l'Institut de Droit Romain, no. 1, Paris

Lewis, C.T. and Short, C. (1962) *A Latin dictionary*, Clarendon Press, Oxford

Lightman, M. and Zeisel, W. (1977) *Univira*: an example of continuity and change in Roman society. *Church History, 46*: 19-32

Lyman, R. (1974) Barbarism and religon: Late Roman and Early Medieval childhood. In L. deMause (ed.), *The history of childhood*, Harper and Row, New York: 75-100

McBride, T. (1978) As the twig is bent: the Victorian nanny. In A.S. Wohl (ed.) *The Victorian family*, Croom Helm, London: 44-58

McDonnell, M. (1987) The speech of Numidicus at Gellius, *NA* 1.6. *American Journal of Philology, 108*: 81-94

MacDonnell, W.R. (1913) The expectation of life in Ancient Rome. *Biometrika, 9*: 366-80

MacFarlane, A. (1979) Review essay of Stone (1977). *History and Theory, 18*: 103-26

Mackenzie, C. (1913-14) *Sinister street*, Macdonald, London, 2 vols

Malinowski, B. (1916) Baloma: the spirits of the dead in the Trobriand Islands. *Journal of the Royal Anthropological Institute, 46*: 353-430

—— (1929) *The sexual life of savages*, Routledge, London

—— (1930) Kinship. *Man, 30*: 19-29

Manson, M. (1975) La *pietas* et le sentiment de l'enfance à Rome d'après les monnaies. *Revue Belge de Numismatique et de Sigillographie, 121*: 21-80

——(1983) The emergence of the small child in Rome (third century BC — first century AD). *History of Education, 12*: 149-59

Marquardt, J. (1886) *Das Privatleben der Römer*, Hirzel, Leipzig, 2 vols

Marshall, A.S. (1975) Roman women and the provinces. *Ancient Society, 6*: 109-27

Marshall, P.K. ed. (1977) *Cornelii Nepotis Vitae cum Fragmentis*, Teubner,

Leipzig

Mattingly, H. *et al.* (1966-76) *Coins of the Roman Empire in the British Museum*, Trustees of the British Museum, London, 6 vols = BMCRE (First published 1928-62. Vols 1-4 by H. Mattingly, vol. 5, 2nd edn 1975, pts. 1-2 by R.A.G. Carson and P.V. Hill, vol. 6 by R.A.G. Carson)

Mattingly, H., Sydenham, E.A., Sutherland, C.H.V. and Carson, R.A.G. (1923-81) *The Roman Imperial Coinage* = *RIC*, Spink, London, 9 vols in 13 parts. (Edited by H. Mattingly and E.A. Sydenham. Later vols, ed. by C.H.V. Sutherland and R.A.G. Carson. N.B.: The revised first volume, by C.H.V. Sutherland (Spink, London, 1984) became available in Australia when this book was in an advanced draft. Dual references have therefore been inserted.)

Mead, M. (1954) The swaddling hypothesis: its reception. *American Anthropologist, 56*: 395-409

―――― (1962) A cultural anthropologist's approach to maternal deprivation. In *Deprivation of maternal care: a re-assessment of its effects*, World Health Organisation Public Health Paper no. 14, Geneva: 45-62

Medick, H. (1976) The proto-industrial family economy: the structural function of household and family during the transition from peasant society to industrial capitalism. *Social History, 3*: 291-315

Minturn, L. and Lambert, W.L. (1964) *Mothers of six cultures: antecedents of child-rearing*, Wiley, New York

Mitchell, J. (1974) *Psychoanalysis and feminism*, Allen Lane, London

Mitford, N. (1980) *The blessing*, Penguin Books, Harmondsworth

―――― (1980) *The pursuit of love*, Penguin Books, Harmondsworth

Moir, K.M. (1983) Pliny *HN.* 7.57 and the marriage of Tiberius Gracchus. *Classical Quarterly, 33*: 136-45

Mommsen, T. (1879) Die Skipionenprozesse. *Römisches Forschungen, 2*, Werdmann, Berlin: 417-510

―――― (1887-8) *Das römisches Staatsrecht (II²)* Hirzel, Leipzig, 3 vols, in 5 parts

―――― (1899) *Das römisches Strafrecht*, Duncker und Humbolt, Leipzig, reprinted Akad. Druck-U. Verlagsanstalt, Graz, 1955

Moretti, L. (1959) Statistica demografica ed epigrafica: durata media della vita in Roma imperiale. *Epigraphica, 21*: 60-78

Morgan, E.S. (1966) *The Puritan family: religion and domestic relations in 17th century New England*, Greenwood, New York

Muensterberger, W. (1951) Orality and dependence: characteristics of Southern Chinese. In G. Roheim *et al.* (eds) *Psychoanalysis and the social sciences, 3*, New York: 37-69

Murdock, G.P. (1949) *Social structure*, Macmillan, New York

―――― (1967) *Ethnographic atlas*, University of Pittsburgh Press, Pittsburgh

Nardi, E. (1971) *Procurato aborto nel mondo greco romano*, Guiffrè, Milan

Neraudau, J.P. (1979) *La Jeunesse dans la littérature et les institutions de la Rome républicaine*, Les Belles Lettres, Paris

Norden, F. (1912) *Apuleius von Madaura und das römische Privatrecht*, Teubner, Leipzig

Nörr, D. (1977) Planung in der Antike. Über die Ehegesetze des

Augustus. In H. Baier (ed.) *Freiheit und Sachzwang. Beiträge zu Ehren Helmut Schelskys*, Westdeutscher Verlag, Opladen: 309-34

—— (1981) The matrimonial legislation of Augustus. An early instance of social engineering. *Irish Jurist*, *16*: 350-64

Oliver, J.H. (1973) Julia Domna as Athena Polias. In *Athenian studies presented to William Scott Ferguson*, Harvard University Press, Cambridge, Mass.: 521-30

Parsons, A. (1964) Is the Oedipus complex universal? In W. Muensterberger and S. Axelrad (eds), *The psychoanalytic study of society*, *3*, Books Demand UMI, New York: 278-328

Patterson, C. (1985) 'Not worth the rearing'. The causes of infant exposure in Ancient Greece. *Transactions of the American Philological Association, 115*: 103-23

Pedley, Mrs. F. (1866) *Infant nursing and the management of young children*, London

Pharr, C., Johnson, A., Coleman-Norton, P.R. and Bourne, F.C. (1981) *Ancient Roman Statues*, University of Texas, Austin

Phillips, J.E. (1978) Roman mothers and the lives of their adult daughters. *Helios, n.s.6*: 69-80

Piaget, J. (1951) *The child's conception of the world*, Littlefield, London

—— (1952) *The origin of intelligence in children*, International Universities Press, New York

Piaget, J. and Inhelder, B. (1958) *The growth of logical thinking from childhood to adolescence*, Basic Books, New York

Pinchbeck, I. and Hewitt, M. (1969-73) *Children in English society*, Routledge and Kegan Paul, London, 2 vols

Polgar, S. (1972) Population history and population policies from an anthropological perspective. *Current Anthropology, 13.2*: 203-11

Pollini, J. (1985) *Portraiture of Gaius and Lucius Caesar*, Brettschneider, Rome

Pollock, L.A. (1983) *Forgotten children. Parent–child relations from 1500-1900*, Cambridge University Press, Cambridge

Pomeroy, S. (1975) *Goddesses, whores, wives and slaves: women in Classical Antiquity*, Shocken Books, New York

—— (1976) The relationship of the married woman to her blood relatives in Rome. *Ancient Society, 7*: 215-27

—— (1983) Infanticide in Hellenistic Greece. In A. Cameron and A. Kuhrt, (eds), *Images of women in Antiquity*, Croom Helm, London: 207-22

Poulsen, V. (1962-74) *Les Portraits romains*, Publications de la Glyptothèque, Ny Carlsberg, Copenhagen, 2 vols

Price, T.H. (1978) *Kourotrophos: cults and representations of the Greek nursing deities*, Studies of the Dutch Archaeological and Historical Society, 8, Brill, Leiden

Quiggin, P. (1986) 'Demographic influences on attitudes to marriage in Victoria and N.S.W. in the 1870s and 1880s', M.A. Dissertation, Australian National University

Rabello, A.M. (1972) Il *ius occidendi iure patris* della *lex Iulia de adulteriis coercendis* e la *vitae necisque potestas* del *paterfamilias*. In *Atti del Seminario Romanistico Internazionale, Perugia Spoleto-Todi*, Libreria Editrice Universitaria, Perugia: 228-42

—— (1979) *Effetti personali della 'patria potestas'*, Università degli Studi di Milano, Istituto di Diritto Romano 12, Giuffrè, Milan, vol. 1

Radcliffe-Brown, A.R. (1950) In A.R. Radcliffe-Brown and D. Forde, (eds), *African systems of kinship and marriage*, Oxford University Press, London: 1-85

Raditsa, L.F. (1980) Augustus' legislation concerning marriage, procreation, love affairs and adultery. In *Aufstieg und Niedergang der römischen Welt*, H. Temporini (ed.) De Gruyter Berlin. Principat, Recht, II, 13: 278-339

Raepsaet-Charlier, M.-Th. (1982) Épouses et familles de magistrats dans les provinces romaines aux deux premiers siècles de l'Empire, *Historia, 31*: 56-69

Rawson, B. (1966) Family life among the lower classes at Rome in the first two centuries of the Empire. *Classical Philology, 61*: 71-83

—— (1974) Roman concubinage and other *de facto* marriages. *Transactions of the American Philological Association, 104*: 279-305

—— (1986a) (ed.) *The family in Ancient Rome: new perspectives*, Croom Helm, London and Sydney, including:

—— (1986b) (ch. 1) The Roman family: 1-57

—— (1986c) (ch. 7) Children in the Roman *familia*: 170-200

Reiger, K. (1981) 'The transformation of Australian childhood in the late nineteenth and early twentieth centuries'. Unpublished paper delivered in Melbourne

—— (1984) 'Mothering deskilled? Australian childbearing and the experts in the twentieth century'. Unpublished paper delivered at the 1984 Congress of the Australian and New Zealand Association for the Advancement of Science, Canberra

Reisman, D., Glazer, N. and Denny, R. (eds) (1950) *The lonely crowd: a study of the changing American character*, Yale University Press, New Haven, Conn.

Renier, E. (1942) *Étude sur l'histoire de la 'Querela inofficiosi' en droit romain*, Imprimérie de l'Académie, Liège

Riccobono, S. (ed.) (1945) *Acta Divi Augusti*, Accademia d'Italia, Rome, vol. 1

Richards, A.I. (1950) Some types of family structure amongst the central Bantu. In A.R. Radcliffe-Brown and D. Forde (eds) *African systems of kinship and marriage*, Oxford University Press, London: 207-51

Rivière, P.G. (1971) Marriage: a reassessment. In R. Needham (ed.) *Rethinking kinship and marriage*, Tavistock Publications, London: Ch. 3

Rodgers, R.H. (1977) The family life cycle concept: past, present and future. In J. Cuisenier (ed.) *The family life cycle in European societies*, Mouton, Hague: Ch. 2

Rose, H.J. (1970) Children. In *Oxford Classical Dictionary*, Clarendon Press, Oxford (2nd ed. repr. 1979): 229

Rotondi, G. (1922) *Leges publicae populi Romani*, Società Editrice Libreria, Milan

Ryder, N.B. (1959) Fertility. In P.M. Hauser and O.E. Duncan (eds), *The study of population: an inventory and appraisal*, University of Chicago Press, Chicago: 400-36

Sacks, D. (1979) *Sisters and wives*, Greenwood Press, Westport, Conn.

Saller, R.P. (1982) *Personal patronage under the Early Empire*, Cambridge University Press, Cambridge

—— (1984a) Roman dowry and the devolution of property in the Principate. *Classical Quarterly, 34*: 195-205

—— (1984b) *Familia, domus* and the Roman conception of the family. *Phoenix, 38*: 336-55

Saller, R.P. and Shaw, B. (1984) Tombstones & Roman family relations in the Principate: civilians, soldiers and slaves. *Journal of Roman Studies, 74*: 124-56

Sanders, H.A. (1938) A Latin marriage contract. *Transactions of the American Philological Association, 49*: 104-16

Schaps, D. (1977) The women least mentioned. Etiquette and women's names, *Classical Quarterly, 27*: 323-30

—— (1979) *Economic rights of women in Ancient Greece*, Edinburgh University Press, Edinburgh

Shackleton Bailey, D.R. (1960) The Roman nobility in the Second Civil War. *Classical Quarterly, 10*: 253-67

—— (1965-70) *Cicero's letters to Atticus*, Cambridge University Press Cambridge, 7 vols

—— (1977) *Epistulae ad Familiares*, Cambridge University Press, Cambridge, 2 vols

Shaw, B.D. (1984) Latin funerary epigraphy and family relations in the Later Roman Empire. *Historia, 33*: 457-97

—— (1987) The age of Roman girls at marriage. Some reconsiderations. *Journal of Roman Studies, 77*

Sherwin-White, A.N. (1966) *The Letters of Pliny: a historical and social commentary*, Clarendon Press, Oxford

Shorter, E. (1979) *The making of the modern family*, reprinted Glasgow, in paperback from 1975 original, Fontana/Collins, London

Sijpesteijn, P.J. (1965) Die ΧΩΡΙΣ ΚΥΡΙΟΥ ΧΡΗΜΑΤΙΖΟΥΣΑΙ in den Papyri. *Aegyptus, 45*: 171-89

Slater, W.J. (1974) '*Pueri, turba minuta.*' *Bulletin of the Institute of Classical Studies of the University of London*: 133-40

Slusanski, D. (1974) Le Vocabulaire latin des *gradus aetatum*. *Revue Roumaine de Linguistique, 19*: 103-21; 267-96; 345-69; 437-51; 563-78

Smith, R.T. (1956) *The negro family in British Guiana: family structure and social status in the villages*, Routledge and Kegan Paul, London

Solazzi, S. (1930) '*Infirmitas Aetatis*' e '*Infirmitas Sexus*'. *Archivo Giuridico, 194*: 3-31

—— (1937) La madre educatrice. *Atti della Romana Accademia di Scienze Morali e Politiche di Napoli, 58*: 1-11 (reprinted in his *Scritti di diritto Romano*, Naples, 1963, vol. 3: 587-601)

Solidoro, L. (1981) La *familia* nell'editto di Lucullo. *Atti della Accademia di Scienze Morali e Politiche della Società Nazionale di Scienze, Lettere ed Arti di Napoli, 92*: 197-229

Spock, B. (1946) *The pocket book of baby and child care*, Pocket Books, New York

Steinwenter (1893) *Ius Liberorum. RE, X.2*: cols 1281-4

Stephens, W.M. (1962) *The Oedipus Complex: cross-cultural evidence,*

Glencoe, New York

Stone, L. (1977) *The family, sex and marriage in England 1500-1800*, Weidenfeld and Nicholson, London

Strong, E. (1907) *Roman sculpture from Augustus to Constantine*, Duckworth and Company, New York

Strong, D.E. (1961) *Roman imperial sculpture*, Alec Tiranti, London

Sussman, G. (1975) The wet-nursing business in nineteenth-century France, *French Historical Studies*, 9: 304-28

Sutherland, C.H.V. (1974) *Roman coins*, Barrie and Jenkins, London

Syme, R. (1939) *The Roman revolution*, Clarendon Press, Oxford

Taylor, L.R. (1949) *Party politics in the age of Caesar*, University of California Press, Berkeley (reprinted 1966)

—— (1961) Freedmen and freeborn in the epitaphs of Imperial Rome. *American Journal of Philology*, 82: 113-32

Tellegen, J.W. (1980) Was There a *Consortium* in Pliny's Letter VIII. 18? *Revue Internationale des Droits de l'Antiquité*, 27: 295-312

Thayer, J.B. (1929) *Lex Aquilia; on gifts between husband and wife*, Harvard University Press, Cambridge, Mass.

Thomas, J.A.C. (1970) *Lex Iulia de adulteriis coercendis*. In *Études offertes à Jean Macqueron*, Aix-en-Provence: 637-44

—— (1975) *The Institutes of Justinian*, North-Holland Publishing Company, Amsterdam

—— (1976) *Textbook of Roman law*, North-Holland Publishing Company, Amsterdam

Thompson, E.P. (1973) Under the rooftree. *Times Literary Supplement*, 3713: 485-87

Toynbee, J. (1980) *Roman historical portraits*, Thames and Hudson, London

Treggiari, S. (1969) *Roman freedmen during the Late Republic*, Clarendon Press, Oxford

—— (1976) Jobs for women. *American Journal of Ancient History*, 1: 76-104

—— (1979) Lower-class women in the Roman economy. *Florilegium*, 1: 65-86

—— (1981) *Contubernales* in *CIL* 6. *Phoenix*, 35: 42-69

—— (1982) Consent to Roman marriage: some aspects of law and reality. *Échos du Monde Classique/Classical Views* n.s. 1: 34-44

—— (1984) *Digna condicio*: betrothals in the Roman upper class. *Échos du Monde Classique/Classical Views*, n.s. 3: 419-51

United Nations Bureau of Social Affairs, Population Branch (1958) *Recent trends in fertility in industrialized countries*, Population Studies no. 27, New York

Veyne, P. (1957-8) La Table des *Ligures Baebiani* et l'institution alimentaire de Trajan. *Melanges de l'école Française de Rome, Antiquité*, 69 81-135; 70; 178-222

—— (1978) La Famille et l'amour sous le haut-empire romain. *Annales: économies, sociétés, civilisations*, 35: 35-63

Vinogradoff, P. (1920) *Outlines of historical jurisprudence*, Oxford University Press, London, 2 vols

Walbank, F.W. (1957-79) *A historical commentary on Polybius*, Clarendon

Press, Oxford, 3 vols

Walker, A.J. and Thompson, L. (1983) Intimacy and intergenerational aid and contact among mothers and daughters. *Journal of Marriage and the Family, 44*: 841-9

Wallace-Hadrill, A. (1981) Family and inheritance in the Augustan marriage laws. *Proceedings of the Cambridge Philological Society* n.s. *27*: 58-80

Warmington, E.H. (1969) *Nero: reality and legend*, Chatto and Windus, London

Watson, A. (1965) The divorce of Carvilius Ruga. *Tijdschrift v. Rechtsgeschiedenis, 33*: 38-50

―――― (1967) *The law of persons in the Later Roman Republic*, Clarendon Press, Oxford

―――― (1971) *The law of succession in the Later Roman Republic*, Clarendon Press, Oxford

―――― (1976) The origins of *usus*. *Revue Internationale des Droits de l'Antiquité, 23*: 265-70

―――― (1979) Two notes on *manus*. In J.E. Spruit (ed.) *Maior viginti quinque annis*, Van Gorcum, Assen: 195-201

Waugh, Evelyn (1982) *Brideshead revisited*, Penguin Books, Harmondsworth

Weakland, J. and Fry, W. (1962) Letters of mothers of schizophrenics. *American Journal of Orthopsychiatry, 32*: 604-23

Weaver, P.R.C. (1972) *Familia Caesaris: a social study of the Emperor's freedmen and slaves*, Cambridge University Press, Cambridge

―――― (1986) The status of children in mixed marriages. In B. Rawson (ed.), *The family in Ancient Rome: new perspectives*, Croom Helm, London and Sydney: Ch. 6

Westrup, C.W. (1934, 1939, 1941) *Introduction to early Roman law: comparative sociological studies. The patriarchal joint family*, Munksgaard, Copenhagen, 3 vols

Whiting, B.B. and Whiting J.M. (1975) *Children of six cultures*, Harvard University Press, Cambridge, Mass.

Willcox, W.F.L. (1937) The length of life in the early Roman Empire: a methodological note. *Actes du Congrès International de Population, 2*: 14-22

Williams, G. (1962) Poetry in the moral climate of Augustan Rome. *Journal of Roman Studies, 52*: 28-46

Wiseman, T.P. (1971) Celer and Nepos. *Classical Quarterly, 21*: 180-2

Wishy, B. (1972) *The child and the republic: the dawn of North American child nurture*, University of Pennsylvania Press, Philadelphia

Wolff, H.J. (1939) Trinoctium. *Tijdschrift voor Rechtsgeschiedenis* 16: 145-83

Wrigley, E.A. and Schofield, R. (1981) *The population history of England, 1541-1871: a reconstruction*, Arnold, London

Young, M. and Willmott, P. (1957) *Family and kinship in East London*, Routledge and Kegan Paul, London

Zannini, P. (1976) *Studi sulla tutela mulierum, I*, G. Giappichelli, Turin

General Index

This index lists both common and proper nouns in alphabetical order. Most Latin terms (e.g. *patria potestas*) and relationships (e.g. Servilia, mother of Brutus) are explained briefly, but full details will be found by looking up the page references.

The name of a Roman male citizen had three elements, e.g. Caius/Gaius (C.) Julius Caesar. Such names are usually listed by their central, gentile name. Cicero is therefore to be found under T for Tullius. Members of the imperial family, however, are listed under the names by which they are usually known, e.g. Tiberius, Germanicus, Livilla. Names usually spelt with a J in English (e.g. Julia, daughter of Augustus) have been listed in the index under I/J. U and V are also listed together so that, e.g., Vitellius and Ulpian could follow each other.

References to ancient authors are to be found in the Conspectus Auctorum. They appear in this index only where details of their own family life appear. Modern authors are listed in the Bibliography.

life chances
  see demography
Livia — wife of the emperor
  Augustus; mother of Drusus and
  Tiberius 25, 33, 63, 73, 75, 77, 78,
  79, 80, 89, 90, 97, 99 n.10, 99
  n.11, 100 n.15, 112, 131, 132, 157,
  167 n.48, 175, 178, 182f., 186, 192,
  194, 198, 205 n.25, 205 n.33, 209
  n.86, 211, 216, 231 n.43, 236
Livia Julia — daughter of Livilla 225
Livilla — daughter of Antonia 25,
  225
love, conjugal *see* marriage
love of children *see* children
Lucilla — daughter of the emperor
  Marcus (Aurelius) 82, 87
Lucius — grandson of the emperor
  ʹAugustus; son of Julia maior 72,
  82, 91, 107, 136 n.8
Lucretia 15

mamma/ae — possibly
  foster-mother(s) 19, 32, 37 n.21,
  39 n.48, 124, 130, 133, 146, 147,
  148, 149, 151, 154, 159, 160, 163
  n.21, 163 n.22, 164 n.27, 164 n.28,
  165 n.32
maus — literally 'hand' 2, 8, 15, 26,
  38 n.27, 45, 46, 47, 48, 51, 53, 61
manus mariti — the authority of a
  husband over his wife in a
  particular category of Roman
  marriage 15, 48, 68 n.12, 173
Marcellus — son of Octavia; nephew
  of Augustus 73, 178, 201
Marcia — a friend of Seneca 12 n.10,
  38 n.38, 138 n.39, 178, 187, 191,
  192, 212, 222
Marciana — sister of the emperor
  Trajan 81
Marcus (Aurelius), emperor Marcus
  (emperor): 38 n.30, 54, 77, 82, 87,
  107, 159, 170, 171, 174, 193, 195,
  198, 204 n.11
marriage 5, 6, 13, 21, 26, 27, 35, 36
  n.4, 38 n.27, 52, 61, 62, 63, 66, 72,
  76, 83, 92f., 98, 135, 174, 177, 180,
  196, 211, 215, 216; 217, 227, 238
  demographic aspects 17, 26, 30ff.
  married love 2, 26, 31, 75, 83, 98,
    218
  purpose 21, 22, 37 n.23, 49f.,
    71ff., 86, 93, 97, 101 n.26
  see also manus mariti; Augustan
    legislation on marriage and

procreation
Martial
  see Valerius Martialis, M.
mater nutrix
  see breast-feeding, maternal
maternal attachment 18, 28, 34-5, 45,
  73, 76, 105, 111, 115f., 120f., 121,
  130, 131, 135, 153, 170, 174, 182,
  183, 186, 190, 192, 195, 198
maternal authority xiii, xiv, 1, 2, 3, 5,
  6, 8, 28, 31-2, 41, 43, 48, 50, 61-5,
  66, 81, 131, 143, 146, 171, 174,
  175, 176, 177, 178, 179, 180, 181,
  183, 185, 186, 187, 188, 194, 197,
  198, 202, 211, 215, 221, 224, 225,
  226, 227
maternal descent 1, 5, 12 n.11, 15,
  24, 36 n.10, 45, 66, 72, 74, 77, 79,
  80, 81f., 174, 175, 176, 184
maternal forcefulness
  see maternal authority
maternal grief 4, 73, 106, 113, 130,
  138 n.39, 178, 196, 201, 212, 214
Matidia the Elder — niece of the
  emperor Trajan 81, 82, 83, 87, 88
Matidia the Younger 87
matrifocal — "mother-centred" 18
matrilineal — reckoning descent
  through the maternal line 1f., 16,
  39 n.52
Mayombe 1
Melissus 19, 34, 40 n.55, 159
Memmia Panther(a) 153
Memmia Tertulla 153
Memmius Charus, Aulus —
  collibertus of Aulus Memmius
  Urbanus 19
Memmius Urbanus, Aulus —
  collibertus of Aulus Memmius
  Charus 19
Messalina — wife of the emperor
  Claudius; mother of Britannicus
  and Octavia 79, 211, 218, 223,
  230 n.35
Metellus Celer 37 n.18
Metilius — son of Seneca's friend,
  Marcia 178, 193, 208 n.61
midwives 91, 106, 108, 238, 240
Minicia Marcella 92, 113, 137 n.11,
  144
Minicius Fundanus 131
miscarriage 33, 96, 144, 239
Monumentum Liviae — memorial
  tomb of the dependants of Livia
  the empress 16
mother substitutes 17, 110, 131, 141,

Author Index

Author Index

Index of Inscriptions